*Also by Michael Shiner*

DEALING WITH DISAFFECTION
Young People, Mentoring and Social Inclusion (*co-authored*)

TEENAGE KICKS?
Young People and Alcohol: A Review of the Literature (*co-authored*)

# Drug Use and Social Change

## The Distortion of History

Michael Shiner
*London School of Economics and Political Science, UK*

palgrave
macmillan

First published 2009 by
PALGRAVE MACMILLAN

Palgrave Macmillan in the UK is an imprint of Macmillan Publishers Limited, registered in England, company number 785998, of Houndmills, Basingstoke, Hampshire RG21 6XS.

Palgrave Macmillan in the US is a division of St Martin's Press LLC, 175 Fifth Avenue, New York, NY 10010.

Palgrave Macmillan is the global academic imprint of the above companies and has companies and representatives throughout the world.

Palgrave® and Macmillan® are registered trademarks in the United States, the United Kingdom, Europe and other countries

ISBN-13: 978-0-230-22272-4 hardback
ISBN-10: 0-230-22272-2 hardback

This book is printed on paper suitable for recycling and made from fully managed and sustained forest sources. Logging, pulping and manufacturing processes are expected to conform to the environmental regulations of the country of origin.

A catalogue record for this book is available from the British Library.

A catalogue record for this book is available from the Library of Congress.

10 9 8 7 6 5 4 3 2 1
18 17 16 15 14 13 12 11 10 09

Printed and bound in Great Britain by
CPI Antony Rowe, Chippenham and Eastbourne

# Contents

future that are so preoccupied by how things have changed that they lose sight of important continuities and forget key lessons from the past. In challenging these tendencies my aim is to provide 'a history of the present', which seeks to understand 'the historical conditions of existence upon which contemporary practices depend' (Garland, 2001: 2).

The immediate focus of the book is on the way things were in Britain at the turn of the century, but the intention is to look beyond the limitations of time and place that this might imply. By linking drug use to broader patterns of social organisation, the analysis seeks to uncover underlying processes of continuity and change. It is not just that the present represents the final stage of the past (Bromley and Shkaratan, 1972) nor that: 'Past, present and future are linked together in the endless chain of history' (Carr, 1961: 129); but that there are general processes at work in any given situation or at any given time. The real value of the analysis, as with historical reconstruction more generally, lies in its ability to identify implications that go beyond the immediate and topical (Cohen, 2002).

What follows, then, is both historical and sociological – historical in the sense that it addresses processes of continuity and change over time and sociological in the sense that it relates such processes to broader patterns of social organisation. In pursuing these lines of inquiry the analysis is simultaneously empirical and theoretical: that is to say, it relates both to the way things are and the way they are understood to be or to what we might call the nature of reality and the nature of representation. The main message is one of continuity within change. Widespread illicit drug use, it is argued, emerged as the result of an extended historical trend which is rooted in the distinctive patterns of social, economic and cultural organisation that came to prominence across much of the late industrial world during the final third of the twentieth century. When viewed historically, it is apparent that drug use is subject to much greater continuity than is generally assumed and that past work has considerably more to offer than is often implied.

## Out with the old?

*The Drugtakers* by Jock Young (1971) was one of the foremost criminological texts of its time and one of the first to consider the social meaning of drug use in 'late industrial societies'. Some 30 years after publication, *The Drugtakers* was installed into Halovine's *Classic Collection*, with Steven Taylor (2002), the collection's founder and editor, noting that it 'not only became a classic in the sociology of crime and deviance but also seems as relevant today as when it was published'. Despite the plaudits, Young's work is barely mentioned in much that is now written on the subject. This is, perhaps, unsurprising, particularly given drug use has become so much more common and apparently new patterns of consumption have emerged. Add in the 'inevitable half-life of sociological fashions' and the 'ingrained impatience with the old which condemns every set of ideas to limited vitality' (Downes and Rock, 2007: 158) and it is perhaps to be expected that a book written almost 40 years ago should have faded from view.

Whatever the precise reason, dissatisfaction with established theories has become increasingly apparent and a new orthodoxy has emerged which emphasises the widespread and widely accepted nature of drug use among ordinary young people. More than anything, perhaps, it was the death of English schoolgirl Leah Betts that prompted the emergence of this new perspective (Collin with Godfrey, 1997; Cohen, 2002). Leah died on November 16 1995, less than a week after taking ecstasy at her 18th birthday party and her death sparked one of the most pronounced moral panics of the decade: tabloid newspapers sought out the 'murderers' who supplied Leah with ecstasy and encouraged their readers to 'shop a dealer'; a video including images of Leah's funeral was distributed to schools as a warning to other young people; and a billboard campaign showed a photograph of Leah accompanied by the word 'Sorted' over the caption, 'Just one Ecstasy tablet took Leah Betts.' The *Sunday Times* (November 19 1995) declared: 'This is a nightmare for parents' and within six months drugs had, indeed, become the major worry for British parents (*The Times Education Supplement*, March 10 1996). Leah's death was not the first to be linked to ecstasy, but had such an impact because it challenged widely held assumptions about the sort of people who take drugs (Collin and Godfrey, 1997: 295–6):

> Leah Betts...was white, affluent, a college student, an English Rose, and lived not in the metropolitan sleaze of London or Manchester, nor the sink estates of Scotland, but in a sleepy village in the heart of the Tory south-east: a daughter of middle England. Anykid...More than anyone, Betts transformed the image of the drugtaker forever. Broadsheet press editors, who for years had been recycling 'Agony of Ecstasy' headlines, realised this, and descended into a miasma of soul-searching. They had discovered that the people who took Ecstasy were their sons and daughters...It was as if they had stumbled on an alien universe that had somehow existed for years,

> unknown and unseen, within their own society. They found a culture that had previously been invisible, a world where drugs were good not bad; normal, not deviant.

The arrival of ecstasy was interpreted in highly iconic terms, prompting widespread talk of the 'chemical generation' and the 'democratisation' of drug use. Through its fusion with house music, ecstasy was credited with having created 'the largest, most dynamic, and longest lasting youth subculture or counterculture of the postwar era' (Martin, 1999: 77) and providing 'the most visible exemplar of an emergent global culture' (Carrington and Wilson, 2002: 74). Under these circumstances it was not just the mass media that was encouraged to rethink old orthodoxies. By itself 'rave culture' was said to have 'revitalised the sociological literature on youth culture' and to have 'provoked a revisionist view of its history challenging the hegemony of the key writers of previous decades' (Shapiro, 1999: 18). In posing this challenge, several commentator posited a link with post-modernity, which they argued demanded a new set of understandings (Redhead, 1993; Parker et al., 1995; Smith and Maughan, 1998). Most notably, perhaps, academics and researchers at the University of Manchester began to develop the claim that drug use was undergoing a process of normalisation that could not be understood using established perspectives and required a new explanatory framework (Parker et al., 1998).

## Thinking about social change

Recent developments in criminology provide a useful starting point for thinking about the position illicit drug use has come to occupy in late industrial societies. *The Culture of Control* by David Garland (2001) is particularly useful in this regard because it provides a template for considering broader processes of social change and their impact on crime. Garland's primary focus is on the historical conditions that gave rise to the punitive turn in crime control and criminal justice in Britain and the United States during the latter part of the twentieth century. His analysis draws attention to important similarities in the recent experiences of these two countries, which he attributes to broader processes of social and cultural change. For want of a better term, Garland refers to these changes as the coming of 'late modernity', which is shorthand for 'late-twentieth century modernity' – an unwieldy phrase that 'indicates an historical phase of the modernization process without suggesting we are coming to the end, or even to the high point, of a centuries old dynamic that shows no signs of letting up' (2001: 77).[1] Such terminology is not meant to imply homogeneity or uniformity across national boundaries. Garland readily acknowledges the importance of national differences, but maintains Britain and the United Sates share strong similarities, which are evidence of underlying patterns of structural transformation. This, in turn, leads him to suppose that many of the associated problems and insecurities facing these nations are, or soon will be, familiar to other late modern societies.

What Garland describes as the 'crime complex' of late modernity is considered, in part at least, to be a response to massive increases in crime. This aspect of the analysis is particularly useful for our purposes because it offers an important reminder that increases in drug use were part of a more general upsurge in criminal activity and because it begins to sketch out the likely parameters of an explanation. According to Garland late modernity has been accompanied by a rapid and sustained increase in recorded crime – not just in Britain and the United States, but in every Western industrialised nation; a trend he describes as a 'massive and incontestable social fact', albeit one that has levelled of in many countries (2001: 90). A heightened susceptibility to crime is not, in Garland's view, an inevitable or inexorable feature of late modern life, but the initial impact of this reconfiguration did serve to make crime much more likely. The particularly high crime rates that were recorded in the 1960s and 1970s were said to be an emergent property of the converging social and psychological changes of the post-war period – 'an unplanned but altogether predictable product of the interaction of these elements' (2001: 90).

The impact of late modernity has, in Garland's view, been a multidimensional one involving increased opportunities for crime, reduced situational controls, an increase in the population 'at risk' and a reduction in the efficacy of social and internal controls. With the consumer boom of the post-war decades, a mass of portable, high-value goods entered the market, generating much greater opportunities for acquisitive crime. At the same time, situational controls began to weaken as shops became increasingly 'self-service' and as densely populated neighbourhoods gave way to more dispersed and/or anonymous forms of living. Added to this, the 1960s witnessed the arrival of a large cohort of teenage males – the demographic group most prone to criminal behaviour – who were more affluent than their predecessors and spent longer outside the disciplines of family and full-time work. As a result of this new found freedom, young people began to enjoy greater access to leisure, particularly in subcultural settings such as clubs, cafes, discos, and street corners. With the emergence of a 'universalistic commercial culture', moreover, the 'baby-boom generation' grew up with a whole new level of desires, expectations and demands for instant gratification.

Finally, Garland identifies the relaxation of informal social controls as a key ingredient in the crime-boom of late modernity. At the very time that society was becoming more heavily laden with criminal temptations and opportunities, social space became more stretched out, more anonymous and less well supervised. This was compounded by the simultaneous questioning of traditional authorities, part of what Ralph Miliband (1978) referred to as 'desubordination', a relaxation of the norms governing conduct in the realm of sexuality and drug use and the spread of a more 'permissive', 'expressive' style of child-rearing. The net result was that (2001: 91):

> For some sections of the population, especially the emerging voices of the new youth culture, 'deviance' came to be a badge of freedom, and 'conformity' a sign of dull, normalised repression. The old categories of 'crime' and 'delinquency' became less obvious in their behavioural reference and less absolute in their moral force.

## The particular and the general

For studies such as this there are inevitable tensions between broad generalisation and the specification of empirical particularities. Some authors, including Garland (2001: vii), have sought to resolve these tensions by operating at a high level of abstraction in the belief that doing so will enable them to identify 'the broad organising principles' that are at work, but such an approach has obvious costs, including excessive simplification, false generalisation and a neglect of variation. My inclination is to lean much more heavily towards the specification of empirical particularities, though this – as we shall see – brings its own problems, which tend to invert those of more abstract approaches.

### Monitoring and analysing drug use

The analysis presented in this book is based largely on two surveys – the 1998 British Crime Survey (BCS) and 1998/9 Youth Lifestyles Survey (YLS), both of which contain detailed information about self-reported drug use.[2] The self-report methodology is the most reliable source of information about drug use currently available and was pioneered in the United States, where it has been used to monitor prevalence rates within the general household population and the high school population since the early-and-mid 1970s respectively (SAMHSA, 2007; Johnston et al., 2007). Self-report surveys have obvious advantages over other sources of information, including criminal justice records and treatment records, but the focus on illegal and stigmatised activities brings difficulties and limitations of its own. Above and beyond the standard difficulties of sampling bias and measurement error, respondents may be reluctant to disclose sensitive information about potentially embarrassing or self-incriminating behaviour or may choose to exaggerate the level of their involvement. Various techniques have been used to assess the extent of misreporting, including comparisons with biological tests based on hair and urine analysis, repeat surveys and the inclusion of non-existent 'dummy' drugs (Harrison, 1997). On the whole these techniques indicate that the self-report methodology offers a reasonably accurate measure of drug use in the general population (early studies routinely produced validity rates of between 70 per cent and 90 per cent), albeit one that tends to underestimate the extent of such use.

Respondent's willingness to disclose illicit drug use is known to vary according to the nature of the drug use, the survey and the setting (Harrison, 1997). The self-report methodology appears to be least reliable in criminal justice settings which is, perhaps, unsurprising given there are clear disincentives to honest reporting in such an environment. Among individuals in treatment, self-reports have been found to be more reliable at intake than follow-up, possibly because respondents do not want to disappoint the service or risk being excluded from future treatment. As a general rule the validity of self-report measures is increased by modes of administration that encourage a sense of privacy and confidentiality: self-administered questionnaires produce higher prevalence rates – and ostensibly more valid data – than interviews where the respondent has to say their answer out loud and computer assisted interviews, which allow respondents to provide answers via a keyboard, yield higher prevalence rates than pencil-and-paper surveys (see also Flood-Page et al., 2000). Rates of disclosure also conform to the social desirability hypothesis, so that respondents are generally more willing to disclose less stigmatised forms of use and that which occurred in the past. Estimates of problematic drug use are further compromised by the tendency to rely on general household surveys.[3] Chaotic habitual users are almost certainly under-represented in such surveys because they are more likely than most to be homeless, in prison or living in residential institutions and are probably less inclined to respond even when they are included in the sample (Ramsay and Partridge, 1999;

Police Foundation, 2000). In short, the self-report methodology is most valid when used to measure recreational drug use within the general population and when administered in ways that promote privacy and confidentiality.

It is only fairly recently that the self-report methodology has been applied in Britain on anything like a systematic basis. The first British survey to include detailed questions about drug use was conducted in 1969 by the Office of Population Censuses and Surveys on behalf of the Home Office (Marks et al., 1973; see also Police Foundation, 2000), but proved to be an isolated exercise. Few such surveys were conducted in the two decades that followed and those that were carried out invariably involved small localised samples. Under these circumstances assessing drug use was said to be 'more like piecing together a jigsaw with most of the pieces missing (and the rest fitting poorly or not at all) than an exercise in statistics' (ISDD, 1993: 6). After years of relative inactivity, the early 1990s witnessed an 'explosion' of drugs surveys and the Home Office began to seriously investigate the possibility of establishing a national monitoring system (Ramsay and Percy, 1996: 3). The feasibility of the self-report methodology was confirmed by the 1992 BCS and 1992 YLS, though doubts were raised about the validity of the pencil-and-paper methods on which these surveys were based. With the subsequent introduction of computer assisted interviewing techniques 'the credibility of the self-report methodology for measuring drug use within the general population of this country' was said to have been 'established beyond doubt' (Ramsay and Percy, 1996: viii). Since 1994 the BCS has used a standardised approach to measure self-reported drug use, initially on a bi-annual basis and then annually since 2000. As such, it provides the main basis on which the government monitors the extent of the 'drug problem' and the effectiveness of the national drugs strategy (Ramsay and Percy, 1996; Ramsay et al., 2001).

The BCS and YLS provide a sound basis for analysis. Both are representative of the general household population of England and Wales and have been administered by specialist research companies according to the highest standards of quantitative social research: the samples are large, the sampling techniques sophisticated and the response rates highly respectable (Hales and Stratford, 1999; Stratford and Roth, 1999). In drawing on these surveys my intention is to look beyond general prevalence rates to explore the social origins of drug use and my main focus is on young adults, defined as those aged 16 to 30 years, as they are the most active users of illicit drugs (and also represent the overlap between the two surveys).

The analysis divided into three distinct phases. At the outset it was necessary to develop an empirically grounded social classification of drug use. This classification was then used to examine variations in use, with particular attention being paid to the influence of demographic characteristics, experiences of deprivation, key life-course events and broader lifestyle orientations. Bivariate techniques were initially used to examine how prevalence rates vary between groups and multivariate procedures were then used to identify which variables are most important in predicting the various types of drug use under consideration. Cannabis, the hallucinants[4] and cocaine were considered separately, while substances such as heroin and methadone were excluded from the detailed analysis on the grounds that they are rarely used by young adults and are therefore tangential to the main aim of the study. For each category of drug use considered distinctions were drawn between recent use (in the last 12-months), past use (not in the last 12-months) and abstinence (never used). Further details about the multivariate procedures, including summaries of the final models, are included in the Technical Appendix.

## The significance of the study

From a strictly technical perspective the analysis may be viewed as an attempt to reconstruct the way things were at a particular time and place, but this is only part of what the study aims to achieve. When the focus is on the specification of empirical particularities, the central problem is one of significance – 'what', in the end, does the analysis tell us about 'the world in which we live?' (Garland, 2001: vii). With this in mind the survey analysis has been used as a platform for thinking more generally about the position that illicit drug use has come to occupy in late industrial societies. As such, the detailed findings are framed within a narrative that has been shaped by my broader historical and theoretical concerns. From this perspective the analysis may be viewed as a case study, which aims to establish what it is about late industrial societies that has given rise to widespread illicit drug use. If Britain is considered illustrative of such societies then much of what follows is likely to be more 'general than particular' with regard to time and place (Laub and Sampson, 2003: 283).

The surveys were well suited to these broader aims, not least because they were conducted at a key point in the development of one of western Europe's most active drug markets. While Britain in the late 1980s and early 1990s witnessed the emergence of increasing, and increasingly diverse forms of, youthful drug use, the period that has followed has largely been one of consolidation, with some evidence of decline (ISDD, 1994; Ramsay and Partridge, 1999; Murphy and Roe, 2007). Overall rates of drug use reached a plateau during the late 1990s, with prevalence rates for most substances levelling off or falling during the ten years or so that have followed (see Table 1.1). Cocaine has proved something of an exception in that its use has continued to rise, but this increase has been off-set by a corresponding decline in amphetamine use: while cocaine use has doubled, amphetamine use has halved, suggesting a shift in taste rather than something more fundamental. Given the general stability of recent trends, the 1998 BCS and 1998/9 YLS provide a reasonable basis for thinking about the position illicit drug use has come to occupy and for assessing the various claims that have been made in this regard.

The rise of illicit drug use across much of the late industrial world has been fuelled by a series of global trends, including the proliferation of the 'ganja complex' (Hamid, 2002), the rise of dance drugs (Hunt and Evans, 2003) and the growing popularity of cocaine (EMCDDA, 2007). With some of the highest rates of drug use in Europe, Britain has been at the forefront of these trends, but is only one of a number of countries to have been so effected (Bauman and Phongsavan, 1999).

**Table 1.1 Recent trends in drug use (percentage of young adults who had used drugs in the last 12 months)**

| | *1994* | *1998* | *2002/3* | *2006/7* |
|---|---|---|---|---|
| Cannabis | 19.8* | 21.9 | 22.8 | 17.6** |
| Amphetamines | 6.4 | 7.6 | 3.3** | 3.0** |
| Ecstasy | 2.8* | 3.7 | 4.9* | 4.4 |
| LSD | 3.6** | 2.0 | 0.7** | 0.6** |
| Magic mushrooms | 2.5 | 2.3 | 1.6* | 1.6* |
| Amyl nitrates | 4.0 | 3.5 | 3.3 | 3.4 |
| Cocaine | 1.1** | 2.8 | 4.7** | 5.9** |
| Glues, solvents, gas or aerosols | 0.6 | 0.6 | 0.3* | 0.6 |
| Crack | 0 | 0.2 | 0.4* | 0.4* |
| Heroin | 0.4 | 0.2 | 0.3 | 0.2 |
| Methadone | 0.3 | 0.3 | 0.2 | 0.1 |
| Any of the above | 21.7* | 24.1 | 24.7 | 19.9** |
| *n* | *3,061* | *2,812* | 5,754 | *7,101* |

*Source*: BCS ** $p < 0.01$ * $p < 0.05$
*Note*: significance tests were used to compare prevalence rates for each of the given years to those that were evident in 1998.

Broadly comparable rates of drug use can be found, for some substances at least, in neighbouring west European countries, such as France, Germany, Italy and Spain, as well as further afield in the United States, Canada, Australia and New Zealand (Vega et al., 2002; United Nations, 2008). Recent British trends are, in addition, illustrative of what has been happening more generally: global drugs consumption has stabilised following a period of sustained growth; rates of cannabis use have levelled off throughout Europe; and cocaine use has increased to the point that it is now the second most widely used illicit drug in the region.

None of this is meant to imply that national differences are unimportant, nor that increasing rates of drug use are an inevitable or inexorable feature of late industrial societies. Some such societies, including Sweden and Japan, have very low rates of drug use, while others differ in their levels and patterns of use: cannabis use is more prevalent in the United States, Canada, Australia and New Zealand than in most European countries; ecstasy use tends to be more prevalent in Britain than elsewhere; and cocaine is used more widely in north America than most other parts of the world (EMCDDA, 2008; United Nations, 2008). These variations are neither fixed nor immutable, however, and there is recent evidence of convergence, with increases in cocaine use in Europe coinciding with increases in ecstasy use in the United States (Hunt and Evans, 2003). Finally, although the general trend has been towards increasing rates of drug use, countries on both sides of the Atlantic have experienced relatively recent periods when prevalence rates have fallen (Silbereisen et al., 1995; Johnston et al., 2007).

The particularities of time and place remain important, but should not blind us to the broader significance of the analysis that follows. The greater use and acceptance of illicit drugs has been described as 'one of the most profound transformations to take place within British youth culture since 1945' (Osgerby, 1998: 179) and the same might be said in relation to many other countries, especially those in western Europe and north America. On this basis Britain may be considered to approximate to Yin's (2003) representative or typical case, where the lessons learned are assumed to be informative about experiences elsewhere. Although we must remain alive to the dangers of overgeneralisation my contention is that the analysis presented here goes some way towards identifying what it is about late industrial societies more generally that has facilitated the rise of illicit drug use over the last half a century or so. Ultimately, of course, this is an empirical claim which may be confirmed or refuted on the basis of further studies.

## Structure of the book

The main body of the book is divided into five chapters, the first of which provides a chronological summary of what are taken to be the main developments in the sociology of drug use. This summary sets the context for the empirical analysis that follows and begins to address some of the book's main analytical themes. In particular it identifies some striking, and largely unacknowledged, parallels between recent work and earlier developments in the field. Chapter 3 presents an empirically-based, social classification of drug use, which, as well as providing the basis for the rest of the analysis, addresses some important substantive issues. Among other things this chapter compares social and medical classifications and explores why young adults use the substances they do, suggesting that the desire to avoid harm and risk are central to their decisions, while legal considerations appear to be less significant.

Chapters 4 to 6 concentrate on the social distribution of drug use, assessing the role of demographic characteristics, lifestyle indicators and life-course influences respectively. The first of these chapters endorses the notion of the 'normalised' drug user in the sense that apparently conventional young adults from privileged backgrounds are shown to be well represented among those who use illicit drugs, but questions whether there is anything particularly novel about this profile. Contrary to recent claims regarding the normative nature of drug use, moreover, significant differences are reported on the basis of sex, ethnicity, religiosity, unemployment and marginalisation from the labour market. The main finding in Chapter 5 is that illicit drug use typically occurs in the context of a distinctly hedonistic leisure style, involving a particular commitment to consumption and intoxication. Such a style, it is suggested, represents a form of subterranean play, which is a response to the central life problems of work, identity and leisure that are characteristic of late industrial societies, and have been since the 1960s. Picking up the thread, Chapter 6 demonstrates that illicit drug use, and other associated lifestyle choices, remain closely related to the ambivalent position of youth. Drawing on recent developments in life-course criminology, the analysis suggests that young adults continue to 'grow out' of drug use, but do so in ways that reflect the changing nature of youth transitions.

Chapter 7 draws the book to a close by focusing on the central theme of continuity within change and teasing out its broader implications. The basis of this theme is provided by the observation that, in Britain and across much of the late industrial world, illicit drug use has increased massively, but has done so over an extended historical period, dating back half a century or so. While the proliferation of drug use, like the upsurge in crime more generally, has been facilitated, and made possible, by broader processes of social change, there are, nonetheless, significant continuities at work here, which are rooted in enduring patterns of organisation. Rather than seeking to develop new perspectives, the theme of continuity within change suggests that the sociology of drug use would be better served by building on the insights provided by earlier work and this means reconnecting with its criminological past. Nowhere are these insights more apposite than in relation to policy. The central problems of drug control are, after all, not so different from those that were evident at the time *The Drugtakers* was published; and nor are the solutions.

# 2
# The Sociology of Drug Use

> ...if ever there was a time when the answers [to the many questions about the past, present and future place of drugs in our society and culture] were straightforward, it is surely not today...Drug use may still represent a route to 'unreality' and a means to slip away from the constraints of routine, but today, in many more different ways for many more different people, drug use is *actually a part* of the 'paramount reality' of everyday life (South, 1999: 1 and 4, original emphasis).

Something like a coherent sociology of drug use began to emerge during the 1960s. This body of work was closely related to broader developments in criminology and was largely formulated under the umbrella of the 'new' deviancy theories, which helped to inspire such seminal contributions as Howard Becker's (1963) *Becoming a Marihuana User* and Jock Young's (1971) *The Drugtakers*. Criminological preoccupations soon shifted, however, and with them interest in the sociology of drug use faded. Remarkably little work was carried out in this field during the next couple of decades and it is only fairly recently that sociologists have begun to make up for their previous lack of engagement. Unsurprisingly, perhaps, given the marked increases in drug use that occurred during the intervening period, much recent commentary has emphasised the extent of change and the need for new forms of understandings. In responding to this apparent need the sociology of drug use has fallen prey to a form of chronocentricism, whereby disciplines forget their past and get caught up in a recurring cycle of new beginnings (Rock, 2005). Nowhere is this more evident than in the critique of deficit based perspectives, which attribute drug use to individual pathology and/or social dysfunction. Recent studies have made much of rejecting such perspectives, but, in so doing, have repeated many of the themes that were central to earlier work.

This chapter begins by reviewing the origins and main tenets of the 'new' deviancy theories, before going on to consider their implications for the sociology of drug use. From here the focus shifts onto more recent developments, with particular attention being paid to the new orthodoxy and its critique.

## The 'new' deviancy theories

Early developments in the sociology of drug use were closely linked to the fluctuating fortunes of the 'new' deviancy theories. These theories came to prominence during the 1960s, but only enjoyed a relatively short period of ascendancy, the end of which represented a watershed in the development of both the sociology of drug use and criminology more generally. By the mid-1970s criminology had been reshaped by neo-Marxist perspectives which were primarily concerned with links between capitalism and crime. Expressive deviance was considered peripheral to such weighty concerns and subjects such as drug use and sexual deviance received little criminological attention. With this development the sociology of drug use pretty much fell into abeyance and was not revived on any significant scale until some 20 years later.

The 'new' deviancy theories were very much a product of their time, sharing in the general spirit of protest and rebellion that characterised the 1960s. Emerging against a background of Civil Rights activism, anti-war demonstrations, student sit-ins and the rise of modern feminism, they presented a serious and sustained challenge to the 'correctionalist' orientation of mainstream criminology (Matza, 1969). 'New' deviancy theorists rejected their allocated role as assistants in the quest to free society from 'troublesome activities' and dismissed the idea that there was a distinct, unambiguously deviant, minority whose behaviour could be explained as a result of individual pathology or social dysfunction. Instead, they advocated an 'appreciative' stance that was committed to faithful representation and to understanding the world as it was seen by the subject. From this perspective, much of what had previously been taken for granted became contested and many of the old certainties began to fall away: deviance was considered to be meaningful behaviour involving choice; rule breaking was viewed as commonplace rather than exceptional; and the continuity between normality and deviance was emphasised (Plummer, 1979).

The 'new' deviancy theories had what Heidensohn (1989: 67) calls 'a pantheon of respectable and ancient founding fathers', including Karl Marx, George Herbert Mead and Alfred Schutz. As a leading exponent of symbolic interactionism, Mead laid the foundations for the social anthropology of deviance, which came to prominence during the early part of the twentieth century under the auspices of the Chicago School and provided the basis for what came to be known as the appreciative stance (Downes and Rock, 2007; Sumner, 1994). Crucially, the Chicago sociologists rejected the widely accepted notion that delinquency was the result of individual pathology, arguing instead that it was a functional response to deprivation and to the experience of growing up in the city. For those living in the 'zone of transition' in particular, deviance was said to provide a surrogate order, replacing the workings of conventional institutions. The Chicago School's legacy owed much to the work of Edwin Sutherland, a one time student at the University, who went on to develop the theory of differential association. According to Sutherland (1939), deviance is a way of life that is passed from generation to generation and is based on norms learned within a delinquent or criminal subculture. While maintaining that deviance emerges out of mundane social settings, he also emphasised that meaning and motive are central to the formation of deviant projects.

The apparently pathological nature of crime was further challenged by the American sociology of deviation which came to fruition in the late 1930s. While the Chicago sociologists shifted the focus away from individual pathology to social disorganisation, the likes of Frank Tannenbaum and Edwin Lemert went further and challenged the idea that crime was the result of social deficits. In so doing, they began to map out the territory that would later be explored by 'new' deviancy theorists. In *Crime and the Community*, Tannenbaum (1938) rejected the common characterisation of the criminal and the community as the embodiments of 'good' and 'evil', arguing that deviation grew out of everyday conflicts of interest and that crime was generated by the values of the community and its methods of social control. Pointing to a variety of criminogenic influences in American society, including a history of endemic conflict, rapid social change and the exaltation of 'pioneer' values such as individualism, competition and acquisitiveness, he argued that the law had come to be experienced as a foreign, external imposition and that distinctions between the legitimate and the criminal had become decidedly blurred. It was, after all, the community that provided criminals with their ideas, purpose and methods – 'whether these be graft, political pull, or the use of the machine gun'

(1938: 25). To make matters worse, attempts at social control – or what Tannenbaum called the 'dramatization of evil' – were deemed counterproductive: 'The young delinquent becomes bad because he is defined as bad and because he is not believed if he is good' (1938: 19).

These themes were subsequently developed by Edwin Lemert (1948, 1951). Emphasising the ubiquity of deviance and the proximity of 'respectable citizens' to criminal activity, Lemert challenged the legitimacy of distinctions between 'normal' and 'abnormal' human behaviour and between 'normal' and 'pathological' personalities. While acknowledging that some rule breaking might be a symptom of 'intrapsychic' conflicts, he argued that deviance was primarily generated by social situations, particularly those involving cultural conflict. In highlighting the importance of social reaction, Lemert famously distinguished between 'primary' and 'secondary' deviance. Primary deviance is ubiquitous and managed within a socially acceptable identity, while secondary deviance is internalised and becomes part of the core definition of the self. Interaction with significant others is central here. On the one hand, it may lead to the normalisation or acceptance of the deviation as peripheral to identity, but, on the other, may stimulate a symbolic reorganisation of the self so that the deviance becomes systematic and significant: 'When a person begins to employ his deviant behavior or a role based upon it as a means of defence, attack or adjustment to the overt and covert problems created by the consequent societal reaction to him, his deviation is secondary' (1951: 76). This analysis had important implications for social control. Arguing that psychiatry was irrelevant or even dangerous to a scientific account of the origin and organisation of most deviations, Lemert concluded that reform movements, along with public reactions, 'may create more problems than they solve' (1951: 4).

The ideas developed by Tannenbaum and Lemert received relatively little attention until David Matza and Howard Becker helped propel them into the mainstream of American sociology. Matza has been credited with providing 'the most developed all-round position possible within the framework of interactionist or phenomenological sociology of deviance' (Sumner, 1994: 241). In his early work, with Gresham Sykes, he criticised the dominant theories of the time for creating the misleading impression that delinquents and wider society exist in an antagonistic relationship with one another. According to Matza and Sykes (1961) delinquents commonly support the same set of norms and values as everybody else and are attracted to delinquency, not because of a deeply held oppositional morality, but because of an exaggerated adherence to widely held 'subterranean' values such as the pursuit of adventure, excitement and thrills. In developing these arguments Matza (1964, 1969) distanced his analysis from subcultural strain theory, which he criticised for being overly deterministic and for over-predicting rates of delinquency. For Matza (1964: 28) delinquency could be characterised as a gradual process of 'drift':

> The delinquent is neither compelled nor committed to deeds nor freely choosing them; neither different in any simple or fundamental sense from the law abiding, nor the same...He is committed to neither delinquent nor conventional enterprise...the delinquent transiently exists in a limbo between convention and crime, responding in turn to demands of each, flirting now with one, now with the other, but postponing commitment, evading decision. Thus he drifts between criminal and conventional action.

The break from strain theory was critical, but nonetheless partial and elements of this approach were retained. Noting that drift may be facilitated by the 'subculture of delinquency', Matza described how failure in the status system of the wider society and feelings of powerlessness may create a mood of fatalism whereby the delinquent is rendered 'irresponsible' and is released to drift in and out of delinquency. That said, he was careful to avoid the determinism of existing approaches and his emphasis on free will, drift and the similarity of delinquents and non-delinquents 'swamped the neat boundaries between this subculture and that which were the hallmark of existing approaches' (Downes and Rock, 2007: 124). While the 'subculture of delinquency' allowed delinquency, moreover, it did not demand it and this sense of ambiguity reflected the role of 'techniques of neutralization' which enabled individuals to violate norms without surrendering allegiance to them. Arguing that deviation requires a mastery of guilt, Sykes Matza and (1957) identified five neutralisation techniques: denial of responsibility, 'it was an accident'; denial of injury, 'no one got hurt'; denial of the victim, 'he was asking for it'; condemning the condemners, 'the police are just as bad'; and appeal to higher loyalties, 'I did it for my mate'. Through the application of these techniques, apparently deviant acts could be rationalised (1957: 668): 'In this sense, the delinquent both has his cake and eats it too, for he remains committed to the dominant normative system and yet so qualifies its imperatives that violations are "acceptable" if not "right"'.

The importance of Matza's work lay partly in its ability to explain aspects of delinquency which defied existing theories. While the emphasis on free-will and drift helped to explain the typically 'mundane' and episodic nature of delinquency, the proposed proximity of the delinquent's values to those of conventional society helped to account for the relative ease with which many individuals mature out of delinquency as they move into adulthood, start to work and have families of their own.

Alongside Matza's work, the labelling perspective raised a number of problems and suggested a few themes that linked together all the main 'new' deviancy enterprises of the 1960s (Plummer, 1979). The labelling perspective did not constitute an explanation or theory of deviance so much as provide a series of sensitising concepts. Labelling theorists were less concerned with addressing the 'causes' of delinquency than with identifying the ways in which social reaction influences deviant phenomena. Howard Becker was hugely influential in the development of this perspective and, in *Outsiders*, produced one of the most widely cited American criminological writings of the time. In Becker's (1963) view the process by which things are defined as deviant is a 'moral enterprise', reflecting the economic, political and organisational needs of 'moral entrepreneurs'. Most famously, he declared (1963: 9):

> *Social groups create deviance by making the rules whose infraction constitutes deviance*, and by applying those rules to particular people and labelling them as outsiders. From this point of view, deviance is *not* a quality of the act the person commits, but rather a consequence of the application by others of rules and sanctions to an 'offender'. The deviant is one to whom that label has successfully been applied; deviant behaviour is behaviour that people so label [original emphasis].

By approaching social reaction as a variable rather than a constant the labelling perspective broke with mainstream criminology. Labelling theorists noted that an audience often reacts to apparently deviant acts in a way which normalises them or accommodates them into the fabric of accepted life and that gross reaction tends to occur only where such acts are deemed inexplicable, disorganised or threatening. Proclamation of a deviant label was considered to be a key moment in this process, for 'when rule-breaking receives a reply from the outside world it must be defended, ended or disguised' (Downes and Rock, 2007: 164). While public labelling may discourage future deviance, as rule breakers feel shame and fear, labelling theorists also highlighted the risk of amplification. Being labelled deviant, they argued, may stimulate a symbolic reorganisation of the self around the deviant label and create problems which the individual resolves by retreating into 'errant subworlds', populated by those who are similarly beset, and which offer 'modest refuge' from a 'hostile discouraging world' (Downes and Rock, 2007: 163). Such insights were not entirely novel, but brought about 'the most fundamental reorientation of the field' because they 'expressed, with exemplary elegance, the sterility of analysing deviance and control as two utterly distinct topics' (Downes, 1988: 181).

Although the 'new' deviancy theories emerged as a very American phenomenon their effects were strongly felt in Britain. The expansion of British criminology during the 1960s saw the emergence of a new generation of academics who, inspired by the American sociology of deviance, challenged the administrative and correctionalist orientation of the discipline (Downes, 1988). The creation of the National Deviancy Symposium in 1968, known subsequently as the National Deviancy Conference, led to the development of the 'sceptical approach to deviance', which drew heavily on the work of Becker and Matza, but was more overtly political and stretched the 'meaning and viability of the radical conception of deviance to its absolute limit' (Sumner, 1994: 262; see also Cohen, 1971).

Most significantly, perhaps, the sceptical approach to deviance generated a much more collective version of deviancy amplification theory than had previously been offered. Leslie Wilkins (1964), a British social statistician, planted the seeds for this development just as the labelling perspective was coming to prominence in the United States. According to Wilkins, deviants tend to become structurally isolated, with the result that information about them is relayed back to the majority over distance and is subject to distortion. This was said to promote inappropriate reactions in wider society, which combine with the response of the deviant minority to create 'spirals of deviancy' that amplify minor indiscretions. Wilkins' model fitted neatly with the 'new' deviancy project and heavily influenced the main architects of the sceptical approach to deviance, such as Jock Young (1971) and Stanley Cohen (1972).

## The 'new' deviancy theories and the sociology of drug use

The rise of 'new' deviancy theories was accompanied by growing interest in the sociology of drug use and the proximity of these developments reflected an underlying compatibility. 'New' deviancy theorists frequently expressed unease about the extension of social control into morally ambiguous areas and tended to focus on examples of rule breaking that were designed to elicit a liberal response (Cohen, 1971). As a 'victimless crime' illicit drug use provided an ideal vehicle for such concerns, while the 'new' deviancy theories were, in turn, particularly well suited to the study of drug use. This symbiosis was evident from the way in which 'new' deviancy theorists absorbed drug use into their general conceptual frameworks (see Matza and Sykes, 1961 and Cohen, 1971) and from the substantial contribution that some made to the emerging sociology of drug use.

Reflecting his experiences as a jazz musician and activist in the campaign to legalise marihuana, Howard Becker (1963; see also 1955) devoted two chapters of *Outsiders* to the moral career of the marihuana user.[1] Both chapters were based on interviews conducted during the early 1950s with 50 users, half of whom were professional musicians. Becker rejected the idea that marihuana use could be explained in terms of psychological traits and developed the hypothesis that users learn to view it as something that can give them pleasure. Focusing initially on the process by which people become marihuana users, he argued that (1963: 58):

> ...an individual will be able to use marihuana for pleasure only when he goes through a process of learning to conceive of it as an object which can be used in this way. No one becomes a user without (1) learning to smoke the drug in a way which will produce real effects; (2) learning to recognize the effects and connect them with the drug use (learning, in other words, to get high); and (3) learning to enjoy the sensations he perceives.

Turning conventional wisdom on its head, Becker maintained that deviant motivations grow out of deviant behaviour: as an individual learns to use marihuana, vague impulses and desires are transformed into a certain motivation which could not have been present earlier because it depends on actual experience. The second chapter of the *Outsiders* to focus on marihuana considered what happens once an individual has learnt to use the drug and identifies three stages of use represented by the beginner, the occasional user and the regular user. Each stage was said to mark a distinct shift in the individual's relationships with the larger society and the subculture within which marihuana is used. In order to continue or increase their use of marihuana, Becker argued, individuals must contend with powerful forces of social control which seek to limit access to the drug, ensure that its use must remain hidden from non-users and define its use as immoral. Participation in the user group helps to disable these attempts at control in the following ways, though it should be noted that the membership of such a group was deemed to make marihuana use possible rather than necessary:

1. A source of supply becomes available through participation in a group in which marihuana is used, 'ordinarily a group organized around values and activities opposing those of the larger conventional society' (1963: 62). As well as offering opportunities for initial and occasional use, participation in such a group provides the basis for regular use as it offers access to a steady source of supply.
2. Through participation with other users and experiences with the drug, users realise they can keep their use secret with relative ease and thus control based on the fear of discovery is undermined. While occasional use is scheduled around situations free of non-users, regular use is not limited in this way, but rests on a confidence that marihuana can be used 'under the noses' of non-users without them knowing or is used as part of a lifestyle in which contact with non-users is minimised.
3. Participation in user groups also offers ways of circumventing conventional moral controls as it provides access to a whole series of rationalisations and justifications – 'conventional society allows much more harmful practices such as the use of alcohol', 'the drug is beneficial not harmful' and 'its use can be controlled'. By acquiring the view that conventional moral notions about drugs do not apply to a specific drug, users may reorganise their moral notions so as to permit its use.

Becker's work was crucial in setting the tone for much of what followed. His focus on subcultural perspectives was developed by Harold Finestone whose essay 'Cats, kicks and colour' has been described as being 'much more important, substantive and prophetic' than Becker's work on marihuana use (Sumner, 1994: 193). Finestone (1964) studied the world of Chicago's young black heroin users and described a section of African American culture which posited 'cool' and 'kicks' as an adjustment to segregation and discrimination. Out of the frustration and rage experienced by the 'sacrificed generation', the 'cat' emerged as the personification of an expressive social movement which rejected the values of the dominant culture and developed a sense of superiority over the 'square' world. Adopting an aesthetic of sharp clothes and cool jazz, the 'cat' chose to live by the 'hustle' rather than work: heroin offered him (the 'cat' was invariably described as being male) the ultimate 'kick' as it provided a vehicle through which he could place himself beyond the comprehension of the 'square'.

Other commentators went on to develop Becker's interest in social control and it was here that the sociology of drug use coincided most strongly with the 'new' deviancy theories. Edwin Schur (1965) argued that for 'crimes without victims', such as homosexuality, prostitution, abortion and drugtaking, laws were bound to meet with very limited success. A claim which was echoed by Troy Duster (1970: 244):

> Drug use is engaged in privately, not publicly, and there is no party to the act who has an interest in being the plaintiff. For these reasons the law will not be effective in bringing about a change in behaviour or morality of the law violators. Thus, millions of dollars are spent in a fruitless attempt to stamp out the problem, that could better be used upon some constructive programme. At the very least, the negative gain would involve the elimination of the pursuit of an impossible task.

Duster described how, in America, moral outrage against drug use was applied selectively against socially vulnerable groups: while the middle-class white addict was regarded as a medical problem, the lower-class black addict was viewed as an object of extreme hostility. Schur (1963, 1969), meanwhile, was particularly concerned with the way in which American drugs policy created illicit heroin markets, arguing that prohibition had secured a kind of monopoly for suppliers who were prepared to break the law. By generating high prices illicit markets were said to have almost completely driven heroin users out of 'respectable' society, pushing them into a subculture of crime and addiction: 'By defining him as a criminal, we have pushed the addict in the direction of becoming one' (1969: 213). Like Alfred Lindesmith (1965), Schur favoured the 'British System' which treated addiction as a sickness and supplied heroin free of charge through legally designated channels. This medically oriented policy, he argued, helped to keep the situation within manageable limits as, in Britain, the number of heroin addicts was relatively small and there was virtually no illicit market in heroin and little or no associated crime. A similar perspective was offered by Wilkins (1965) who used his notion of deviancy amplification to explain differences in heroin use in Britain and the United States.

Building on the foundations provided by Becker and others, Jock Young (1971) formulated the most fully developed analysis of drug-taking from the 'new' deviancy perspective. In *The Drugtakers*, he was principally concerned with the 'social meaning of drug use' and set about challenging the 'absolutist monolith' which dominated contemporary thinking and which portrayed drug use as a disease found at the edges of society among the 'sick' and undersocialised. According to Young such a perspective exaggerated the importance of drugtaking to those involved and mistakenly sought to explain users' behaviour solely in terms of the pharmacology of the substances that they used. Far from being 'limited to the psychologically abnormal or perverse few', demand for psychotropic drugs (including alcohol and tobacco) was said to be 'part and parcel of our day-to-day social life', and 'as ingrained in the average respectable citizen as it is in the most way out hippie' (1971: 10). Adopting a relativist position, Young (1971: 50) rejected the idea that there is anything inherently deviant about drug use:

> To act in a certain way then can be simultaneously deviant and normal depending on whose standards you are applying. In this perspective, the smoking of marihuana may be normal behaviour amongst young people in Notting Hill and deviant to, say, the community of army officers who live in and around Camberley.

Because of its preoccupation with pharmacological effects and emphasis on the role of pathology, the absolutist monolith was said to divest drug use of any meaning. As an alternative, Young developed a subcultural perspective based on a socio-pharmacological approach, which explained 'drug-induced behaviour in terms of the interaction between the physiological effects of the drug and the norms of the group of which the drugtaker is a member'. Society, he argued, is made up of a large number of groups or subcultures offering solutions to the problems that are generated by the social position of their members. While different groups have different problems, drugs offer a common means of problem solving. Psychotropic or mood-altering substances are valued because they are pharmacologically suited to realising certain culturally defined aspirations: they may, for example, provide a source of relaxation and enjoyment or may help users forget their workday worries. A specific form of drug use starts because it is available and pharmacologically suited to a given problem, but, thereafter, its effects are restructured by the relevant subculture, so that: 'The meaning of drugtaking has to be sought in the context of the group's values and worldview' (1971: 124). Where a problem has no apparent solution individuals may start to use substances in a way which differs from that envisaged within their culture of origin. Crucially, however, any new solutions will be related to the culture of origin as the old provides a 'moral springboard' for the new.

While emphasising the importance of the group's values and worldview, Young noted that a broader focus is required if the phenomenon of drugtaking is to be explained. We must, he argued, look beyond the 'immediate origins' of such behaviour to identify its 'structural origins'. That is, we should relate the subculture to the 'total society' and seek to explain the 'immediate origins' of drugtaking in terms of broader social processes. In developing this analysis, Young (1971: 124) focused on the notion of subterranean values, arguing that 'drugtaking is almost ubiquitous in our society...it is only the type and quality of psychotropic drugs used which varies'. Alcohol, he argued, is commonly used to gain access to that area of subterranean values which is typically integrated into, and subsumed within, the cycle of productivity, while other drugs, in the hands of those who disdain the work ethic, provide a route to 'more radical accentuations of subterranean reality' (1971: 137).

Drawing heavily on the labelling perspective, Young placed social reaction at the centre of his theory of drugtaking. Modern industrial societies, he argued, are prone to deviancy amplification because they are highly segregated and specialised. The police, psychiatrists and other 'experts' mediate contact between the community and deviant groups, leaving 'normal' citizens with little direct contact with such groups and dependent on the mass media for information about them. This introduces an important source of misperception because the mass media is shaped by an institutionalised need to create moral panics. The media, along with 'moral crusaders', experts and law enforcement agencies play a leading role in initiating social reactions against drugtakers. Motivated by a mixture of self-interest, moral outrage and apparently 'humanitarian' impulses, these groups approach drug use from an absolutist perspective. Crucially, they either have little direct contact with drugtakers or have the type of contact that reinforces stereotypes. Consequently social reaction is 'phrased in terms of stereotyped fantasy rather than accurate empirical knowledge of the behavioural and attitudinal reality of their [deviant] lifestyles' (1971: 182). Accordingly, the fantasy stereotypes of the powerful have a self-fulfilling quality and may be translated into reality as a result of deviancy amplification. Amplification may occur as social reactions increase the problems faced by deviants (anomie induced), inspires a sense of gross social injustice among them (rebellion induced) or increase their isolation from 'normal' society, thereby freeing them to develop their own norms and values (isolation induced).

The final chapter of *The Drugtakers* is given over to policy considerations and, in effect, provides an early formulation of what we now know as harm reduction.[2] Young accepted that, in the final analysis, the most 'fundamental criterion of drug abuse is health risk', but argued this did not mean people should be forced to avoid actions which endanger their lives: 'I am', he noted, 'in complete agreement with J.S. Mill's dictum here. Namely that the only purpose for which power can be rightly exercised over any member of a civilized community against his will is to prevent harm to others. His own good, either physical or moral, is not sufficient warrant' (1971: 222). From here, Young went on to call for the restriction of legislation on the grounds that drugs law had proved damaging and unworkable. To legislate against victimless acts carried out privately and willingly, he argued, is fruitless and counter productive as it creates a black market, increases drug prices and adulteration and invites criminal involvement. While recognising that laws may be useful in protecting the consumer, Young emphasised that they cannot direct or stamp out consumer demand or illicit supply. In order to avoid a vast amount of unnecessary misery and hardship, he concluded, policy should concentrate on adjusting drug users' habits by suggesting alternative drugs or safer methods of use: 'We must learn to live with psychotropic drug use; it is only by treating citizens as responsible human beings that any sane and long-lasting control can be achieved' (1971: 222). Among the rules he laid down for a 'sane and just policy', Young included the following:

- *Maintain cultures*: subcultures which involve drug use often have a body of stipulations and controls which govern such behaviour and it is vital that drug use is enmeshed in a system of norms and controls if negative effects are to be avoided. To control the amount, type and administration of drugs requires sound knowledge accumulated over time and it is strongly dysfunctional to harass and undermine existing drug subcultures. In the cure of addiction or the treatment of bad trips, non-professional people from the respective subcultures are often more successful than medical professionals whose values are alien and knowledge sadly inapplicable.
- *Positive propaganda*: most information fed to the public about the nature and effects of drugs is inaccurate and this results in widespread scepticism. As young people learn from the experience of friends that the dangers of drug use are routinely exaggerated the credibility of much of the literature and of traditional authority figures is lost. Members of drug subcultures become cynical about

outside information. Given that law enforcement has failed to curb drug use authoritative facts about the effects of drugs should be fed into the drug subculture itself, for it is this subculture that has the only viable authority to control the activity of its members. Information aimed at controlling drug use must be phrased in terms of the values of the subculture, not in terms of the values of the outside world.

## From scepticism to normalisation

*The Drugtakers* represented the culmination of 'new' deviancy theories engagement with the sociology of drug use. Once these theories were displaced by more overtly political perspectives, criminological interest in illicit drug use began to fade. Such was the extent of this collective disengagement that the chapter on drugs in the first edition of the *Oxford Handbook of Criminology* began with a quote lamenting the dearth of sociological research in the area (South, 1994). Just a few years later, however, in the equivalent chapter for the second edition, it was noted that this 'deficiency has been greatly remedied in the intervening period' (South, 1997: 925). From the early 1990s a plethora of national and local surveys began to show that, in Britain, somewhere between a quarter and a half of young adults had used an illicit drug at some time in their life (ISDD, 1994). While cannabis was by far the most widely used illicit drug, these surveys also began to chart the influence of 'rave', which was evident in the increasing use of amphetamines, particularly ecstasy, and the return of the psychedelics, such as LSD. With widespread and increasingly diverse forms of drug use, numerous commentators began to emphasise the need for new perspectives (Ruggiero and South, 1995; Shapiro, 1999; South, 1997, 1999).

Such calls were developed most fully by Howard Parker, Fiona Measham and Judith Aldridge on the basis of the North West Cohort Study (Measham et al., 1994, 1998 and 2001; Parker et al., 1995, 1998 and 2002; Williams and Parker, 2001). These authors have been particularly critical of dominant psychological perspectives, which, they contend, have little to offer because they were developed at a time when drug use was atypical and tended to be limited to delinquent and disordered young people. Although their rejection of 'positivist psychology' and its preoccupation with 'risk factors' is reminiscent of the 'new' deviancy theories and related developments in the early sociology of drug use, Parker et al., pay very little attention to such work. Neither Howard Becker nor Jock Young are specifically mentioned in their review of sociological perspectives, although the general value of the appreciative stance is noted. Ultimately, established theories are said to struggle to function in the context of widespread recreational drug use, with the result that (Parker et al., 1998: 20–1):

> ...we have no tailor-made theoretical perspective to answer the *why* questions... The disciplines which would have been expected to explain such significant increases in adolescent drug use have simply been left behind by the pace of social and behavioural change. We thus face the daunting task of attempting to construct such an explanatory framework ourselves.

In their attempts to provide such a framework, Parker et al., went on to develop the claim that illicit drug use is undergoing a process of normalisation. Their position was stated in its most authoritative and straightforward form when they claimed: 'Over the next few years, and certainly in urban areas, non drug-trying adolescents will be a minority group. In one sense they will be the deviants...for many young people taking drugs has become the norm' (1995: 26). A revised and more cautious formula was provided subsequently based on the claim that (1998: 153):

> Normalisation in the context of recreational drug use cannot be reduced to the intuitive phrase 'it's normal for young people to take drugs'; that is both to oversimplify and overstate the case. We are concerned only with the spread of deviant activity and associated attitudes from the margins *towards* the centre of youth culture where it joins many other accommodated 'deviant' activities such as excessive drinking, casual sexual encounters and daily cigarette smoking...So normalisation need not be concerned with absolutes; we are not even considering the possibility that most young Britons will become illicit drug *users*. It is quite extraordinary enough that we have so quickly reached a situation where the majority will have tried an illicit drug by the end of their teens and that in many parts of the UK up to a quarter may be regular recreational users.

With this move the authors of the normalisation thesis became more circumspect about the breadth of the processes they described. At first normalisation was linked to the rise of ecstasy culture, with claims that drug taking 'appears to be starting at a very early age, and involves a wide range of drugs, *especially* dance drugs' (Measham et al., 1994: 310, original emphasis) and suggestions that the arrival of the 'rave' and 'pay party' scene in the late 1980s was 'the watershed whereby drugs moved from subcultural status to become part of mainstream youth culture' (Parker et al., 1995: 24). Subsequently, however, the thesis was said to refer primarily to the use of cannabis, nitrates and amphetamines and only 'equivocally' to LSD and ecstasy (Parker et al., 1998: 152). The previous emphasis on the 'normalization of recreational drug use' (Measham et al., 1994: 310) gave way to the 'normalization of "sensible" recreational drug use' as it was noted that stimulant-dance drugs are consumed sparingly and that the excesses of recreational poly-drug use, which are accepted in the partying – clubbing scene, 'are not as acceptable outside this semi-private setting' (Parker et al., 2002: 941 and 960). Regular users who move onto combination drug repertoires were said to form a 'a discrete minority' (Parker et al., 1998: 154) and to present a 'conundrum' for the normalisation thesis: 'outside club land, their poly-drug use and "risky" nights out potentially clash with the notions of responsible, sensible recreational drug use which is at the core of our conceptualization' (Parker et al., 2002: 947). Nonetheless, the dance drug scene continued to be considered part of the normalisation process, 'not in its origins but because it is now sustained by migration from the adolescent drugs pathways we have described' (Parker et al., 1998: 154).

As they refined their arguments, Parker et al., delineated the main elements of the thesis more clearly than before. Reflecting the behavioural focus of their earlier work, they noted that significant increases in availability and accessibility had provided the basis for unprecedented increases in drug trying and drug use: 'young Britons have become, in less than a decade, such determined consumers of 'recreational' drugs that we can begin to talk about the normalisation of *this* type of drug use' (1998: 151, original emphasis). That a quarter of the young people in the North West cohort had become regular drug users was considered to be 'a remarkable proportion and a robust measure of normalisation' (1998: 154). The normative nature of drug trying was also said to be evident from the disintegration of traditional distinctions between users and non-users based on social class, sex and ethnicity. While socio-demographic characteristics were no longer considered to serve as strong predictors of illicit drug use, it was also argued that such behaviour cannot be explained in terms of academic failure, delinquency or low self-esteem. Rather than viewing drug use as the result of individual pathology, the authors of the thesis emphasised the rational nature of young people's decision making processes, which, they claimed, are based on recognisable cost-benefit assessments.

Alongside the continued behavioural focus, the authors of the thesis came to pay much greater attention to attitudinal and cultural dimensions. According to Parker et al. (1998) the extent to which abstainers and ex-triers accommodate recreational drug use is an essential dimension of normalisation. Because drugs no longer belong to an unknown subcultural world, abstainers cannot simply escape encounters with drugs and drug users. As a result, nearly all young people are 'drugwise' and most abstainers become pragmatic, accommodating their peers' drug use providing it does not cause harm to others. Apparent changes were also noted in relation to young people's future intentions. Occasional drug trying in adolescence by well-adjusted young people has traditionally been interpreted as an example of 'normal' adolescent experimentation, rule testing and rebelliousness (see, for example, Plant and Plant, 1992). While recognising that these notions still have some value, the authors of the normalisation thesis claim that recreational drug use within the North West cohort continued to escalate into young adulthood and persisted beyond traditional markers (Parker et al., 1998; Williams and Parker, 2001). They thus identify open mindedness about future drug use, often by young adults who abstained throughout their adolescence, as a further dimension of normalisation. The apparent liberalism of youth is, moreover, contrasted with the 'shock' and 'outrage' that is said to characterise adult reactions (Measham et al., 1994: 311; see also Parker et al., 1998).

In the more recent versions of the normalisation thesis considerable emphasis has been placed on the cultural and social accommodation of the illicit. According to Parker et al. (1998, 2002) British youth culture has accommodated and, perhaps, even facilitated recreational drug use by absorbing and accommodating the language and imagery of drugs via the fashion, media, music and drinks industries. The blurring of the licit and the illicit, which is exemplified by young people's 'pick-and-mix' approach to drinking and recreational drug use, constitutes an important aspect of normalisation. There are, in addition, said to be multiple indicators that recreational drug use is being accepted as a 'liveable with' reality by wider society: the use of illicit substances such as cannabis and cocaine alongside alcohol as part of weekend relaxation is now routinely referred to in television dramas and serials; drug-taking adventures are a key source of inspiration for stand up comedy and youth movies; drugs realities are discussed in youth magazines in wholly practical ways; and drug-taking by film and popular music stars is increasingly described in neutral rather than condemnatory ways.

## Theorising change and explaining normalisation

The normalisation thesis contains clear echoes of some well established criminological themes, which can be traced back through 'new' deviancy theories and the American sociology of deviation to the Chicago School: the rejection of explanations rooted in individual pathology and social dysfunction; the emphasis on the meaningful and goal-oriented nature of deviance; and the focus on consumption and pleasure-seeking were all central to the 'new' deviancy theories and related developments in the early sociology of drug use. Such are the nature of these parallels that the normalisation thesis has been characterised by some as an attempt to combine Becker's insights with post-modern theory (Blackman, 2004). Although there are notable similarities between these bodies of work, the focus on post-modern theory represents a significant departure from the sociology of deviance and has given rise to a very different understanding of normalisation.

According to the labelling perspective normalisation represents one of a number of possibilities when an audience is confronted with instances of rule-breaking: condemnation, expressions of moral outrage and stigmatisation being among the others. By virtue of its reaction, an audience *may* redefine stigmatised or 'deviant' behaviour so that it no longer needs to be managed as deviant. As a result, rule-breaking may take the form of 'normal trouble', whereby 'improper activities' are frequent enough to be 'simply shrugged off or ignored' (Cavan, 1966: 18) or may even become 'the standard, taken-for-granted substance and form of acts within the setting' (Rock, 1973: 84). Such is the ability of the audience to redefine deviant phenomena that it generates possibilities for subcultural formation: being labelled 'deviant' creates problems which those who have been so labelled may solve by joining together to form subcultures that provide social support for deviant behaviour and protection against the outside world (Downes and Rock, 2007; Braithwaite, 1989). This is precisely what Becker (1963) had in mind when he described how membership of a marihuana-using-group provides access to the drug, as well as to rationalisations and justifications that enable members to circumvent conventional moral controls.

What Parker et al. (1998 and 2002) describe is different, not least because they reject the link with subcultural formations. Drawing on developments in Cultural Studies (see Redhead, 1993 and 1997), these authors argue that the 1950s to 1980s were, if anything, characterised by 'subcultural' drug use, but that new patterns of consumption reflect the fragmentation of subcultural youth scenes. Because recreational drug use has gone from being a small minority activity to a majority activity, subcultural theory is said to struggle and, because normalisation concerns the accommodation of previously 'deviant' activities into the mainstream, it is said to sit uncomfortably with subcultural explorations. Whereas the labelling perspective and early sociology of drug use view normalisation as a contingent process based on negotiation between social actors in bounded situations, Parker et al., seem to view it as a pre-given product of macro-social forces. Given the 'moribund' nature of existing perspectives, they felt 'obliged to turn to more general perspectives on adolescence and social change' (1998: 30) and this led to the link with post-modernity.

Post-modern theory has been described as complex, diverse and as lacking a critical consensus (DeKoven, 2004). While some theorists maintain that the term post-modern should be reserved for a particular aesthetic style or form of representation, others insist that it should be used as a 'periodising concept'. Even among those who hold to the latter view there is considerable disagreement over the timing of this development, with the emergence of post-modernity being variously ascribed to the early twentieth century, to the aftermath of the second world war, to the 1970s or 1980s. To some theorists, moreover, post-modernity represents a new historical era, which signifies a change that is just as radical as the transition from traditional to modern society; to some it marks the collapse or exhaustion of modernity; while to others key elements of modernity are assumed and incorporated within post-modernity (DeKoven, 2004). Despite the lack of a critical consensus, it is possible to identify common themes in post-modern social theory. Post-industrialism and the rise of the information society, the growth of consumerism, and the apparent triumph of liberal-democratic capitalism in the wake of the Cold War all feature strongly in this body of work and are heavily implicated in the proposed shift from modernity to post-modernity (Dodd, 1999). From a sociological perspective, moreover, post-modernity may be understood in terms of fragmentation and de-differentiation. Whereas modernity was predictable and uniform, post-modernity is fluid and diverse: boundaries and distinctions created through social differentiation have been blurred and structural analysis, based on concepts such as class and sex, is said to have lost validity.

Some of the tensions in post-modern social theory are also evident in the distinctions that are drawn between post-modernity and late modernity. The concept of post-modernity implies a break with modernity and this has been viewed by some as a radical break which signifies the start of an entirely new epoch. Others have been more cautious, preferring to use terms such as 'high modernity' or 'late modernity' to emphasise that recent developments represent changes within modernity, rather than its end (Giddens, 1990, 1991; Beck, 1992). As well as challenging the idea of a radical break with the past, these theorists question the emphasis on de-differentiation. Social structures, they maintain, continue to play an important role, though collective ties based on work, class and family are said to have weakened considerably. The demise of these ties, it is claimed, has given rise to a process of individualisation which means that people must now reflexively construct their own social identities. As work, occupation and family have receded into the background, consumption and lifestyle are said to have become increasingly central to our sense of self.

The finer points of debates about post-modernity versus late modernity need not detain us here. What is of most concern is the way these concepts have been used to explain the changing nature of illicit drug use. In the initial formulation of their thesis Parker et al. (1995) linked normalisation to post-modernity, which, they noted, revolved around the question of whether advanced post-industrial societies are being reshaped into a new formation that is so different from what came before, in the 1960s and 1970s, that we can usefully talk about the end of an epoch rather than the evolution and development of the same sort of social structure. They went on to suggest that post-modernity is characterised by a fracturing of moral authority, increased globalisation, an emphasis on consumption rather than production and a reshaping of class and gender relations. Given the apparent disintegration of traditional distinctions between users and non-users they concluded that: 'perhaps drugs consumption best depicts what is under way; for illegal drugs have become products which are grown, manufactured, packaged and marketed through an enterprise culture whereby the legitimate and illicit markets have merged' (1995: 25). In their subsequent work, Parker et al. (1998: 157) sought to side-step theoretical debates about the nature of modernity, preferring to concentrate on the 'universally agreed implications of growing up in modern times'. At this stage, they suggested the normalisation of recreational drug use was consistent with Beck's (1992) notion of individualisation and the risk society, though their emphasis on the 'dramatic' and 'unprecedented' nature of recent trends, as well as the disintegration of traditional gender and social class distinctions, arguably sat more comfortably with the concept of post-modernity than late modernity. Within a few years, moreover, they were again talking about 'post modern times' (Parker et al., 2002: 959).

## A critique of the normalisation thesis

The normalisation thesis has been challenged on a number of fronts, with criticisms being levelled in five main areas: the prevalence of drug use, trends in drug use, attitudes to drug use, decision making processes and political/ideological implications (Shiner and Newburn, 1996, 1997, 1999; Shiner, 2000; Pearson and Shiner, 2002). Some early criticisms were implicitly absorbed into later versions of the thesis and may seem less pertinent now than when they were first made. Much of the critique has gone unanswered, however, and areas of disagreement remain, though recent evidence of convergence has raised the possibility of a rapprochement (Measham and Shiner, 2008).

One of the main criticisms of the thesis is that it exaggerates the extent of illicit drug use. Using data from the North West cohort study, the BCS and YLS, Shiner and Newburn (1997, 1999) showed that young people were fairly evenly divided between those who had used illicit drugs and those who had not. They also highlighted the dynamic nature of drug use, demonstrating how lifetime measures – which indicate whether an individual has ever used a drug – exaggerate the extent of such behaviour. When measures based on shorter timeframes were used evidence of normalisation inevitably became more elusive and regular use, however defined, remained a minority activity (see also, Ramsay and Percy, 1996). This pattern was more pronounced in relation to some substances than others and early versions of the thesis were criticised for downplaying distinctions between drugs and for simplifying the decisions that young people make about what to use and what not to use. In particular, it was suggested that the impact of the 'rave' scene had been overstated because the associated forms of drug use were limited to a relatively small proportion of the youthful population.

Critics of the normalisation thesis have also rejected the proposed link with post-modernity on the grounds that it fails to make sense of recent and longer term trends. Drawing on the international evidence, Shiner and Newburn (1999) note that rates of youthful drug use fell in the United States throughout much of the 1980s and that a similar decline was evident in some European countries. The example of the United States also illustrates the point that widespread drug use has a much longer history than is allowed for by the normalisation thesis. Youthful drug use reached 'epidemic' proportions in America during the 1960s and the use of marihuana, as well as other illicit substances, peaked during the late 1970s to early 1980s (Johnston et al., 2007).

Although the subsequent decline was followed by a brief period of increasing use during the mid 1990s prevalence rates have remained fairly stable since the turn of the century, though they remain lower than in 1975 when monitoring began. At the peak of the American 'epidemic' almost two-in-three twelfth grade high school students had used illicit drugs at some point and more than half had done so during the last year. Although less prevalent now, it remains the case that almost half of twelfth grade students have used illicit drugs at some point and approximately two-in-five have done so in the last year.

The situation in Britain is more difficult to assess because of the lack of long term trend data, but even so it is clear that increases in drug use have not taken the sudden or spectacular form that is sometimes suggested. The YLS has been credited with providing the 'most persuasive evidence of increased drug use' (Parker et al., 2002: 946), yet actually points to a fairly modest increase and even this is likely to be an exaggeration. Separate waves of the YLS were administered in 1992/3 and 1998/9, but were not strictly comparable because the second survey focused on a slightly wider age group than the first and was based on a different method of data-collection that encouraged higher rates of disclosure (Graham and Bowling, 1995; Flood-Page et al., 2000).[3] Even so, there was little evidence of a striking increase in drug use: the 1992/3 survey found that 24 per cent of 14 to 25 year olds had used an illicit drug in the previous year, while the 1998/9 survey found that 27 per cent of 12 to 30 year olds had done so. Far from pointing to ever increasing levels of use, moreover, subsequent surveys indicate that drug use reached a plateau during the late 1990s and then began to fall (Murphy and Roe, 2007; see also Chapter 1).

A lack of comparable data for previous decades makes it difficult to assess change over a longer period, but critics of the normalisation thesis have argued that recent surveys can be used to make some comments about the likely nature of long term trends. Assuming that most people who use drugs do so during adolescence and early adulthood – and all the indications are that they do – then changes over time will be reflected in differences between age cohorts. According to Shiner and Newburn (1999: 149) the trend implied by such differences 'is one of evolution over an extended period rather than of a sharp, fundamental structural shift' and does not support the contention that changes in patterns of drug use since the late 1980s are indicative of major epochal change. This interpretation is further supported by the limited historical evidence that is available. In its initial report, published in 1961, the Inter-Departmental Committee on Drug Addiction, headed by Sir Russell Brain, concluded that drug supply in Britain was almost negligible, but then gave a revised opinion four years later when it noted a marked increase in use. This increase was based largely on marihuana and continued through to the end of the decade and beyond. As Young (1971: 11) reflected:

> ...ten years ago the occurrence of marihuana-smoking [in Great Britain] was minute and largely limited to first generation West Indian immigrants. Since that time there has been an unparalleled growth in use, occurring largely among young people, to such an extent that the Wootton Report estimated that between 30,000–300,000 people in Britain had used marihuana. There can be little doubt that the actual number is considerably larger than the latter figure and that this number is steadily growing.

By the early 1970s, marihuana use had become sufficiently common for Young (1971: 50) to suggest it 'may be normal behaviour amongst young people in Notting Hill'. From around this time a handful of surveys also began to document evidence of fairly widespread drug use among young people in various locations. An early survey of higher education students in Leicester found nine per cent reported having used an illicit drug at some time in their lives (Binnie and Murdock, 1969). A few years later, a survey of 17 to 24 year olds in Cheltenham indicated that a fifth had used cannabis, LSD or amphetamines (Plant, 1973) and a study of medical students in Glasgow reported that 14 per cent had used illicit drugs (McKay et al., 1973). Another university-based study found that a third of respondents had used illicit drugs (Kosviner and Hawks, 1977) and a second Glaswegian study of 16 to 24 year olds contacted through schools, hospital casualty departments and sexual health clinics reported that 31 per cent had done so (Fish et al., 1974). In 1982 the first BCS indicated that 12 per cent of 20 to 29 year olds in England and Wales had used cannabis, a figure which doubled by 1992 (Mott and Mirrlees-Black, 1995), while a survey commissioned by the *Daily Mail* newspaper reported that 28 per cent of 15 to 21 year olds in London had used cannabis and 10 per cent had used amphetamines (NOP Market Research Ltd, 1982). By the second half of the 1980s national data suggested that around a quarter to a third of young people had tried solvents or illegal drugs by their twentieth birthday (ISDD, 1993 and 1994).

None of this is to deny that the second half of the twentieth century saw very substantial increases in illicit drug use throughout much of the late industrial world; nor that, in Britain at least, the late 1980s and early 1990s witnessed a significant degree of diversification, whereby increases in the use of established drugs like cannabis and amphetamines were accompanied by the rise of ecstasy use and LSD use, albeit from a very low baseline (ISDD, 1994). What it does illustrate, however, is that the emergence of widespread illicit drug use has taken the form of an extended historical trend. To suggest that developments in the 1980s or 1990s were unprecedented is to ignore the very substantial increases in use that occurred in previous decades.

As well as challenging the normalisation thesis on the basis of levels and trends in drug use, critics have also emphasised the importance of the normative context within which such behaviour occurs. According to Shiner and Newburn (1997: 519):

> At the heart of the normalisation thesis, we would suggest, is a confusion between normalcy and frequency. There has been a tendency for self-reported behaviour to be taken at face value and for insufficient emphasis to be placed on the normative context of that behaviour. Normative behaviour is not necessarily the most frequently occurring pattern, but is that which conforms to popular expectation. This distinction is, however, often ignored in discourse about youthful drug use. It is important to recognise that social norms, as prescriptions serving as common guidelines for social action, are grounded in values and attitudes rather than behaviour... From this perspective, what young people think is at least as important as what they do.

The normative context of drug use was initially explored on the basis of depth interviews with young people conducted as part of an evaluation of a drug education project in the London borough of Newham. According to Shiner and Newburn (1996, 1997) the young people they spoke to generally viewed drug use with concern and managed it as a problematic, or potentially problematic, activity. Although some made positive associations between drug use and, for example, increased confidence, many expressed the kind of restrictive views which are often held to be characteristic of the adult world. Such views were strongest among non-users and reflected concerns about health implications, fear of addiction and losing control, financial cost, potential damage to relationships with significant others (including parents) and the perceived link with criminal activity. Although non-users generally felt that challenging drug using behaviour by their peers was inappropriate and likely to be counter-productive, there was considerable evidence of peer selection: that is, of young people seeking out and developing friendships with people that are like them (Coggans and McKellar, 1994) and of non-users avoiding meaningful relationships with their drug using peers.

Surprisingly, perhaps, the young people who had used drugs expressed similar views to those who had not. Users revealed many of the same concerns as non-users and described clear rules about what, where, why, and how much people should use. According to Shiner and Newburn (1997) the principal difference between young drug users and non-users was the development, by the former, of neutralisation techniques which allowed them to continue using drugs without abandoning their affiliation to consensus values. These neutralisation techniques commonly focused on the differences between substances – the substances being used are not harmful, are not really drugs and not enough is being used to get addicted. What was implied by such claims was that there are no serious consequences from the drug(s) being used and that, by extension, the user was making rational and responsible choices.

Whilst highlighting the embedded rationality of young people's decisions about drug use, Shiner and Newburn (1996, 1997 see also Shiner, 2000) went on to challenge the idea that such decisions involve rational calculation of costs and benefits. In doing so, they drew on the phenomenology of Alfred Schutz (1966, 1972). Schutz emphasised the habitualised nature of human action, claiming that choice, involving dramatic rehearsal and calculation, only occurs rarely and almost never in the context of everyday life. As well as being costly, calculation is superfluous because knowledge about the world is 'automatically at hand' and offers a limited number of relatively rough but sufficient rules of thumb, or recipes, for typical behaviour in repeated typical situations. Because most situations are familiar, typical courses of action are generated routinely and individuals only begin a formal process of information collection when, and if, their existing rules of thumb break down. This does not mean that human behaviour is irrational, however, because recipes involve the 'automatic' anticipation of consequences and are, therefore, pre-calculated. As such, they can, and should, be traced back to the logic of selection embedded in the meaningful orientation of action (Srubar, 1993). In their application of these ideas, Shiner and Newburn argued that young people make decisions about drugs without dramatic rehearsal and calculation based on 'rules of thumb', which are generated routinely as part of everyday life. These rules of thumb are, they noted, based on images, ideas and information from a variety of sources including magazines, newspapers, television programmes, parents and friends.

In his later work, Shiner (2000) describes how young people's rules of thumb change as they move through their teenage years and become more familiar with drugs and drug users. Although some of the youngest participants in this study – who were 12 years old – knew older people who used drugs, such behaviour was very unusual within their peer networks and their rules of thumb were based on a normative perspective within which drug use was viewed in wholly negative terms and drug users were considered to be dangerous outsiders. From the early teens, increased contact with drugs and drug users provided young people with new information which challenged this normative perspective. As a result some of the older participants in the study adapted their rules of thumb and incorporated neutralisation techniques which accommodated their own drug use and/or that of their friends.

The normative context of drug use has also been examined on the basis of public attitude surveys. Pearson and Shiner (2002) focused on perceptions of drug-related harm and found that not all adults conform to the conservative characterisations presented in some of the sociological literature. Indeed, their analysis called into question the very idea of a generation gap because it suggested that young people's judgments about harmfulness come to resemble those of adults ever more closely as they move through adolescence. As familiarity with drug users increased, cannabis was more clearly distinguished from other illicit drugs so that, by the mid-teens, young people's perceptions of drug-related harm were remarkably similar to those of adults. Both groups appeared to be thoroughly convinced of the harmfulness of heroin, cocaine and ecstasy and considered cannabis to be considerably less harmful than other illicit substances. On this basis, Pearson and Shiner noted that young people who use any other illicit drug than cannabis do so in a general context in which the vast majority of their peers, as well as their elders, are thoroughly convinced of the potential harmfulness of their actions. As such, they concluded that any shift towards normalisation has been much more limited and ambiguous than is allowed for by the existing literature. Gould and Stratford (2002) also considered perceptions of harm, but did so as part of a more general focus on legal and moral dimensions. They found that attitudes to cannabis are becoming more liberal and pragmatic, but that this is not the case in relation to heroin and ecstasy. While suggesting there is some evidence to support the normalisation thesis in relation to cannabis, these authors noted that attitudes are becoming more liberal across all age cohorts, including adults – a pattern they explain in terms of increasing levels of use and familiarity, dating back to the 1960s.

Finally, while the normalisation thesis has primarily been challenged on the basis of empirical considerations, concerns have also been raised about its political or ideological implications. Based on their empirical observations, Shiner and Newburn (1999) argued that the discourse of normalisation reinforces adult concerns about the problematic nature of youth and runs the risk of feeding 'respectable fears' (Pearson, 1983). Similarly, given that increases in drug use have been used to justify the need for government intervention, it has been claimed that the normalisation thesis sits comfortably within the 'framework of control' (Blackman, 2004: 138), though this is not what its authors intended. Ultimately, the main critique of the normalisation thesis concluded by calling for a set of ideas, and a way of expressing them, that is sensitive to changing patterns of drug use and differences between youth subcultures, while also taking seriously the non-user and the concerns many young people continue to have about illicit drug use (Shiner and Newburn, 1999).

## Reactions to the normalisation 'debate'

Reactions to the normalisation 'debate' have tended to divide into two distinct positions. While many commentators have readily accepted the idea that illicit drug use is undergoing a process of normalisation, others have sought to negotiate a middle path between this thesis and its critique. Despite the attempts that have been made to find a compromise, the first position predominates and the normalisation thesis has become something of an academic orthodoxy (see Coffield and Gofton, 1994; Hirst and McCamley-Finney, 1994; 6 et al., 1997; Hammersley et al., 2003). With the diffusion of this thesis, moreover, some of its more tentative aspects are in danger of being forgotten and a much fuller and more far-reaching process of change has sometimes been envisaged, leading to claims that 'drug use is a normal part of the adolescent experience' (Furlong and Cartmel, 2007: 99); 'that illicit drugs now constitute a normal feature of young adult life in Britain' and that, among the young, the use of ecstasy and cocaine, has 'become normalised' (Hough, 2001: 431); that: 'For British youth Ecstasy has become a milestone on the road to adulthood like cutting your teeth, riding a bike and losing your virginity' (Wright, 1998: 231); and that the 'normalization of youth drug experiences' is a 'new social fact' (Seddon et al., 2008: 821).

It is, perhaps, even a little misleading to talk of a 'debate' in this context because to do so implies a degree of exchange that has, until recently, been largely absent. The authors of the normalisation thesis 'scarcely addressed' the detailed criticisms of their work (Ramsay and Partridge, 1999: 57) and, though elements of the critique do appear to have been taken into account, this has not been made explicit. On the few occasions the authors of the thesis directly considered their critics' work they drew attention to what they felt were its methodological weaknesses, rather than addressing the substance of the argument (see Parker et al., 1998, 2002). Similar silences can be found outside the immediate confines of the 'debate'. Those who have drawn on the thesis have sometimes presented it as though it were uncontested, with little, if any, mention of alternative positions (see, for example, Shapiro, 1999; Hammersley et al., 2003). Even when the evidence might be thought to challenge aspects of the thesis, moreover, there appears to have been little pause for thought. Recent increases in drug use have, as noted in Chapter 1, levelled out and prevalence rates have been largely stable over the last ten years or so, with some recent evidence of decline, but this has done little to interrupt the momentum behind the new orthodoxy. Despite these trends and regardless of the warnings that have been made about reliance on global measures of lifetime use, a recent review concluded (Barton, 2003: 122):

> ...it may be that the critical voices raised against the normalization thesis have been overtaken by events...non-drug-adolescents are now in a minority. It may be the case that the work of the Manchester group identified the beginnings of a social change, and one that seems to be gathering pace at a rapid rate.

The possibility of synthesis was first raised by Nigel South. He considered the critique to be 'convincing', but was equally persuaded by the 'intellectual and cultural dimensions' of the normalisation thesis and of the need for a 'new perspective' (1999: 6). The apparent tensions in this position were eased by his description of what the 'essentials' of such a perspective might be:

- drug use is, undeniably, of enormous contemporary importance, whether as symbol, social problem or fashion accessory;
- data, however challenged, indicate socially significant changes in patterns and degree of use over the past 20 years;

- while prevention efforts, peer influence and other factors will probably restrain and perhaps even stabilise rates of increase in drug use it is unlikely that they will reverse recent changes;
- the availability of drugs will not be significantly diminished;
- hence, the whole issue and persistence of drugs as a feature of everyday life has become and will remain 'normalised'. While drug use has not itself become the true norm, it has moved some way from the status captured by the term 'exception to the norm': from 'exceptionality' to being part of everyday life.

For South, the most significant thing about illicit drugs in late modernity is not simply the question 'how many people actually use them?', but is the sheer volume of related social activity. Regardless of whether we use drugs, he argues, we all live in an environment saturated by references to, and images of, them. As a result drugs 'are simultaneously officially damned yet dragged ever more firmly into the everyday discourse of social life' (1999: 7).

Christopher Wibberley and Jason Price (2000) also challenged what they considered to be the unduly polarised nature of the normalisation debate. Suggesting that individuals have tended to take one 'side' or the other, they argued: 'Both sides of the debate over-egg the pudding in order to strengthen their case – leaving room for both sides to criticize the other's argument' (2000: 161). Based on the results of a school survey conducted in the Greater Manchester area, these authors went on to note: 'The conclusion that can be drawn is rather ambiguous in that it is *not abnormal* to have either tried or not tried an illicit drug by the end of compulsory schooling in the UK' (2000: 160). In a further development, such ambiguity has given rise to talk of 'differentiated normalisation', which, it is argued, 'allows for the ways in which different types of drugs and different types of drug use may be normalized for different groups of young people' (Shildrick, 2002: 36; see also: Pilkington, 2005).

## Beyond academia

Elements of the normalisation thesis have gained currency well beyond the boundaries of academia. Most notably, perhaps, an emphasis on the widespread and widely accepted nature of illicit drug use among young people has become a familiar feature of our cultural commentary more generally. Around the time that the normalisation thesis was first published, Irvine Welsh began to chronicle the adventures of the 'chemical generation' in a series of novels and short stories under such titles as *The Acid House* and *Ecstasy*. More or less simultaneously, a series of eye witness and journalistic accounts of ecstasy culture began to appear, among the most notable of which were those produced by the late Nicholas Saunders (1993 and 1995) and Matthew Collin with John Godfrey (1997). The interest of the mainstream media in this phenomenon also started to increase as a new generation of young writers entered the profession having worked on a range of specialist magazines such as *i-D, Mixmag, Jockey Slut* and *Muzik*. Dance pages were introduced into the weekly music press, club reviews appeared in newspapers, dance resources were posted on the Internet and new legal dance radio stations such as *Kiss FM* were established in London and Manchester. Crucially, this growing familiarity with ecstasy culture began to be reflected in mass media representations of drugs and drug users. *The Guardian* (July 25 1995) noted the 'opening of a generation gap', claiming that 'drug taking has become an integral part of youth culture and a significant part of the lives even of schoolchildren'. A message which it repeated following the death of Leah Betts (November 17 1995):

> An underground movement, which started in 1988 with the advent of house music in this country, has almost invisibly expanded into a giant culture. The secret is out; the adult world has had thrust upon it the attitudes and the lifestyle of a generation it does not understand.

The events of January 1997 provided a further milestone in the development of this new media perspective. The New Year revelry had barely died down when Brian Harvey, then member of British band *East 17*, sparked one of the biggest drugs stories of the decade by speaking openly about having used 12 ecstasy tablets in one night, claiming that the drug is 'harmless' and 'makes you a better person' (*The Mirror*, 17 January 1997). The backlash against Harvey was swift and unforgiving. He was criticised by the Prime Minister in the House of Commons, furiously condemned by much of the media and isolated by the pop-music establishment. *East 17*'s records were banned by several radio stations and, ultimately, Harvey was sacked from the group. Amidst the controversy Noel Gallagher, mastermind of super-group *Oasis*, made the following statement to the press: 'As soon as people realise that the majority of people in this country take drugs, then the better off we'll all be...Drugs is like getting up and having a cup of tea in the morning' (*New Musical Express*, January 29 1997). Although condemned by some,

Gallagher received considerable support for his intervention, some of it from unlikely quarters. In an article in the *London Evening Standard* (January 31 1997) entitled 'Why Noel is right about Drugs' A.N. Wilson, the normally conservative commentator, wrote:

> Whatever we would like to be the case, what he says is actually right. For the generation under the age of 40, drug-taking *is* normal. You do not need to watch 'concerned' television documentaries about housing estates in the North of England where tabs of LSD change hands for less than a small round of drinks, nor watch police raids at 'raves' where the dancers have all taken Ecstasy, to know this is the case.

In subsequent media coverage normalisation has tended to provide the assumptions around which reports are constructed, rather than providing the main substance of the story. In the week that three members of the pop group *S Club 7* were cautioned for smoking cannabis, *The Guardian* (March 23 2001) claimed: 'Out in the real Britain, you'd be struggling to find a 21-year-old who hadn't puffed on a reefer at least once.' Almost as if to endorse this claim, revelations soon followed that Prince Harry had smoked cannabis when he was 17 years old. Under the headline 'Prince Harry Drugs and Drink Shock' *The Sunday Express* (January 13 2002) noted that: 'It is all a long way from the innocent days when the Prince of Wales himself made headlines all over the world after he sneaked out of Gordonstoun for a small glass of cherry brandy.' The article concluded:

> [Prince William and Prince Harry] were both the sons of a mother who wanted them brought up as normal children....The revelation that Harry last year dabbled in soft drugs may ironically be the best evidence that he is a truly normal wayward teenager.

## Conclusion

The sociology of drug use has developed sporadically since its first stirrings more than half a century ago. Two decades – the 1960s and 1990s – stand out as periods of particular activity and, to some extent, this reflects the importance of what was happening in relation to drug use at the time. After all, the 1960s witnessed the beginnings of widespread youthful drug use in Britain, the United States and elsewhere, while the 1990s witnessed the growth of ecstasy culture into a global phenomenon.

For sociologists in both decades, the developments they observed highlighted the folly of trying to explain drug use in terms of individual or social deficits and emphasised the need for explanations that recognise the meaningful, goal-oriented nature of such behaviour. These continuities have been all but lost, however, obscured by recent calls for new perspectives and the notion that prior theorising has been rendered obsolete by the pace of change. The irony, of course, is we have been here before, or somewhere very similar at least, and much of what has recently been written about drug use can be found in earlier work. By positing a radical break with the past, the new orthodoxy raises important questions about both the nature of social reality and the representation of this reality; questions which provide a key focus for what is to come in the following chapters.

# 3
# A Social Classification of Drug Use

> It is not then the study of drugs in a vacuum, as isolated pharmacological effects, which will help us understand drug addiction; rather it is the social *meanings* ascribed to a particular drug in a specific society or culture that we must analyse (Young, 1971: 34).

Established ways of classifying drugs cannot be assumed to provide a suitable basis for sociological analysis because they are typically rooted in medical or pharmacological perspectives. One of the best known pharmacological classifications distinguishes between stimulants, hallucinogens and depressants, but these categories are not readily applicable to the most commonly used illicit drugs. Cannabis and ecstasy, for example, defy precise pharmacological classification because they contain both stimulant and hallucinogenic properties. An alternative approach is offered by the Misuse of Drugs Act 1971, which classifies controlled substances according to their perceived dangerousness or harmfulness. Although this classification is sometimes used as a basis for sociological analysis its suitability for such a role remains open to doubt. As Sellin (1938: 23–4) noted some 70 years ago:

> The unqualified acceptance of the legal definitions of the basic units or elements of criminological enquiry violates a fundamental criterion of science. The scientist must have freedom to define his own terms, based on the intrinsic character of his material...the acceptance of the categories of specific forms of 'crime' and 'criminal' as laid down in law renders criminological research theoretically invalid from the point of view of science.

The aim of this chapter is to develop an empirically valid classification of drug use based on social dimensions of use. As well as providing the basis for the subsequent analysis, the classification addresses some important substantive issues in its own right. Building on previous work, it highlights the limited and transient nature of most young adults' involvement in illicit drug use. It also explores the role of self-regulation, with particular reference to the law and perceptions of harmfulness. As part of the analysis, social dimensions of drug use are compared to medico-legal classifications based on the principle of harmfulness.

## Legal classification in context

International law, in the form of various United Nations conventions, aims to restrict the use of controlled substances to 'legitimate' medical, industrial and scientific purposes. Among other things, the conventions arrange these substances in schedules which determine the level of control to be applied and impose limitations on manufacture, production, cultivation, importation and possession. The specifics of implementation are left to individual states, but the UN conventions set the tone, so that differences between states are largely variations on a set of themes. The issue of classification, for example, is dominated by a medico-legal perspective, with substances being largely classified on the basis of their medical use and/or perceived harmfulness. In some countries, such as Britain and the Netherlands, classification is directly related to maximum legal penalties, though elsewhere, as in the United States, for example, it is left to the courts to reflect the harmfulness of the drug in the sentence passed. The practical significance of legal classification is also evident in claims that it offers a means of channelling resources towards substances that pose most risk and of conveying drug prevention messages (see Police Foundation, 2000; House of Commons Science and Technology Committee, 2006). This normative dimension is well illustrated by the Dutch system which distinguishes between two main classes: i) drugs that pose unacceptable risks, including opiates, coca derivatives, ecstasy and amphetamines; and ii) other drugs, including cannabis and tranquillisers.

### The Misuse of Drugs Act

The Misuse of Drugs Act 1971 provides the main basis of British drug law and was introduced as part of a broader reorientation of policy. For much of the last century, the 'British system', which was formalised by the 1924 Rolleston Committee, fell well short of outright prohibition and permitted lawful possession of opium and cocaine under prescription from a general medical practitioner (Spear and Mott, 2002). This arrangement was not the liberal experiment that is sometimes suggested, but was tolerated on the basis that it offered a pragmatic solution to what was then considered to be a small and declining problem. When drug use increased sharply during the 1960s a revised, and much more explicit control-led, approach was formulated: the United Nations Single Convention on Narcotic Drugs was ratified; strict legal controls were imposed on possession, supply and production of a wide range of illicit substances; and treatment was much more tightly regulated (South, 2002). In short, the revised approach took a system that was internationally renowned for its apparent liberalism and turned it into one of the harshest drugs regimes in Europe (Dorn and Lee, 1999; Police Foundation, 2000).

The introduction of the Misuse of Drugs Act represented a significant milestone, but did not signal a major change of philosophy. Although the balance shifted, the revised response continued the fusion of medical and legal perspectives: the principle of medical authorisation was retained, albeit in a restricted form, and legal penalties were tied to a new system of classification based on the notion of harmfulness, which has been described as a normative notion grounded in a paternalistic view of the law that is linked to a judgement about the wrongness of drug use (Ruggiero, 1999). This new system divided controlled substances into three classes that are subject to progressively harsher penalties and did so on the basis of the following criteria: whether they are being misused; whether they are likely to be misused; and whether the misuse in either case is having or could have harmful effects sufficient to constitute a problem. The classes, allocation and associated penalties are:

- Class A: includes heroin, cocaine, ecstasy, LSD and magic mushrooms etc. Maximum penalty for possession is seven years imprisonment and/or an unlimited fine; and for possession with intent to supply is life imprisonment and/or an unlimited fine.
- Class B: includes amphetamines and cannabis etc. Maximum penalty for possession is five years imprisonment and/or an unlimited fine; and for possession with intent to supply is 14 years imprisonment and/or an unlimited fine. If prepared for injection substances in this category are treated as Class A.
- Class C: includes anabolic steroids and benzodiazepines etc. Maximum penalty for possession is two years imprisonment and/or an unlimited

fine; and for possession with intent to supply is five years imprisonment and/or an unlimited fine.

When the new legislation was introduced the allocation to classes was said to be provisional and open to review, but has remained largely intact, albeit with a few additions and revisions: most notably, ecstasy was added in 1977, cannabis was transferred from Class B to C in 2004 though this decision was subsequently reversed[1] and methamphetamines were transferred from Class B to Class A in 2007.

## The contested nature of classification

The notion that drugs have an inherent degree of harmfulness which can be readily classified is less straightforward than it may seem. There is no one generally accepted method of assessing harm and no explicit criteria appear to have been used for this purpose when the Misuse of Drugs Act was being framed (Police Foundation, 2000). The potential for harm is mediated by external factors, moreover, including the socio-legal arrangements governing supply, and varies with the disposition and susceptibilities of individual users, while dosage and tolerance provide further complicating factors (Best et al., 2001). Even apparently innocuous substances, including water and common salt, can be fatal when used to excess, while regular use of some apparently harmful substances, such as heroin, produces increased tolerance enabling experienced users to survive doses that would prove fatal to non-users. None of this is to deny that drugs have different pharmacological properties, nor that these properties can be understood in terms of degrees of harmfulness, but it does make the point that developing a harms-based classification is far from straightforward and that the results will vary depending on the criteria that are given priority.

Comparing the legal classifications of various countries shows that differences can result even when similar criteria are used. The binary system used in the Netherlands puts 'clear blue water' between cannabis and heroin, as does the three class system enshrined in British law (Police Foundation, 2000: 47), but this is not the case everywhere. In the United States, for example, substances subject to regulation under federal law are divided into five schedules depending on their medicinal value, harmfulness and potential for abuse or addiction: Schedule I is reserved for substances with a high potential for abuse and no recognised medicinal use; Schedule II is for substances with a high potential for abuse, some (but often marginal) medical use, and a high incidence of physical or psychological dependence; while, at the other end of the scale, Schedule V is for substances deemed to have the lowest potential for abuse and a small incidence of physical or psychological dependence (Faupel et al., 2004). Marihuana is placed in Schedule I, alongside heroin and ecstasy, while cocaine is placed in Schedule II, alongside amphetamines. For the purposes of legal classification then, the United States makes no distinction between marihuana and heroin or between cocaine and amphetamines. Britain, by contrast, like the Netherlands, separates cannabis from heroin and also separates cocaine from amphetamines.

The contested nature of classification is evident from various calls for reform. Since the early 1970s, lobby groups in the United States have campaigned against existing legal arrangements, coming together to form the Coalition to Reschedule Cannabis (see: www.drugscience.org). In Britain, the Advisory Council on the Misuse of Drugs (ACMD), which has a statutory duty to advise government, recommended that cannabis be transferred from Class B to Class C for the first time in 1979 (Home Office, 1979). Although the recommendation was rejected, the issue came to prominence once again, some 20 years later, when legal classification was subject to an unprecedented level of public scrutiny. The momentum behind this development came from the Independent Inquiry into the Misuse of Drugs Act, which prompted a series of interventions that culminated in the reclassification of cannabis in what was the first significant – albeit temporary – move towards liberalisation in over 30 years.[2] As the process of reform gathered pace, the whole issue of classification was put firmly on the political agenda: the then Home Secretary, Charles Clarke, announced his intention to undertake a 'root and branch' review of the existing system (*The Guardian*, January 20 2006), while the House of Commons Science and Technology Committee (2006) focused on the issue as part of its general review of evidence based policy making.

The Independent Inquiry was convened in 1997 with the aim of establishing whether the law should be revised to make it more effective and responsive. It concluded that 'demand will only be significantly reduced by education and treatment, not by the deterrent effect of the law' (Police Foundation, 2000: 8). This conclusion was reflected in calls for a less punitive approach to possession offences and detailed recommendations that cannabis be transferred from Class B to C, ecstasy and LSD be transferred from Class A to B, prison sentences be abolished for most possession offences and the power of arrest be removed for most cannabis possession offences. Although far-reaching in their implications, these recommendations were developed within the framework and philosophy of existing legislation: the Inquiry endorsed the three-tiered legal framework and the role of dangerousness as the main criterion for classification, proposing the reclassification of cannabis, ecstasy and LSD in order to ensure that 'the classes provide a more accurate hierarchy of harm and commensurate sanctions' (Police Foundation, 2000: 4). These proposals were subsequently endorsed by the Select Committee on Home Affairs (2002) and/or the ACMD (2002).

The House of Commons Science and Technology Committee (2006) reiterated much of what the Independent Inquiry had to say, but was more damning in its conclusions. Like the Inquiry, the Committee found no convincing evidence for the deterrent effect of the existing classification and identified significant anomalies in the allocation of individual substances. Whereas the Inquiry endorsed the three-tiered approach, the Committee talked of 'serious failings of the ABC classification', concluding that the current system 'is not fit for purpose and should be replaced with a more scientifically based scale of harm decoupled from penalties for possession and trafficking' (2006: 3). Significant moves have been made towards developing a scale of harm (see below), but such an approach may be considered problematic because it requires a greater degree of precision than a broad class based system. The Committee's preference for a scale rather than classes is all the more odd given its conclusion that determining harm scores 'is almost as much an art as a science' (2006: 43).

## The state of the art

Developing a 'scientific' scale of harm is made difficult by the lack of definitive data marking clear levels of harm. Indeed, in the absence of such data, it may be impossible to move beyond the most general observation that there are dangers associated with drug use without encountering disagreement and controversy (Best et al., 2001). Nonetheless, recent work, conducted under the auspices of the Independent Inquiry and ACMD, has generated a 'systematic' framework for assessing harm based on 'fact' and 'scientific knowledge' (Nutt et al., 2007; see also Police Foundation, 2000). This system identifies three major categories of harm – personal harm, made up of dangers for individual users; the tendency of the drug to induce dependence; and social harm, made up of the effects on families, communities and society in general. Each category is divided into three, producing an assessment matrix based on nine parameters of risk. Two independent groups of experts, made up primarily of addiction specialists but with some representation from the legal and police services, were then asked to use this matrix to rate individual substances, including alcohol and tobacco. Results from the two groups were similar, which was taken to suggest that the process is robust and that the scores have some validity.

The first group of experts was consulted by the Independent Inquiry and its ratings helped give rise to the recommendations regarding the reclassification of cannabis, ecstasy and LSD. Responses from the second group also highlighted a 'surprisingly poor correlation' between the established legal classification and harm score, with particularly striking discrepancies in relation to 'psychedelic-type' drugs (Nutt et al., 2007). Another key message to emerge from the matrix based assessment is that, in terms of their harmfulness, alcohol and tobacco could reasonably be placed in Class A and B respectively, alongside heroin and amphetamines.[3] Unlike most controlled substances, alcohol and tobacco are physiologically addictive and also have significant health risks: together they account for approximately 90 per cent of all drug related deaths in the United Kingdom, while tobacco is estimated to cause up to 40 per cent of all hospital illness and alcohol is involved in over half of all visits to casualty departments and orthopaedic admissions (Nutt et al., 2007). It is on the basis of such figures that the World Health Organisation (2002) considered tobacco to pose the most serious risk to health in developed countries followed, in order, by blood pressure, alcohol, cholesterol, obesity, low fruit and vegetable intake, physical inactivity and illicit drugs.

The matrix based system has gone some way towards establishing a more accurate hierarchy of harm, but has left some anomalies unchallenged and has created one or two of its own. Magic mushrooms have not been included in the assessment procedure and no recommendations have been made regarding their reclassification, which is odd given that their current status as a Class A drug is disproportionate to the potential for harm and is not based on scientific evidence (House of Commons Science and Technology Committee, 2006). By proposing the reclassification of LSD, but not magic mushrooms, moreover, the Independent Inquiry created an anomaly all of its own: these substances are very similar in their pharmacological effects and there is no obvious scientific rationale for distinguishing between them (Best et al., 2001). The continued separation of cocaine (Class A) and amphetamines (Class B) may also be challenged on similar grounds. None of the recent inquiries or reports have suggested anything other than that cocaine is sufficiently harmful to justify its continued inclusion in Class A, alongside heroin. But the juxtaposition of these substances has been described by one leading addictions expert as a 'legal quirk' on the grounds that they have 'next to nothing in common' (Gossop, 1996: 148). Cocaine certainly carries significant health risks, including the potential for fatal overdose, but is much closer in actions and effects to amphetamines than heroin: it is not physiologically addictive in the same way as heroin and is far less widely implicated in drug-related deaths – between 2003 and 2007 cocaine was linked to 845 deaths officially attributed to drug-related poisoning in England and Wales, compared with figures of 3,831 for heroin and morphine and 453 for amphetamines (Gossop, 1996; ACMD, 2000; Office for National Statistics, 2008).[4]

## Social dimensions of drug use

Although the established harms perspective has come through recent policy reviews relatively unscathed, this does not mean it provides a suitable starting point for sociological analysis. In the year that the Misuse of Drugs Act was introduced, Young (1971: 45–6) complained of 'myopic' approaches to drug use which concentrate on pharmacological effects and disregard the cultural context and social meanings of behaviour:

> To describe adequately a particular form of drug use, then, we must use what I will term a socio-pharmacological classification. Thus we will need to divide drug users up into categories which describe patterns of drug use involving similar social meanings and beliefs, on the one hand, and drugs with closely related pharmacological effects on the other...The problem of proper classification of drug use is, in this light, not a mere academic whim, but a necessity if we are to create meaningful categories with which to explain the reasons why certain groups take drugs and the likely consequences of such behaviour.

Social scientists have shown surprisingly little interest in establishing what such a classification might look like, preferring instead to classify substances according to their legal status (MacDonald, 1999; Roe and Man, 2006) or 'apparent' social attributes (Ramsay and Percy, 1996). The aim of this chapter is to construct an empirically meaningful social classification of drug use based on prevalence rates, underlying patterns of use, age of onset, extent of users' repertoires and motivations for non use.

As well as distinguishing between different types of drug use, the analysis explores related decision making processes, paying particular attention to the role of legal deterrents and normative considerations based on the notion of harmfulness. It is reasonably well established that the global distribution of drug use is not straightforwardly related to drug policy, since countries with stringent regimes do not have lower rates of use than those with liberal regimes (Degenhardt et al., 2008; see also United Nations, 2008). Illustrating this discrepancy, the United States has some of the world's highest rates of recorded drug use and one of its strictest regimes of control, which has resulted in an imprisonment rate for drug offences that is higher than that in most Western European countries for all crime put together (MacCoun and Reuter, 2001). A similar paradox is evident in Britain, which has some of Europe's highest rates of drug use as well as one if its harshest regimes of control (EMCDDA, 1999, 2008). Conversely, the Netherlands combines lower rates of drug use with a more liberal approach to control, which includes licensed cannabis outlets in some parts of the country (Degenhardt et al., 2008; United Nations, 2008; EMCDDA, 2008).

Patterns of drug use raise further doubts about the efficacy of legal deterrents. Despite marked differences in legal classification, Britain, the United States and the Netherlands share broadly similar patterns of use: cannabis is comfortably the most widely used illicit drug in all three countries, followed by a range of hallucinogens and stimulants, with heroin and crack cocaine being used by a very small proportion of the respective populations. If legal considerations were primary we might expect to see a degree of symmetry between patterns of use and the law, but the extent to which substances are used cuts across legal distinctions: cannabis, for example, is the most widely used illicit drug in the United States despite being included in Schedule I alongside other substances considered to have a high potential for abuse and no recognised medicinal use. The importance of extra legal factors is further implied by variations in the extent to which substances with the same legal status are used: in the United States cannabis is used much more widely than ecstasy or LSD, which are, in turn, used much more widely than heroin; in the Netherlands ecstasy and cocaine are used much more widely than heroin; and similar variations are evident in Britain (see below). What these patterns indicate is that the extent to which illicit drugs are used is more closely aligned to the potential for harm than to legal classification: cannabis is consistently the most widely used illicit drug, in part at least, because it is also the least harmful, while heroin is consistently one of the least widely used because it is one of the most harmful.

## The extent of illicit drug use

Prevalence rates suggest a certain ambiguity in the position that illicit drug use has come to occupy; one that is, perhaps, best captured by the notion of primary deviance. It is far from unusual for young adults to have used illicit drugs at some point in their lives, but much of this use remains hesitant, tentative and short-lived. Both the 1998 BCS and 1998/9 YLS indicate that young adult drug users have, on average, only ever used two substances and that between a third and a half have only ever used one.[5] The tentative nature of much illicit drug use is further evident from the extent to which it is, or is not, evident during the last year. Based on this measure, between a quarter to a third of young adults are recent users, while almost as many are ex-users. The extent of past use increases with age, moreover, so that young adults in their late twenties include more ex than recent users (see Chapter 6).

The prevalence of drug use varies markedly between substances and such variations point towards three distinct categories of use (see Table 3.1). Cannabis forms a category of its own because it is, by some distance, the most widely used illicit drug, both in terms of lifetime use and recent use. The second category might be said to include the hallucinants (i.e. amphetamines, ecstasy, LSD, magic mushrooms, and amyl nitrate), plus cocaine because they are fairly widely used, albeit considerably less so than cannabis. Finally, the third category might be said to include heroin, crack and methadone on the basis that their use, even on a lifetime basis, is limited to a very small proportion of the population. This leaves solvents in an ambiguous position because they are similar to the hallucinants in terms of lifetime use, but are closer to heroin, crack and methadone in terms of recent use. Significantly, the three categories identified here do not equate to clear legal distinctions, but are more closely aligned to the potential for harm. Such an alignment is consistent with previous research which indicates that young people take account of risks when making decisions about drug use (Coffield and Gofton, 1994; Measham et al., 1998) and that lay attitudes reflect a hierarchy of harms, which broadly resembles existing 'scientific' evidence (Pearson and Shiner, 2002). On this basis it seems that normative judgements about harmfulness are a more important source of self-regulation than symbolic or instrumental concerns about the law.

Table 3.1 shows that prevalence rates are more closely aligned to the classification developed by the Independent Inquiry than that contained in the Misuse of Drugs Act. The different rates at which cannabis and amphetamines are used, for example, cannot be explained in terms of legal distinctions because both were Class B drugs when the surveys

**Table 3.1 Prevalence of drug use among young adults and medico-legal classification**

| | *Ever used (percentage)* | | *Used in last year (percentage)* | | *Legal classification* | |
|---|---|---|---|---|---|---|
| | *BCS* | *YLS* | *BCS* | *YLS* | *Misuse of Drugs Act* | *Independent Inquiry* |
| Cannabis | **41** (39–44) | **49** (47–51) | **22** (20–24) | **30** (28–32) | **B** | **C** |
| Amphetamines | **19** (17–21) | **27** (24–29) | **8** (6–9) | **11** (10–12) | **B** | **B** |
| Ecstasy | **10** (8–11) | **13** (12–15) | **4** (3–5) | **6** (5–7) | **A** | **B** |
| LSD | **10** (9–11) | **15** (14–17) | **2** (1–3) | **2** (2–3) | **A** | **B** |
| Magic mushrooms | **10** (9–11) | **13** (11–14) | **2** (2–3) | **3** (2–4) | **A** | **None** |
| Amyl nitrates | **16** (14–17) | **21** (19–22) | **4** (3–4) | **4** (3–5) | **Unclassified** | **None** |
| Cocaine | **6** (5–7) | **11** (8–12) | **3** (2–4) | **6** (5–7) | **A** | **A** |
| Glues, solvents, gas or aerosols | **6** (5–7) | **9** (7–10) | **1** (0–1) | **1** (1–2) | **Unclassified** | **None** |
| Crack | **1** (1–2) | **2** (1–2) | * | * | **A** | **A** |
| Heroin | **1** (0–1) | **2** (1–2) | * | **1** (0–1) | **A** | **A** |
| Methadone | **1** (0–1) | **1** (1–1) | * | * | **A** | **A** |
| Any drug | **49** (47–52) | **54** (52–56) | **25** (23–27) | **33** (30–35) | – | – |

*Source*: 1998 BCS, 1998/9 YLS, Police Foundation (2000) * < 0.5 per cent n = 2846 (BCS) and 3,544 (YLS)

*Notes*:

1. 95 per cent confidence intervals are given in brackets.
2. The classification given for cannabis based on the Misuse of Drugs Act refers to the situation that existed at the time the surveys were administered.
3. The higher prevalence rates reported by the YLS may be linked to the context within which the questions were asked. Because the YLS focused on various forms of delinquency it may have the effect of 'normalising' illegal activities, thereby making respondents more willing to admit drug use (Flood-Page et al., 2000).

were conducted, but may be explained by differences in harmfulness. Similarly, both ecstasy and LSD are more widely used than heroin even though they share the same legal status and this may, once again, be explained by differences in harmfulness. The apparent fit between prevalence and harmfulness is evident in various ways: cannabis is both the least harmful and most widely used illicit drug; the hallucinants tend to occupy an intermediate status in terms of their relative harmfulness and the degree to which they are used; and the most harmful substances – heroin, methadone and crack – are the least widely used. The relatively widespread use of cocaine may be thought to challenge the general pattern, but existing medico-legal classifications arguably overstate the harmfulness of this drug. As such, cocaine may be used more widely than heroin, in part at least, because it is less harmful.

While less harmful drugs tend to have higher prevalence rates, a similar fit is evident in relation to the intensity with which illicit drugs

**Table 3.2 Frequency of recent drug use (as a percentage of those who had ever used, young adults)**

| | *Desisted* | *Ad-hoc use* | *Occasional use* | *Regular use* | *Frequent use* |
|---|---|---|---|---|---|
| Cannabis | **39** (36–42) | **21** (18–24) | **9** (7–11) | **11** (9–13) | **20** (18–23) |
| Amphetamines | **59** (54–63) | **24** (20–28) | **8** (6–11) | **6** (3–8) | **3** (2–5) |
| Ecstasy | **56** (49–62) | **19** (14–24) | **12** (8–16) | **11** (7–15) | **3** (1–5) |
| LSD | **86** (82–90) | **9** (6–13) | **2** (0–3) | **2** (0–4) | **1** (0–2) |
| Magic mushrooms | **76** (69–82) | **21** (15–26) | **2** (0–3) | **1** (0–3) | **1** (0–3) |
| Amyl nitrate | **81** (76–85) | **14** (11–18) | **3** (1–4) | **2** (0–3) | **1** (0–2) |
| Cocaine | **44** (35–52) | **34** (26–42) | **10** (4–15) | **9** (4–14) | **3** (0–6) |
| Solvents | **87** (82–92) | **11** (6–15) | **1** (0–2) | **1** (0–2) | **1** (0–3) |

*Source*: 1998/9 YLS n = 1,615 (cannabis) to 293 (solvents)

*Key*:
Frequent use – once a week or more;
Regular use – between once and three times a month;
Occasional use – once every couple of months;
Ad-hoc use – once or twice in the last year; and
Desisted – not used in last year.

*Notes*:
1. 95 per cent confidence intervals are given in brackets.
2. Questions about frequency of use were not included in the BCS, but desistance rates were broadly in line with those shown here.

are used.[6] As the least harmful illicit drug, cannabis is not only the most widely used, but is also the most intensely used (see Table 3.2). According to the YLS approximately one-in-five young adults who had ever used cannabis had done so on a weekly basis or more during the last year, although a similar proportion had used it on an ad-hoc basis and twice as many had not used it at all during this period. The tentative and hesitant nature of drug use is more marked in relation to the hallucinants and cocaine, which suggests that desistance and moderation after a period of experimentation are particularly important in managing the risks associated with these more harmful forms of recreational use. It may be, as the British Medical Association (2003) has argued, that the 'binge' use of amphetamine-type stimulants presents the greatest public health risk associated with adolescent recreational drug use, but self-regulation appears to play an important role in moderating this risk. More than half the young adults who had ever used amphetamines had not done so during the last year and a quarter or so had done so on no more than an ad-hoc basis during this period. The situation regarding ecstasy was similar, while rates of desistence were even more marked for LSD, magic mushrooms and amyl nitrate. Finally, although cocaine had a relatively low desistence rate this did not reflect particularly intense forms of use: in terms of frequency of use cocaine was similar to amphetamines.

## Underlying patterns of use

While prevalence rates provide some support for the idea that illicit drugs can be grouped together on the basis of social attributes, this possibility was assessed more formally by looking at underlying patterns of use. Such patterns were identified by examining the way in which various forms of drug use are associated with one another. Analyses were restricted to young adults who had used at least one illicit drug at some point and, for each substance, distinctions were drawn between abstinence (never used), desistance (used but not in the last year) and recent use (used in the last year). All possible comparisons were made between the various substances and this revealed a high degree of consistency between the BCS and YLS as well as considerable stability over time.[7]

Throughout the period 1994 to 2006/7 young adults' illicit drug use was organised around three distinct groupings or families of drugs, which confirm the validity of the three categories described above based on variations in prevalence rates. Cannabis formed a group on its own and was not strongly associated with any other specific substance:

although most strongly associated with ecstasy, amphetamines and LSD, these relationships were fairly modest in strength (i.e. Kendall's tau was consistently less than 0.30).

Underlying patterns of use also confirm the validity of the hallucinant category. In general, the substances included in this category were fairly strongly associated with one another and weakly associated with other drugs. With one possible exception, all of the hallucinants were most strongly associated with another substance in this category,[8] though the strength of the relationships varied: the strongest associations were evident between amphetamines, ecstasy and LSD (tau lay in the range 0.49 and 0.59) and between LSD and magic mushrooms (tau was 0.49 or 0.46 according to the BCS and YLS respectively), while those relating to amyl nitrates were somewhat weaker (tau lay in the range 0.22 to 0.40).

The third, and final, group was made up of heroin, methadone and crack, reflecting the low levels of use of these substances and their status as 'hard' drugs. Methadone and crack were both most strongly associated with heroin. The BCS and the YLS indicated that for heroin and crack tau was 0.55 and 0.44 respectively and for heroin and methadone it was 0.41 and 0.44 respectively. The relationship between methadone and crack was somewhat weaker at 0.30 (BCS) and 0.25 (YLS).

Although underlying patterns of use appear to have been remarkably stable during the period covered, notable changes were evident in relation to ecstasy and cocaine. While ecstasy consolidated its place among the hallucinants, the position of cocaine appeared to undergo quite a fundamental shift. Ecstasy use was already most closely associated with the use of LSD and amphetamines at the beginning of the period, but these relationships became notably stronger in the next few years (see

**Table 3.3 The changing status of ecstasy (Kendall's tau, young adults)**

| | *Ecstasy* | | | |
|---|---|---|---|---|
| | *1994* | *1998* | *2003/4* | *2006/7* |
| Amphetamines | 0.39 | 0.50 | 0.53 | 0.60 |
| LSD | 0.43 | 0.59 | 0.49 | 0.42 |
| Magic mushrooms | 0.24 | 0.37 | 0.37 | 0.42 |
| Amyl nitrates | 0.27 | 0.40 | 0.40 | 0.39 |

Source: BCS

*Note*: the 1998/9 YLS indicated that ecstasy use was associated with other forms of hallucinant use at the following rate: amphetamines (0.49), LSD (0.51), magic mushrooms (0.33) and amyl nitrates (0.33).

Table 3.3). Even allowing for the more mixed picture that emerged after 1998, the general pattern is consistent with the claim that ecstasy defined the prevailing mood of the 'rave' scene during the late 1980s and early 1990s, before taking its place alongside amphetamines and LSD in what became a poly-drug using culture (Collin with Godfrey, 1997).

The position of cocaine in 1994 was consistent with its image as a 'hard' drug, but changed markedly over the next few years. Increases in cocaine use appear to have been part of a broader process whereby it drifted away from the most marginalised forms of use towards the 'club' scene. Such has been the nature of this transformation that cocaine use has gone from being most strongly associated with heroin use to being most strongly associated with ecstasy use (see Table 3.4). According to the BCS the proportion of young adult ecstasy users who had also used cocaine increased from 28 per cent in 1994, to 41 per cent in 1998 (56 per cent according to the YLS), to 56 per cent in 2002/3 and to 70 per cent in 2006/7. Conversely, the proportion of cocaine users who had also used heroin fell from 19 per cent in 1994 to eight per cent in 1998 (12 per cent according to the YLS), since when it has remained fairly stable.[9]

## Age of onset

Underlying patterns of use reflect significant differences in the age at which substances are first used. The mid-to-late teens have been identified as a key period in the onset of illicit drug use and this was confirmed by the YLS,[10] which indicated that a slight majority (54 per cent) of young drug users first used an illicit substance when they were 13 to

**Table 3.4 The changing status of cocaine (Kendall's tau, young adults)**

| | *Cocaine* | | | |
|---|---|---|---|---|
| | *1994* | *1998* | *2002/3* | *2006/7* |
| Amphetamines | 0.25 | 0.37 | 0.42 | 0.54 |
| Ecstasy | 0.28 | 0.45 | 0.54 | 0.60 |
| LSD | 0.28 | 0.36 | 0.41 | 0.40 |
| Crack | 0.22 | 0.24 | 0.29 | 0.25 |
| Heroin | 0.38 | 0.21 | 0.16 | 0.20 |

*Source*: BCS

*Notes*: the 1998/9 YLS indicated that cocaine was associated with the following substances at the following rate: amphetamines (0.39), ecstasy (0.52), LSD (0.40), crack (0.31) and heroin (0.26).

16 years of age and that the average age of first use was 16. The earliest age of onset was evident in relation to solvents which were first used at an average age of 14 years, with nearly two-thirds of users using them before the age of 15. At the other end of the spectrum, cocaine was first used at an average of 19 years of age, with almost two-fifths of users waiting until they were 21 or older before using this substance.

The average age at which specific substances were first used suggests a fairly tightly compressed pattern of onset, with the figure for cannabis, most of the hallucinants and heroin being 16 or 17 years. This is somewhat misleading, however, because it is based on all users, including a large number who had only ever used one illicit drug – mainly cannabis – and had started to do so fairly late on. More detailed analysis of poly-drug use revealed a clearer, extended, career of onset, in which specific substances were markers for different stages of development (see Figure 3.1). This analysis was based on comparisons between the age at which specific substances were first used. Paired tests were used and comparisons were made on the basis of individuals who had used both substances of interest. Figure 3.1 shows the average difference in years of age between the first use of one substance and another. Thus, for example the relationship between solvents and cannabis was assessed on the basis of individuals who had used both drugs. On average, these individuals had first used solvents when they were approximately one year younger than when they first used cannabis. Similar comparisons revealed that, on average, solvents were first used almost two years earlier than amyl nitrates. Where no significant differences were evident, substances have been grouped together.[11]

A degree of orderliness is evident in the way poly-drug use typically unfolds, though drug-using careers can begin, end, or stall at any point and few users progress to the later stages. In their fullest form, poly-drug users' careers of onset typically developed over a period of approximately four years and broadly confirmed the underlying patterns of use described above. The distinctiveness of cannabis was reflected in its position towards the beginning of users' careers. Cannabis use typically predated hallucinant use by an average of one year (for amyl nitrates) to almost three years (for ecstasy). Although solvents were not widely used, they were the only illicit substance that tended to be used before cannabis. At the other end of the spectrum, users' careers confirmed the coherence of the crack, heroin and methadone category as use of these substances tended to start at around the same time and constituted the final phase of onset.

The hallucinants tended to be located towards the middle of a fully developed career, though there were notable differences between the

*Figure 3.1* Career of polydrug use (mean difference in years of age when first used, all users aged 12–30 years)

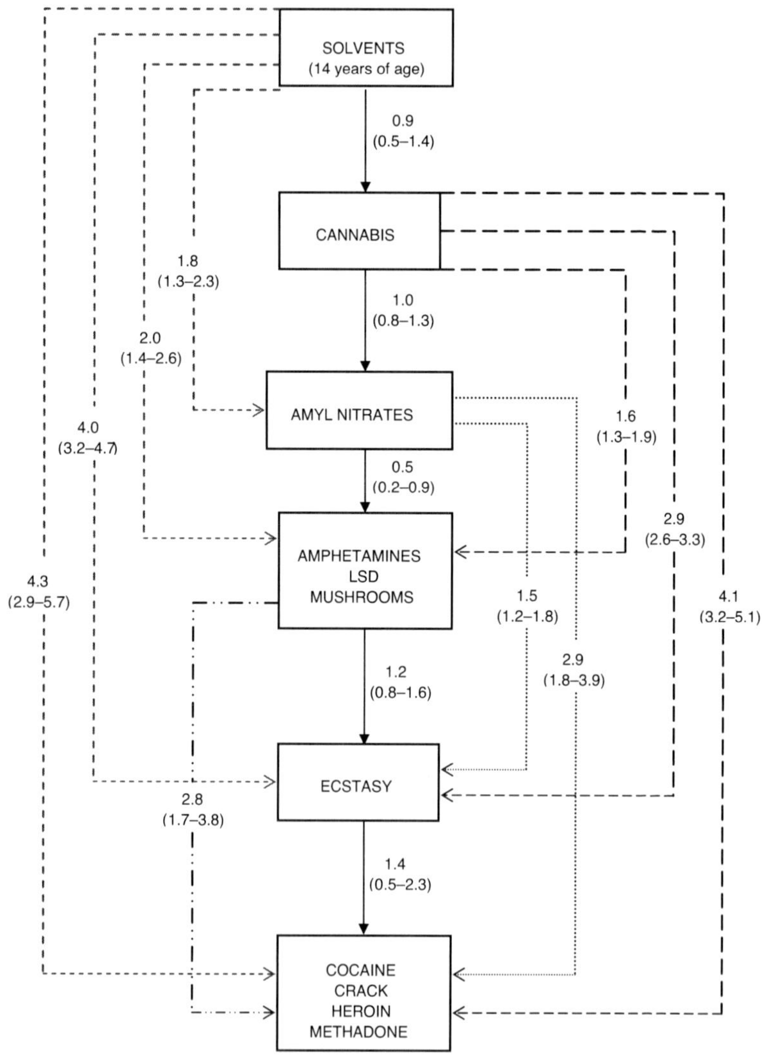


*Source*: 1998/9 YLS

*Note*: 95 per cent confidence intervals are given in brackets.

substances that made up this category. Amphetamines, LSD and magic mushrooms were grouped together, but tended to be used slightly later than amyl nitrates and somewhat earlier than ecstasy. Given that LSD, amyl nitrates and magic mushrooms were characterised by particularly ad-hoc patterns of use and high rates of desistance, this pattern supports the suggestion that they, along with solvents, tend to provide the basis for 'early experimentation' (Measham et al., 1998: 13).

Finally, the position of cocaine suggests a degree of ambiguity in its overall status. It was noted earlier that this substance has drifted away from the most marginalised forms of drug use towards those most closely associated with the 'club' scene, particularly ecstasy. According to Figure 3.1, however, cocaine tends to be first used somewhat later than the hallucinants, including ecstasy, and at about the same time as heroin and methadone. While this suggests a degree of uncertainty, the status of cocaine was clarified by variations in the extent of users' repertories.

## Variations in the extent of users' repertoires

Although illicit drug use is typically tentative and hesitant, specific substances are markers for different levels of involvement (see Table 3.5). The differences that are evident in this regard point towards a very similar classification to that suggested by underlying patterns of use and careers of onset. While cannabis use typically starts early on in poly-drug users' careers, it also tends to take place in the context of highly restricted repertoires. As such, it has a very limited role as a gateway to more harmful substances. Both the BCS and YLS indicated that young adults who had used cannabis had, on average, only ever used one other illicit substance and that between a third and two fifths were single susbtance users. Put another way, slightly more than a quarter of all young adult drug users had only ever used cannabis. At the other end of the spectrum, crack, heroin and methadone were indicative of fully developed, mature, repertoires. Young adults whose drug using careers extended this far had, on average, used a total of nine or ten illicit substances.

Once again, the hallucinants occupied the middle ground, as they were generally used in the context of moderately well-developed repertoires. There was, moreover, little evidence of variation between these substances. Although amphetamines tended to be used in the context of significantly narrower repertoires than ecstasy and LSD, no other significant and consistent differences were apparent between the hallucinants. More importantly, perhaps, cocaine was used in the context of repertoires that were very similar to those associated with ecstasy, LSD

**Table 3.5 Extent of young adult drug users' repertoires (number of drugs used)**

| | Median number of substances used | |
|---|---|---|
| ***If used...*** | *BCS* | *YLS* |
| Cannabis | **2** (2–2) | **2** (2–3) |
| Amphetamines | **4** (4–5) | **4** (4–5) |
| Amyl nitrates | **4** (4–5) | **5** (4–5) |
| Ecstasy | **6** (5–6) | **6** (5–6) |
| LSD | **6** (5–6) | **6** (5–6) |
| Magic mushrooms | **5** (5–6) | **6** (5–6) |
| Glues, solvents, gas or aerosols | **5** (4–6) | **5** (4–6) |
| Tranquillisers | **6** (5–7) | **7** (6–8) |
| Cocaine | **6** (5–7) | **6** (6–7) |
| Crack | a | **9** (8–10) |
| Methadone | a | **10** (8–11) |
| Heroin | a | **9** (8–10) |
| Any drug | **2** (2–2) | **2** (2–3) |

*Source*: 1998 BCS and 1998/9 YLS a = insufficient cases
n = 1,266 (any drug) to 18 (methadone) for the BCS and 1,804 (any drug) to 63 (methadone) for the YLS

*Notes*:
1. 95 per cent confidence intervals are given in brackets.
2. The figures presented here are based on individuals who had ever used the particular substance in question. Steroids have not been included as they had been used by very few respondents (< 40) and the confidence intervals were very wide. While the number of methadone users was also very small the confidence interval was reasonably narrow for the estimate based on the YLS.

and magic mushrooms and which were significantly, and fairly substantially, narrower than those associated with heroin, crack and methadone. When combined with the analysis described earlier, this indicates that cocaine is best viewed as a late feature of 'recreational' drug-using careers.

Finally, it is worth noting the position of solvents, as their use appears to be an early indicator of relatively extensive repertoires. Solvent use tended to occur in the context of fairly well developed repertoires and was typically located at the beginning of users' careers. That said, underlying patterns of use indicate that use of solvents was not particularly strongly linked to use of any other specific substance.[12]

## Reasons for non-use

The reasons people give for not using illicit drugs have received relatively little attention, but help to clarify the nature of the relationship between medical, legal and social dimensions of use. A useful starting point for discussion in this area is provided by American research into why people obey the law. Tyler (1990) compared 'instrumental' and 'normative' influences and concluded that normative issues are more important than dominant 'self-interest' models allow for. In essence, he suggested that people evaluate laws in normative terms and obey them if they consider them to be 'legitimate and moral'.

One of the few British studies to consider young people's reasons for not using illicit drugs found that, while motivations varied between substances, lack of interest in the effects was the most commonly given reason, while fear of addiction and harm were also frequently mentioned (Fountain et al., 1999). By contrast, lack of opportunity was not quoted as the major reason for non-use of any drug, references to legal deterrents were notable by their absence and cost only appeared to be a barrier to the use of cocaine.

Motivations for non-use were also explored in the YLS. In this context use and non-use were defined separately in relation to cannabis, the hallucinants and cocaine/opiates. Attempts to assess the extent to which people had not used these drugs 'because it is illegal', 'because I might get caught by the police' or 'because they might harm me' were particularly relevant to the analysis presented here as they help to separate out the influence of legal deterrents and normative considerations related to the potential for harm. Overall, these considerations appeared to have an important role in discouraging illicit drug use and were cited by the vast majority of young adult non-users (83 per cent to 92 per cent depending on the substance). Table 3.6 shows the number of young adults who indicated they had never used certain drugs

**Table 3.6 Reasons for non-use among young adults (percentages)**

| | *Never used because concerned about…* | | | | |
|---|---|---|---|---|---|
| *A.* | *…illegality* | *…police detection* | *…harm* | *…other issues* | *have used* |
| Cannabis | **30** (28–32) | **19** (17–21) | **36** (34–38) | **9** (7–10) | **50** (47–52) |
| Hallucinants | **40** (38–42) | **27** (25–29) | **53** (51–55) | **7** (6–8) | **36** (34–39) |
| Cocaine/opiates | **52** (50–54) | **39** (37–41) | **78** (76–80) | **7** (6–8) | **12** (10–13) |

| *B.* | *…illegality and police detection* | *…illegality but not police detection* | *…police detection but not illegality* | *…other issues* | *have used* |
|---|---|---|---|---|---|
| Cannabis | **16** (14–18) | **14** (12–15) | **3** (2–4) | **17** (16–19) | **50** (47–52) |
| Hallucinants | **24** (22–26) | **16** (14–18) | **3** (2–4) | **21** (19–23) | **36** (34–39) |
| Cocaine/opiates | **33** (31–35) | **19** (17–21) | **6** (5–7) | **30** (28–32) | **12** (10–13) |

| *C.* | *…illegality and harm* | *… illegality but not harm* | *…harm but not illegality* | *…other issues* | *have used* |
|---|---|---|---|---|---|
| Cannabis | **25** (23–27) | **5** (4–6) | **11** (10–12) | **9** (8–11) | **50** (47–52) |
| Hallucinants | **36** (34–39) | **3** (3–4) | **16** (15–18) | **7** (6–8) | **36** (34–39) |
| Cocaine/opiates | **49** (47–51) | **3** (2–4) | **29** (27–31) | **7** (6–8) | **12** (10–13) |

*Source*: 1998/9 YLS n = 3,474 (cannabis); 3,404 (hallucinants) and 3,428 (cocaine/opiates)

*Notes*:

1. The figures given here show the percentage of all young adults who had not used certain substances and whose non-use was, in part at least, motivated by the specified deterrent or combination of deterrents.
2. 95 per cent confidence intervals are given in brackets.

for the reasons given expressed as a percentage of *all* young adults (including those who had used the drugs in question).[13]

Responses to the YLS indicate that concern about the law is reasonably widespread. Almost a third of young adults had not used cannabis, in part at least, because they were concerned about breaking the law and this increased to two-fifths in relation to the hallucinants and to half in relation to cocaine/opiates. Fear of being caught by the police was not so apparent, however, and legal considerations were less widely implicated in young adults' decisions not to use illicit drugs than was the potential for harm (Table 3.6, section A).

Concern about the law and fear of being caught by the police did not act independently of one another (Table 3.6, section B). A sizeable proportion of young adults indicated that they had not used specific drugs, in part at least, because they were concerned about the law and were afraid of being caught by the police. The deterrent effect of the law seems to be only partially based on fear of punishment, however: depending on the substance, between 14 per cent and 19 per cent of young adults had not used illicit drugs because they were concerned about breaking the law even though they did not appear to be worried about being caught by the police. It is also notable that a sizeable proportion of young adults had not used illicit drugs even though they did not appear to be concerned about breaking the law or being caught by the police: 17 per cent in relation to cannabis, 21 per cent in relation to the hallucinants and 30 per cent in relation to cocaine/opiates.

Finally, the deterrent effect associated with harmfulness highlighted the importance of normative values (Table 3.6, section C). Depending on the substance, between a quarter and a half of young adults had not used illicit drugs because they did not want to break the law and because they were concerned about the potential for harm. Very few, five per cent or less, appeared to be motivated out of respect for the law in the absence of concern about harm, however, which suggests that the purely symbolic value of the law is very limited regardless of the legal status of the drug(s) involved. By contrast, harmfulness had a sizeable deterrent effect which was independent of concern about breaking the law and increased markedly with the potential for harm: 11 per cent of young adults had not used cannabis because they were concerned about the potential for harm even though they did not appear concerned about breaking the law and this increased to 16 per cent in relation to the hallucinants and 29 per cent in relation to cocaine/opiates.

## Conclusion

In the course of developing a social classification of drug use, this chapter has touched on a series of well established criminological themes. Prevalence rates and patterns of drug use, it has been argued, reinforce longstanding doubts about the efficacy of legal deterrents and prohibitionist

**Table 3.7 Social and harms-based classification of illicit drugs use**

| *Medico-legal classification (Independent Inquiry)* | *Social classification (patterns of use and key characteristics)* |
|---|---|
| **Class C – least harmful**<br>Cannabis | **Group 1**<br>Cannabis<br>• Most widely and intensively used illicit drug.<br>• Typically used in context of very limited repertoires.<br>• In the context of polydrug use, starts towards the beginning of users' careers.<br>• Concern about harm has relatively weak deterrent effect. |
| **Class B–moderately harmful**<br>Amphetamines, LSD and ecstasy | **Group 2**<br>Amphetamines, LSD, ecstasy, amyl nitrates, magic mushrooms and cocaine<br>• Fairly widely used.<br>• Infrequently used and high levels of desistance – especially for magic mushrooms, amyl nitrates and LSD.<br>• Markers for moderately well-developed repertoires.<br>• Typically start to be used after cannabis but before heroin, methadone and crack. Use of ecstasy tends to start after use of other hallucinants and use of cocaine tends to start after use of ecstasy.<br>• Concern about harm has fairly strong deterrent effect. |
| **Class A – most harmful**<br>Heroin, methadone, crack, cocaine and magic mushrooms | **Group 3**<br>Heroin, methadone and crack<br>• Least widely used illicit drugs.<br>• Markers for fully-developed mature careers:<br>– extensive repertoires;<br>– basis for final phase of onset.<br>• Concern about harm has very strong deterrent effect. |

policies more generally. International comparisons reveal relatively high rates of drug use in countries with punitive systems of control and highlight broadly similar patterns of use that transcend differences in legal classification. In Britain, as elsewhere, there is little symmetry between the extent to which illicit substances are used and their legal status. Far from ushering in a period of increased use, moreover, the recent liberalisation of the law in relation to cannabis was followed by a continued reduction in its use.

The widespread nature of illicit drug use presents a serious challenge to deficit based explanations, but it does not necessarily follow that such behaviour has been normalised in the way that has been suggested. Recent trends have not altered the essential ambiguity surrounding drug use, a position that is neatly encapsulated by the notion of primary deviance. Although it is far from unusual for young adults to have used illicit drugs, much of their use remains tentative, hesitant and short-lived. This, in turn, highlights the significance of normative concerns about managing risk and reducing the potential for harm. Such concerns are strongly implied by high rates of desistance, widespread evidence of moderation and the decisions that young adults make about what to use and what not to use.

While not clearly aligned to legal distinctions, patterns of drug use show considerable congruence with the potential for harm (see Table 3.7). Put simply, most young adults who use illicit drugs focus on less harmful substances. This tendency is reflected in the unique position of cannabis which, as well as being the least harmful illicit drug, is also the most widely and intensively used. Use of more harmful recreational drugs (i.e. the hallucinants and cocaine) is less widespread and tends to be more tentative and fleeting. Magic mushrooms and cocaine may appear to confound the general pattern, because they are fairly widely used even though they are included among the most harmful controlled substances, but their harmfulness has arguably been overstated. As such, the position of these substances may be considered consistent with the general pattern.

The way that harmfulness shapes young adults' decisions about drug use is made explicit by their reasons for not using certain substances. Concern about the potential for harm features more prominently in their reasoning and has a greater deterrent effect than the law. While the potential for harm discourages drug use independently of the law, the law appears to discourage drug use only in so far as its underlying philosophy is accepted: that is, that it is there to protect people from harm. It can be inferred from this that young adults' responses to the law are driven by normative, rather than instrumental, concerns.

# 4
# The Folk Devil Next Door

> It is clear from the rates of drug use, smoking and, especially, drinking among adolescents that these activities are not confined to the margins of adolescent life. Of the three activities, drug use is most commonly associated with social disadvantage. From reviewing recent studies however it is evident that no specific personality type, family background, socio-economic grouping or environmental situation categorically predicts drug use...contrary to common stereotypes, adolescents using recreational drugs are found predominantly among the young, studious, employed and relatively affluent (British Medical Association, 2003: 17).

In *Folk Devils and Moral Panics* Stanley Cohen (1972) documents the sensitivities that began to coalesce around youthful drug use during the 1960s. Groups like the Mods and Rockers, he notes, were identified by particular events (such as demonstrations) or particular disapproved forms of behaviour (such as drug-taking or violence) and occupied a constant position as folk devils, providing 'visible reminders of what we should not be' (1972: 2). Although finding little evidence of such behaviour himself, Cohen noted that the Mods' use of amphetamines or 'purple hearts' gave rise to 'one of the first big scares about drug use among juveniles' (1972: 112). Writing some 30 years later, in the introduction to the third edition of his book, Cohen reflected that psychoactive drugs had proved to be a remarkably consistent source of moral panics. Like many commentators, he was particularly struck by the reaction to the ecstasy related death of Leah Betts, noting: 'The warning was symbolically sharpened by Leah's respectable home background: father an ex-police officer, mother had worked as a drug counsellor...Leah was the girl next door' (2002: xiii).

Cohen's observations reflect a significant shift in the way illicit drug use is commonly perceived. According to the new orthodoxy that dominates academic and cultural commentary, drug use has been transformed by a process of 'democratisation', whereby increases in use have been accompanied by profound changes in the types of people involved. What was once an 'atypical' pursuit of the mainly 'delinquent and disordered' has, it is claimed, become commonplace and the normative nature of such behaviour is said to be demonstrated by the disintegration of traditional distinctions between users and non-users (Parker et al., 1998: 20). Sex, social class and ethnicity have all been implicated in this process and the 'withering of traditional sociological predictor variables' has been identified as the politically 'most challenging aspect of normalisation' (Parker et al., 1998: 154). The following analysis explores the demography of drug use and considers whether we can reasonably talk about the normalised drug user. Reflecting the claims that have been made in this regard, particular attention is paid to the role of sex, social class and ethnicity, alongside a range of other variables, including religiosity, income, area of residence and various deprivation indicators. The influence of these variables is considered separately in relation to cannabis, the hallucinants and cocaine. Although fairly closely associated with one another, the hallucinants and cocaine have been kept apart on the grounds that cocaine tends to feature later on in users' careers. Heroin, methadone and crack cocaine were excluded from the more detailed analysis presented here because they are rarely used and because of the particular limitations of household surveys in measuring their use.

## Social class

According to the authors of the normalisation thesis the normative nature of drug trying is demonstrated by the closure of traditional social class differences: being 'middle class' is said to no longer predict school-based abstinence, so that the children of professional and managerial parents are often found to have the highest rates of drug trying, followed by young people from the lowest socio-economic backgrounds (Parker et al., 1998). The BCS and YLS confirm that drug use is only weakly related to family background.[1] There was some suggestion that cannabis use and cocaine use were most prevalent among young adults from relatively privileged backgrounds, but it was not clear that these differences could be attributed directly to family background. Once other variables had been taken into account, the multivariate models indicated that parental occupation was associated with a limited range of effects, which suggested little by way of a clear pattern (see Technical Appendix for details).

Drug use was no more closely related to young adults' own occupational status. The findings from both surveys were very similar in this regard and pointed to a consistent pattern: the prevalence of cannabis use and hallucinant use was only weakly associated with respondents' occupational class, while the prevalence of cocaine use was not subject to any significant variation across the classes. The multivariate models did identify a number of significant effects associated with young adults' occupational class, but they tended to be fairly modest in size and did not form a clear or consistent pattern (see Technical Appendix for details). This is broadly consistent with the international evidence which indicates that illicit drug use is only weakly related to social class (measured by educational level) once other socio-demographic characteristics have been taken into account (Degenhardt et al., 2008).

Having noted that the relationship between drug use and social class is weak raises the question of whether this represents a significant departure. The BCS has repeatedly found drug use to be fairly evenly distributed among young adults regardless of their social class, though such findings only date back to the early 1990s (Mott and Mirrlees-Black, 1995; Ramsay and Percy, 1996; Ramsay and Spiller, 1997; Ramsay et al., 2001). The absence of comparable data for previous decades creates obvious difficulties in assessing the situation over a longer period, but recent surveys can be used to make some comment about the likely nature of any changes that have taken place. Based on the assumption that most people who use drugs do so during adolescence and early adulthood, changes over time will be reflected in differences between age cohorts (Shiner and Newburn, 1999). Using age cohorts to assess the influence of social class over time also assumes that individual's social position remains stable throughout the life-course, which may seem questionable given the general trend towards upward social mobility over the last 50 years or so. This trend has largely been concentrated within an expanding middle class, however, and has typically involved modest changes in social position (Heath and Payne, 2000). Consequently, class destinations continue to be strongly related to class origins and educational attainment (Jackson et al., 2005), which means occupation and qualifications provide a reasonable basis for assessing the impact of social class across age cohorts. The normalisation thesis implies that drug use was once largely restricted to 'delinquent' working class subcultures and has only recently been widely embraced by middle class youth. If this is the case then we would expect to see marked class differences among older adults that converge sharply among younger adults.

Previous analysis of the BCS confirms that differences between social classes are more pronounced among older than younger adults, but such differences have not taken the form that might be expected. Far from being concentrated among the working classes, drug use has been found to be most prevalent among older adults who remained in education beyond the official school-leaving age or lived in a household headed by somebody in a non-manual occupation (Mott and Mirrlees-Black, 1995). A similar pattern was evident on the basis of the 1998 BCS, which suggested that class distinctions have become less marked, and that, among older adults, illicit drug use was most widespread among those who had participated in higher education or were employed in professional, managerial or technical occupations. The percentage of respondents in their twenties who had ever used cannabis, the hallucinants or cocaine did not vary significantly according to their highest qualification or occupational class, but significant variations were evident among older groups: those in their fifties who had a degree or teaching qualification reported having ever used drugs at two and a half times the rate of those who had not attained this level of qualification (20 per cent compared with eight per cent), while significant, albeit less striking, differences were also found among those in their forties (28 per cent compared with 19 per cent). A very similar pattern was evident on the basis of occupational class and, taken together, these findings support the claim that middle class bohemian youth cultures provided the major growth area for drug use during the mid-to-late 1960s. Middle-class youths, particularly students, were said to be the most 'active aficionados' of marihuana during this period, while the use of LSD was thought to be 'almost entirely limited' to such groups (Young, 1971: 22 and 204).

## Income

The impact of social class on youth lifestyles is often said to have been blunted by the restructuring of the labour market and the consequent marginalisation of young people from full-time paid employment. With so few school leavers going straight into full-time work, British youth culture is no longer oriented towards working class wage-earners in the way it once was and new patterns of inclusion and exclusion have been created. Access to the means of consumption, it has been suggested, may now be more significant than traditional class differences in explaining cultural identification because those 'who have access to the necessary resources are able to participate in youth cultures which cut across class boundaries' (Furlong and Cartmel, 2007: 84–5). Despite being largely excluded from full-time work, young people continue to constitute a key segment of the consumer market and display a distinctive pattern of spending, which combines a high discretionary element with a particular orientation towards leisure products consumed away from the home (Jones and Martin, 1997).

The YLS found young adults had an average of £59 a week to spend after meeting housing costs, paying bills and buying food, though this figure varied sharply from £29 among 16 and 17 year olds to £75 among 27 to 30 year olds, while the 2004/5 Expenditure and Food Survey reported that households headed by somebody aged 30 years or below spent an average of £66 a week on alcohol, tobacco, recreational and cultural services, restaurants and hotels (Gibbins and Julian, 2006). Viewed in this context, illicit drugs would appear to be a reasonably affordable commodity, at least when used recreationally. With falling prices (see http://www.idmu.co.uk/), it has been claimed that, unit for unit, ecstasy is cheaper than Sainsbury's cherries (*The Guardian*, September 24 2005) and cocaine costs less than a cappuccino (*The Observer*, January 9 2005).[2] In itself, then, financial cost does not appear particularly prohibitive, but if drug use forms part of a broader lifestyle based on intensive consumption then some young people may be priced out of the market. On this basis, we might expect such behaviour to be related more strongly to income than social class.

Previous analysis has pointed to a paradoxical relationship between drug use and income. The 1994 BCS indicated that drug use was most common within the poorest households, followed by the richest households and was least common in middle-income households (Ramsay and Percy, 1996). Further analysis of the 1998 BCS showed that, for young adults at least, this paradox is linked to housing transitions. Among young adults who lived with their parents drug use tended to be more prevalent in higher income households, whereas among those who lived independently it tended to be more prevalent in lower income households. These tendencies were not particularly marked, however, as household income was only weakly related to cannabis use and hallucinant use and was not significantly related to cocaine use. The YLS provided a potentially more useful measure of personal disposable income (rather than household income), but, once again, this measure was only weakly related to drug use: prevalence rates did increase with disposable income, but only at a very modest rate.[3]

The multivariate models confirmed that income, like social class, is a poor predictor of illicit drug use. According to the final YLS models, personal disposable income had no significant effects on the probability of cannabis use, hallucinant use or cocaine use, while the final BCS models revealed that household income had a small number of fairly ambiguous effects (see Technical Appendix for details). These effects were concentrated among young adults who lived with their parents and indicated that higher income parental households were associated with an increased probability of past and recent cannabis use, as well as an increased probability of past hallucinant use. Among young adults who were living independently, the only significant effect associated with income indicated that high-income households reduced the probability of past hallucinant use. It is, perhaps, particularly notable that neither household income nor personal disposable income had any significant effects on the probability of cocaine use.

## Sex

Comparative studies, based on countries from various parts of the world, have found that men tend to use illicit, as well as licit, substances in greater numbers than women, but that prevalence rates for both sexes vary sharply by country (Vega et al., 2002; Degenhardt et al., 2008). Such studies also suggest that differences between the sexes are becoming less marked as, in terms of their substance use at least, women are catching up with men. Sex, like social class, has been heavily implicated in the normalisation thesis, with claims that the gender gap closed rapidly during the 1990s and that many studies, including the North West Cohort Study, no longer recorded significant differences between the sexes (Parker et al., 1998). At around the same time the normalisation thesis was being formulated a separate body of feminist work began to emerge which shared an emphasis on the similarities between male and female drug use (see Henderson, 1997, 1999 and Hinchcliff, 2001). Reflecting long-standing feminist concerns about the marginalisation of women, this work sought to give women a 'voice' and emphasised the need to escape from traditional representations which were considered to bear little resemblance to women's actual experiences. In a neat summary of the feminist position, Sheila Henderson (1999: 37) noted:

> This, predominantly medical and psychological, literature presented a picture of drug use in which drug users just happened to be male

> (if you bothered to notice) and women hardly figured. When they did, they appeared as sicker, more deviant, more psychologically disturbed than their male peers: as weak and pathetic creatures. Women's drug use figured as a 'deviation' from 'normal' femininity due to mental or physical deficiencies, or disease...It was worthy of attention only when it affected others: through childbirth and child rearing.

When Henderson (1999: 41) began to consider gender and drug use in the context of dance culture in the early 1990s she found a 'somewhat empty tool-kit': the young women who participated in dance events were 'like the chalk to the cheese of the prevailing images of femininity within other studies of drug use'. This mismatch was said to highlight the need for new perspectives which allow for the possibility that women are active social agents and not merely passive subjects of male power. As a counterpoint to the puritanical (female) victim mentality, Henderson and others emphasised the similarities between male and female drug use: women, they noted, 'have achieved the (dubious) equality of consuming as many illegal mind-changing substances as the next man' (Henderson, 1999: 36); have 'participated in dance events as often as men' (Hinchcliff, 2001: 456); and 'use drugs in ways which have previously been considered predominantly male' (Hinchcliff, 2001: 466). In their attempts to explain this apparent equality, feminist commentators have drawn on developments within Cultural Studies, arguing that certain types of drug use can best be understood as a form of consumption. Where traditional explanations of women's drugs use emphasised coercion and unhappiness, recent feminist accounts emphasise choice and pleasure. Young women, we are told, do not use drugs in the context of dance culture because they are forced to by men, nor are they leading unhappy lives as a result. They are, rather, 'self-confident' women who choose to use drugs as part of a lifestyle which involves a commitment to consumption and mass pleasure seeking, through which they make sense of their place in the world (Henderson, 1999; Hinchcliff, 2001).

What then of the evidence from the BCS and YLS? Both surveys confirm that illicit drug use has become fairly widespread among young women, while also pointing to significant differences between the sexes (see Table 4.1). Approximately one-and-a-half times as many young men as young women had recently used cannabis, twice as many had recently used a hallucinant and two or three times as many had recently used cocaine. Less striking differences were evident in relation to past use, though the ratio of past-to-recent users did suggest female users

**Table 4.1 Prevalence of drug use by sex (percentages, young adults)**

| | *Cannabis* | | | *Hallucinants* | | | *Cocaine* | | |
|---|---|---|---|---|---|---|---|---|---|
| | *Never* | *Past* | *Recent* | *Never* | *Past* | *Recent* | *Never* | *Past* | *Recent* |
| *BCS* | | ** | | | ** | | | ** | |
| Male | 49 | 22 | 29 | 66 | 20 | 14 | 92 | 4 | 4 |
| Female | 63 | 20 | 17 | 78 | 15 | 7 | 96 | 2 | 2 |
| *YLS* | | ** | | | ** | | | ** | |
| Male | 44 | 19 | 37 | 58 | 23 | 19 | 86 | 6 | 9 |
| Female | 57 | 19 | 24 | 72 | 18 | 10 | 94 | 3 | 3 |

*Source*: BCS (1998) and YLS (1998/9) ** $p < .01$ ** $p < .05$ ns $p < 0.05$

*Notes*:
1. BCS: Cramer's V = 0.16 (cannabis); 0.14 (hallucinants) and 0.08 (cocaine).
2. YLS: Cramer's V = 0.14 (cannabis); 0.16 (hallucinants) and 0.13 (cocaine).

were more likely to have stopped using drugs than their male counterparts. Further analysis, which compared the rate of recent use to past use, confirmed the statistical significance of these differences in relation to cannabis and the hallucinants, though not cocaine.

Differences between the sexes persisted even when other factors were taken into account. Being female reduced the probability of recent use across all three drug-types at each stage of the multivariate analysis and across both surveys. Even in the final models, when other lifestyle differences were taken into account, sex had a marked effect on the probability of recent use (see Table 4.2). The BCS indicated that being female roughly halved the probability of recent cannabis and hallucinant use, while the effect on cocaine use was even more striking. For all three drug-types, the YLS indicated that being female reduced the probability of recent use by about a third. According to both surveys sex had a much less marked effect on past use. The multivariate models indicated that the heightened rate of desistance women displayed in relation to the hallucinants could be explained by broader life-course and lifestyle differences, but that which they displayed in relation to cannabis could not be fully explained in this way.[4]

Although drug use continues to be less prevalent among young women than young men gender differences may have become less marked over time. Some sense of whether this is the case can be gained by comparing the various sweeps of the BCS. Figures from the 1992 sweep show that almost one-and-a-half times as many males as females in the 16 to 29 year age group had used an illicit drug at some point and almost twice

**Table 4.2 Probability of drug use by sex (multivariate analysis, young adults)**

| | *Cannabis* | | | *Hallucinants* | | | *Cocaine* | | |
|---|---|---|---|---|---|---|---|---|---|
| | *Never* | *Past* | *Recent* | *Never* | *Past* | *Recent* | *Never* | *Past* | *Recent* |
| *BCS* | | | | | | | | | |
| Male† | 0.49 | 0.21 | 0.30 | 0.62 | 0.22 | 0.16 | 0.88 | 0.04 | 0.08 |
| Female | 0.63 | 0.21 | **0.17** | 0.77 | **0.16** | **0.07** | 0.96 | 0.03 | **0.01** |
| *YLS* | | | | | | | | | |
| Male† | 0.46 | 0.20 | 0.34 | 0.60 | 0.23 | 0.17 | 0.88 | 0.06 | 0.06 |
| Female | 0.59 | **0.18** | **0.23** | 0.72 | **0.18** | **0.11** | 0.93 | **0.03** | **0.04** |

*Source*: BCS (1998) and YLS (1998/9) †reference category *Model*: Lifestyle model

*Notes*:
1. Statistically significant effects are highlighted in bold.
2. Effects on past or recent use were estimated vis-à-vis the probability of never having used. A statistically significant effect changed the probability of past or recent use *relative* to the probability of never having used.

as many had done so in the previous 12-months (Mott and Mirrlees-Black, 1995). Subsequent sweeps have continued to report very similar differences, suggesting that the gender gap is an enduring and stable feature of early adulthood: the 1994, 1998, 2002/3 and 2006/7 surveys all indicate that the percentage of young men who had ever used cannabis, the hallucinants or cocaine was 1.3 or 1.4 times greater than the percentage of young women and that the percentage who had used these substances in the previous year was 1.6 or 1.7 times greater. Comparing age cohorts from the 1998 BCS reinforces the conclusion that the gender gap has been more or less maintained over time. Among respondents in their twenties, thirties, forties and fifties respectively, between one-and-a-half to two times as many men as women had used cannabis, the hallucinants or cocaine, while further analysis confirmed that the size of the gender gap did not vary significantly across the cohorts (see also Shiner, 2006).[5]

## Ethnicity and religion

Anxieties about illicit drugs have long been linked to the politics of 'race', with drug-related images often relying on racist constructions of criminality and assumptions of 'ethnic welfare' (Khan, 1999). The nature of this imagery varies sharply between minority groups, so that African Caribbean communities tend to be equated with wanton and reckless drug use, while Asians are thought to be immune from such behaviour due to specific cultural barriers (Murji, 1999). In challenging such stereotypical images recent studies have tended to emphasise the similarities that are shared across ethnic groups. People from minority groups, it has been noted, start to use drugs in much the same way as whites, draw on a similar range of substances, use drugs for broadly the same reasons and display very similar patterns of use (Patel et al., 1996; Pearson and Patel, 1998; Fountain et al., 2003). While these claims are consistent with the notion that drug use can no longer be predicted on the basis of socio-demographic characteristics, ethnicity has been specifically implicated in the process of normalisation on the basis that 'being black or Asian does not predict higher than average rates of adolescent drug use' (Parker et al., 1998: 154).

The BCS and YLS revealed significant variations between ethnic groups (see Table 4.3). Although discrepancies were evident between the surveys, the analysis supports some general observations that are consistent with other national surveys. On balance, cannabis use seems to be most widespread among young adults from white and black Caribbean backgrounds. This is suggested by the figures shown below and is more clearly established by the 1996 BCS, which included a much larger number of respondents from minority backgrounds (Ramsay and Spiller, 1997; Sangster et al., 2002) and the 2001/2 BCS (Aust and Smith, 2003).

The relatively widespread nature of cannabis use among white and black Caribbean young adults is consistent with Ansley Hamid's (2002) analysis of the 'ganja complex'. This complex was carried to the British Caribbean by indentured Indian labourers during the nineteenth century, where it took root among the African population in rural Jamaica. It was then codified by Rastafarianism and spread across the region, before being exported to Europe and North America by migrant Caribbean communities, 'who planted it among their local neighbours, such as African Americans, Latinos, Canadians, the British, and North Europeans' (Hamid, 2002: xv). In Britain, as elsewhere, the bohemian hippie movement provided a ready-made conduit through which marihuana was introduced into the host community (Young, 1971; Donnelly, 2005). Official statistics for the period 1963 to 1967 show that cannabis use went from being largely restricted to first generation Caribbean migrants to being increasingly associated with white middle-class youth. Not only was there a marked general increase in the number of arrests for cannabis possession during this period, but the

**Table 4.3 Prevalence of drug use by ethnicity (percentages, young adults)**

| | *Cannabis* | | | *Hallucinants* | | | *Cocaine* | | |
|---|---|---|---|---|---|---|---|---|---|
| | *Never* | *Past* | *Recent* | *Never* | *Past* | *Recent* | *Never* | *Past* | *Recent* |
| *BCS* | | ** | | | ** | | | ns | |
| White | 56 | 22 | 23 | 72 | 18 | 10 | 94 | 3 | 3 |
| Black Caribbean | 66 | 3 | 31 | 79 | 21 | 0 | 98 | 2 | 0 |
| Black African | 88 | 4 | 8 | 96 | 0 | 4 | 96 | 4 | 0 |
| Indian | 73 | 13 | 15 | 84 | 15 | 1 | 99 | 0 | 1 |
| Pakistani or Bangladeshi | 81 | 11 | 8 | 95 | 0 | 5 | 97 | 3 | 0 |
| Other | 54 | 29 | 17 | 77 | 12 | 11 | 85 | 9 | 6 |
| *YLS* | | ** | | | ** | | | * | |
| White | 49 | 20 | 31 | 63 | 22 | 16 | 89 | 5 | 6 |
| Black Caribbean | 59 | 21 | 21 | 83 | 15 | 3 | 97 | 3 | 0 |
| Black African | 81 | 0 | 19 | 91 | 0 | 9 | 91 | 9 | 0 |
| Indian | 86 | 8 | 6 | 95 | 3 | 2 | 100 | 0 | 0 |
| Pakistani or Bangladeshi | 90 | 2 | 9 | 100 | 0 | 0 | 100 | 0 | 0 |
| Other | 67 | 13 | 19 | 85 | 9 | 6 | 93 | 2 | 6 |

*Source*: BCS (1998) and YLS (1998/9) ** $p < .01$ * $p < .05$ ns $p < 0.05$

*Notes*:
1. BCS: Cramer's V = 0.09 (cannabis), 0.08 (hallucinants) and 0.05 (cocaine).
2. YLS: Cramer's V = 0.12 (cannabis), 0.12 (hallucinants) and 0.06 (cocaine).
3. Significance tests for cocaine were based on comparisons between two groups – white and other versus the various minority groups. This amendment was required to ensure the validity of the test. Figures for cocaine use based on the BCS have been reported because they were very close to the cut-off indicating statistical significance ($p = .06$) and were similar to those highlighted by the YLS.

proportion of arrestees who were white also increased sharply, from 45 per cent to 73 per cent. While recognising the limitations of the data, Young (1971: 13) maintained that they do 'not in any way detract from the conclusion that there has been a considerable increase in use and that this is concomitant with the spread of use to young white offenders'. Generational comparisons based on the BCS, point in a similar direction having shown that, among older groups, cannabis use is more widespread among African Caribbeans than whites, but that among younger groups whites have 'caught up with or rather overtaken' African Caribbeans (Ramsay and Percy, 1996: 59).

The role of cultural exchange has also been implicated by international studies which suggest that assimilation into societies with high rates of drug use may accelerate rates of drug use among migrant communities towards the normative rates of the host nation (Vega et al., 2002). Thus, it has been noted, that 'long stay' migrants report higher rates of use than 'short stay' migrants and that second generation migrants report higher rates of use than even 'long stay' migrants. That said, the BCS and YLS indicate that young adults from black and minority ethnic groups are considerably less involved in hallucinant use and cocaine use than their white counterparts. Such differences are particularly pronounced in relation to recent use, which reflects the heightened rates of desistance and abstinence that are evident among minority groups. These patterns are broadly consistent with what is known about the development of 'rave', which, though influenced by African, Caribbean and Asian musical forms, started out as 'a predominantly white dance culture in terms of both organisation and participation' (Measham et al., 2001: 54). When the jungle scene brought an increased 'black' presence during the early 1990s, moreover, ecstasy and amphetamines were replaced by 'the new dance drugs of choice' – cannabis, cocaine, alcohol and, to a lesser extent, crack (Measham et al., 2001: 55). Although the 'Asian Underground' also came to greater prominence during this period, its development does not appear to have been accompanied by widespread use of the hallucinants or cocaine among young adults from Indian, Pakistani or Bangladeshi backgrounds.

Differences between ethnic groups proved fairly robust and continued to be evident throughout most stages of the multivariate analysis. The life-course models indicated that such differences could not be explained by the influence of demographic characteristics, deprivation indicators, neighbourhood characteristics or life-course indicators: even when all these factors were taken into account, being from a black and minority ethnic group was generally associated with a reduced probability of recent use and a heightened probability of both abstinence and past use (see Table 4.4).

The effects associated with ethnicity may well reflect the influence of informal social controls. In *Crime, Shame and Reintegration*, John Braithwaite (1989) identified shaming as one of the factors that helps societies to maintain low crime rates, noting that it is more potent when carried out by proximate communities than the state. Braithwaite also noted that cultural groups differ in their traditions of shaming, with some groups shaming more forcefully and effectively than others, and implied that these differences may help to explain the relatively low rates of offending found among some migrant groups. Several British studies have noted the distinct role that informal community controls play among South Asians, particularly those of Pakistani and Bangladeshi origin, pointing to an on-going commitment among younger members of these groups to the extended family system, to the notion of izzat or family prestige and to the desire to avoid bringing shame on the family name (Mawby and Batta, 1980; Webster, 1997). Although the drugs literature has tended not to pay great attention to such factors, various cultural influences have been identified which may serve to limit the extent of drug use among minority ethnic

**Table 4.4 Probability of drug use by ethnicity (multivariate analysis, young adults)**

| | *Cannabis* | | | *Hallucinants* | | | *Cocaine* | | |
|---|---|---|---|---|---|---|---|---|---|
| | *Never* | *Past* | *Recent* | *Never* | *Past* | *Recent* | *Never* | *Past* | *Recent* |
| *BCS* | | | | | | | | | |
| White† | 0.55 | 0.22 | 0.22 | 0.71 | 0.19 | 0.10 | 0.92 | 0.03 | 0.05 |
| Black Caribbean | 0.71 | **0.07** | 0.22 | 0.82 | 0.17 | **0.01** | | | |
| Black African | 0.92 | **0.03** | **0.05** | | | | | | |
| Indian, Pakistani or Bangladeshi | 0.73 | 0.15 | **0.12** | 0.90 | **0.06** | **0.04** | 0.98 | 0.02 | **0.01** |
| Other | 0.55 | 0.22 | 0.22 | 0.19 | 0.19 | 0.10 | 0.92 | 0.03 | 0.05 |
| *YLS* | | | | | | | | | |
| White† | 0.50 | 0.20 | 0.30 | 0.63 | 0.22 | 0.15 | 0.90 | 0.04 | 0.06 |
| Black Caribbean | 0.73 | **0.12** | **0.15** | 0.85 | 0.13 | **0.03** | | | |
| Black African | 0.84 | **0.03** | **0.13** | | | | | | |
| Indian | 0.84 | **0.09** | **0.07** | 0.97 | 0.01 | **0.02** | **0.98** | **0.02** | **<0.01** |
| Pakistani or Bangladeshi | 0.89 | **0.04** | **0.07** | | | | | | |
| Other | 0.64 | 0.17 | **0.19** | 0.78 | 0.13 | 0.09 | 0.90 | 0.04 | 0.06 |

*Source*: BCS (1998) and YLS (1998/9) †reference category *Model*: Life-course model

*Notes*:
1. Ethnicity was classified differently in the different models because its effects varied between substances. In the cannabis model categories were combined according to the procedure outlined in the Technical Appendix. In the remaining models it was not possible to estimate separate effects for each ethnic group because some categories included too few users. Under these circumstances minority groups were combined on the basis that they tended to be associated with low levels of use.
2. Statistically significant effects are highlighted in bold. Effects on past or recent use were estimated vis-à-vis the probability of never having used.
3. The 'other' category was included in the YLS hallucinant model even though it was not statistically significant because it had a sizeable effect, because excluding it would have masked some of the effects associated with other ethnic groups and because it was close to the cut-off point for significance (p = .06 for past use and .10 for recent use).

groups, including those of African Caribbean as well as south Asian origin. These factors include particular conceptions of shame and honour, an emphasis on respectability and reputation, high levels of parental/ adult surveillance, the role of religion and a certain 'mentality' associated with economic migration that involves an over-riding ambition to better oneself and one's family (Abdulrahim, 1998; Sangster et al., 2002; see also Bradby, 2007).

Of these influences, the YLS provides a reasonable basis for assessing the impact of religious orientation. Religiosity is strongly linked to reduced levels of crime and deviance (Tittle and Welch, 1983; Ellis, 1985; Butts et al., 2003) and there are good reasons for supposing it may serve to limit the extent of drug use. Most major world religions oppose the use of drugs to modify states of consciousness (Plant and Plant, 1992; Gossop, 1996) and recent research has confirmed that religiosity is associated with restrictive attitudes to drugs and reduced levels of use (Gould and Stratford, 2002; Butts et al., 2003). In the United States, evidence of such links has prompted suggestions that religion may help to explain differences between ethnic groups and studies have specifically shown that the high degree of religiosity found among African American adolescents goes some way towards accounting for their relatively high rates of abstinence (Wallace et al., 2003).

The YLS confirmed the link between drug use and religiosity. Cannabis use, hallucinant use and cocaine use were all most prevalent among young adults who did not identify with any particular religion and were least prevalent among those who did identify with a religion and had recently attended a religious service or activity. These differences proved to be largely independent of the other variables included in the analysis, moreover, so that being actively religious – as opposed to having no religion – substantially reduced the probability of recent use in relation to all three drug-types: on average, and all other things being equal, it reduced the probability of recent cannabis use from 0.33 to 0.19; of recent hallucinant use from 0.14 to 0.07; and of recent cocaine use from 0.06 to 0.01. Religious identification in the absence of active participation had much less effect (see Technical Appendix for details).

The YLS also confirmed that the effects of religiosity are felt most widely within black and minority ethnic groups, though they are also evident among whites.[6] Religious differences between ethnic groups are closely bound up with tradition, yet continue to be an important source of identity and experience among young people (Cassidy et al., 2006; Bradby, 2007). While noting important generational differences and changes over time, the Fourth National Survey of Ethnic

Minorities in Britain concluded that: 'Religion is perhaps the key area where the minority groups manifest a cultural dynamic which is at least partly at odds with native British trends' (Modood et al., 1997: 356). Such differences are certainly evident from the YLS, which pointed to a greater degree of religiosity among young adults from minority groups than among whites: most notably, one-in-ten white young adults had recently attended a religious service or activity compared with approximately half the black Africans, two-in-five Pakistanis, Bangladeshis and Indians and slightly more than one-in-four black Caribbeans.

The extent to which the greater religiosity of young adults from minority ethnic groups helps to explain their more limited drug use was formally assessed on the basis of the multivariate models. If religiosity fully explains ethnic differences then its inclusion in the models would reduce the effects of ethnicity to the point that they cease to be statistically significant. The inclusion of religiosity did reduce the effects of ethnicity, but only by a fairly modest amount and these effects continued to be statistically significant (see Table 4.5). While helping to mediate the effects of ethnicity, therefore, religiosity provides no more than a partial explanation for the differences that were evident between whites and minority groups. The effects of ethnicity were reduced further, and rather more sharply, by the inclusion of lifestyle indicators, particularly those relating to alcohol and tobacco consumption. In relation to cannabis, for example, the effects of ethnicity became less marked when religiosity was added into the model and ceased to be significant once lifestyle indicators were taken into account. Although ethnic differences were more persistent in relation to the hallucinants and cocaine they too were substantially reduced by the addition of lifestyle variables. The BCS models also indicated that the effects of ethnicity were, in part at least, mediated by broader lifestyle factors. Despite the relatively limited range of lifestyle indicators available for this analysis, their inclusion in the models brought about quite marked reductions in the effects associated with ethnicity (see Technical Appendix for details).

In light of these findings ethnic differences relating to drug use are, perhaps, best viewed as manifestations of more general, culturally distinct, orientations to consumption and intoxication. Young adults from black and minority ethnic backgrounds are less likely to use illicit drugs than their white counterparts, in part at least, because they are less likely to drink alcohol, get drunk and/or smoke tobacco. Almost all the Pakistanis and Bangladeshis included in the BCS indicated they

**Table 4.5 Changing effects of ethnicity – YLS (regression coefficients, multivariate analysis, young adults)**

| | *Past use* | | | *Recent use* | | |
|---|---|---|---|---|---|---|
| | *Life-course model* | *Life-course model + religiosity* | *Lifestyle model* | *Life-course model* | *Life-course model + religiosity* | *Lifestyle model* |
| *Cannabis* | | | | | | |
| White† | – | – | – | – | – | – |
| Black Caribbean | **–0.92** | –0.81 | –0.37 | **–1.08** | **–0.89** | –0.37 |
| Black African | **–2.46** | **–2.22** | –1.02 | **–1.37** | –0.99 | 0.74 |
| Indian | **–1.32** | **–1.13** | –0.27 | **–1.98** | **–1.71** | –0.92 |
| Pakistani or Bangladeshi | **–2.13** | **–1.95** | 0.52 | **–2.00** | **–1.71** | 0.35 |
| Other | –0.41 | –0.44 | –0.58 | **–0.66** | –0.54 | –0.02 |
| *Hallucinants* | | | | | | |
| White† | – | – | – | – | – | – |
| Black Caribbean, black African, Indian, Pakistani or Bangladeshi | **–1.92** | **–1.75** | **–1.04** | **–2.38** | **–2.11** | **–1.10** |
| Other | –0.76 | –0.65 | –0.17 | –0.75 | –0.62 | 0.20 |
| *Cocaine* | | | | | | |
| White† | – | – | – | – | – | – |
| Black Caribbean, black African, Indian, Pakistani or Bangladeshi | **–1.22** | –1.11 | –0.34 | **–2.88** | **–2.61** | –2.03 |
| Other | –0.71 | –0.68 | 0.08 | 0.09 | 0.24 | 1.07 |

*Source*: YLS (1998/9) †reference category

*Key – types of model*:

1. Life-course models included demographic characteristics, deprivation indicators, neighbourhood and regional measures and life-course indicators.
2. Lifestyle models included all of the above plus lifestyle indicators.

*Notes*:

1. For the purposes of the analysis shown here ethnicity was included at each stage of the models regardless of its statistical significance and was included in the same form at each stage to ensure comparability (this form was determined by the final model).
2. Statistically significant effects are highlighted in bold. Effects on past or recent use were estimated vis-à-vis the probability of never having used.
3. The effect of ethnicity on recent cocaine use in the final lifestyle model was close to the cut-off denoting statistical significance ($p = 0.09$).

never drank alcohol, while slightly more than three-in-five of those included in the YLS indicated they had never had an alcoholic drink. Although young adults in the remaining minority ethnic groups reported greater contact with alcohol they generally drank more moderately than whites. Almost three-in-four white young adults included in the YLS indicated they had been 'very drunk' in the previous 12 months, compared with none of the Pakistanis and Bangladeshis, one-in-ten black Africans, less than one-in-three black Caribbeans and approximately two-in-five Indians. Similar differences were evident in relation to tobacco consumption: almost two-in-five white young adults smoked on a daily basis or thereabouts, which was between two and nine times greater than the rate among minority ethnic groups.

Patterns of alcohol and tobacco consumption were also linked to religious orientation, with actively religious young adults showing a particular propensity towards abstinence and moderation.[7] Consequently, the extent to which drinking and smoking habits help to explain differences in drug use between ethnic groups cannot be readily separated from the role of religion. The broader, culturally distinct, orientations to consumption and intoxication, of which drug use is a part, are themselves shaped by religious influences. Most, if not all, major world religions impose some sort of strictures on the use of alcohol and tobacco, varying from the highly stringent to the relatively liberal (World Health Organisation, 1999; Wallace et al., 2003; Cook, 2006). Islam and Hinduism are particularly restrictive in this regard, though certain branches of Christianity, including some traditional black churches, have also adopted a strict prohibitionist stance. Even the more liberal religions and denominations typically oppose the vices of intoxication and addiction, while promoting the virtues of abstinence and restraint. There is, moreover, some evidence that religious influences operate differently between ethnic groups. Research in the United States has found that religion promotes abstinence among white adolescents at an individual level whereas for black adolescents its influence seems greatest at the group level (Wallace et al., 2003). This observation has prompted the suggestion that, in the context of highly religious communities, the influence of religion may extend to those who do not consider it to be personally important.

## Region and neighbourhood

The idea that drug use, or at least certain forms of drug use, are concentrated in particular environments – namely high crime areas facing multiple forms of deprivation and exclusion – provides one of the central themes in British drugs policy (Seddon, 2005). This is, of course, a reworking of an old idea which has been much criticised. Drawing on the 'new' deviancy theories, early sociological studies challenged the widespread assumption that drug use arises in disorganised areas of society characterised by anomie and a lack of behavioural norms, while similar misgivings have been expressed more recently in relation to the identification of 'wild zones' in official talk about drugs and crime: 'Tales of the city and of particular places, fears about racial ghettos and drugs and crime are mixed in with concerns about vice and moral decline through discourses of contagion and pollution' (Murji, 1999: 56). The empirical evidence regarding the environmental distribution of drug use is rather mixed and highlights important differences between problematic and more general forms of use. Several studies dating back to the 1980s heroin epidemics identified clear links between problematic drug use and urban deprivation (Pearson, 1987; Parker et al., 1988; ACMD, 1998). Where the focus has been on more general forms of drug use, however, there has been little evidence of any such link (Leitner et al., 1993; Ramsay and Percy, 1996).

While providing little evidence of a link with environmental deprivation, the BCS did indicate that rates of drug use vary according to certain area-based characteristics. Region of residence, for example, was significantly linked to the use of cannabis and cocaine, though not the hallucinants. Young adults in London displayed the highest rates of cannabis use and cocaine use, with 30 per cent and nine per cent having recently used these substances respectively, compared with 16 per cent and less than one per cent in some other parts of the country. The multivariate models confirmed the significance of the London effect even when life-course and broader lifestyle factors were taken into account: on average, and all other things being equal, living in the capital almost doubled the probability of recent cannabis use (from 0.19 to 0.31) and more than quadrupled the probability of recent cocaine use (from 0.02 to 0.09). Few other regional effects were evident, though it is worth noting that living in the South East or East Anglia increased the probability of recent cocaine use (see Technical Appendix for details).

Rates of drug use also varied according to neighbourhood characteristics, though there was, once again, little to suggest a link with deprivation or community disorganisation. As in previous sweeps of the BCS, the highest prevalence rates were associated with 'rising' neighbourhoods – that is neighbourhoods with large numbers of young, single people who do not have children (Ramsay and Percy, 1996). The effects associated with such neighbourhoods became much less marked, however, once life-course and lifestyle factors were taken into account: though moderately increasing the probability of recent cannabis use, 'rising' neighbourhood had no discernible effect on the use of hallucinants or cocaine. While more affluent, family oriented 'expanding' neighbourhoods were consistently associated with a reduced probability of recent drug use, the remaining neighbourhood-types did not give rise to any other statistically significant effects. As such the effects associated with the most deprived 'striving' neighbourhoods were similar to those associated with the most prosperous 'thriving' neighbourhoods.

None of the remaining area-based characteristics included in the BCS had anything other than a weak or ambiguous relationship with illicit drug use. Inner city living was only associated with minor variations in use, which ceased to be significant once other factors were taken into account, and a similar pattern was evident in relation to neighbourhood incivility. Young adults who felt their community was one where people helped one another did report lower levels of drug use than those who felt differently, but the final multivariate models revealed an inconsistent picture: living in a 'helpful' neighbourhood reduced the probability of past, though not recent, cannabis use; reduced the probability of recent, though not past, hallucinant use; and had no discernible impact on past or recent cocaine use (see Technical Appendix for details). It is also worth noting that the effects that were evident may simply reflect the extent to which young adults who use drugs are integrated into local networks.

Broadly similar results were evident from the YLS. The final multivariate models confirmed that living in London increased the probability of cannabis use and cocaine use, though not hallucinant use. Other significant regional effects indicated that living in the North West increased the probability of recent use for all three drug-types, while living in Wales and East Anglia reduced the probability of recent cannabis use and past hallucinant use respectively. The YLS also confirmed that neither inner city living nor deprived neighbourhoods are associated with particularly widespread drug use. Rates of use were highest among residents of 'rising' neighbourhoods, but this pattern could be explained by individual life-course and lifestyle differences. The only neighbourhood effects that were significant in the final models indicated that living in 'expanding' or 'aspiring' neighbourhoods reduced the probability of recent and/or past cannabis use (see Technical Appendix for details).

## Social deprivation and risk factors

The idea that illicit drug use is the result of certain deficits has given rise to a well established literature on 'risk' and 'protective' factors. Research in this tradition is closely associated with developmental psychology and has been subject to considerable, and longstanding, criticisms from sociologists. The 'new' deviancy project was, to a large extent, developed in opposition to mainstream psychology (see, for example, Cohen, 1971), while more recent developments have explicitly rejected the idea that youthful drug use can be understood in terms of risk factors (Parker et al., 1998). Given that most young people who use drugs do so in the absence of any obvious risk factors and in the context of apparently 'normal' backgrounds (EMCDDA, 2002), the risk paradigm is perhaps best reserved for attempts to understand problem drug use (Lloyd, 1998). Various risk factors have been identified in relation to such forms of use and a range of 'vulnerable' groups have been identified, including homeless young people, those leaving local authority or foster care, truants and school excludees and those in contact with the criminal justice system (Health Advisory Service, 1996; Lloyd, 1998; British Medical Association, 2003). Although clearly distinct, the aetiology of problem use and recreational use are not unrelated. Research in the United States has demonstrated an 'irrefutable' link between drug use and drug abuse, with early and/or frequent experimentation having been identified as a 'risk' factor for subsequent problem use (Glantz and Pickens, 1992; Lloyd, 1998; Dillon et al., 2007). Such a link has also been implied by several recent British studies of 'vulnerable' groups of young people, which have reported heightened rates of use across a wide range of substances that transcends any obvious distinction between the recreational and problematic (Goulden and Sondhi, 2001; Hammersley et al., 2003; Ward et al., 2003; Wincup et al., 2003; see also Newburn and Shiner, 2005).

General household surveys are not particularly suited to the study of risk factors and vulnerable groups. By virtue of their focus on residential households such surveys routinely exclude some of the most vulnerable members of society and tend not to address the notion of risk in any detail. Consequently the BCS and the YLS provided a very limited basis for assessing the impact of risk factors, though they did contain various indicators of social deprivation, based on unemployment, low income, financial difficulty and poor educational outcomes, which were incorporated into the analysis.[8] Of these indicators, unemployment was most strongly related to drug use. According to the BCS unemployed young adults had recently used cannabis, the hallucinants and cocaine at approximately twice the rate of those who were working and also had considerably higher rates of past hallucinant use. Among young adults who were otherwise marginalised from the labour market[9] rates of use were very similar to those reported by the unemployed. The relationship between labour market status and drug use became less clear-cut when other variables were taken into account. According to the latter stages of the multivariate analysis unemployment and marginalisation from the labour market increased the probability of recent cannabis use but had little by way of a clear effect on the probability of hallucinant use or cocaine use (see Technical Appendix for details).

There was also some suggestion from the BCS that drug use is linked to financial difficulty, though the nature of this relationship remained unclear. Evidence of such a link was absent or ambiguous in relation to cannabis and cocaine and was only clearly apparent in relation to the hallucinants. Living in a low-income household was associated with a heightened rate of recent hallucinant use, particularly where the household was in considerable financial difficulty. Even allowing for the influence of other variables financial difficulty continued to be associated with an increased probability of recent and past hallucinant use (see Technical Appendix for details). It does not necessarily follow that these substances are used in response to financial deprivation as their use may well be a marker for a relatively expensive lifestyle which places a strain on those with low income.

Educational failure is often identified as a risk factor for drug use, but evidence of such a link is fairly specific. While poor school performance has been shown to predict drug use among adolescents, doubts have been raised about the durability of this relationship over the life-course. Such doubts were reinforced by the BCS which provided very little evidence that drug use among young adults is linked to educational failure. Respondents who left school without any qualifications reported a slightly reduced rate of recent cannabis use compared with young adults in general and very similar rates of hallucinant use and cocaine use. Multivariate analyses confirmed that educational failure had no direct effect on any of the categories of drug use considered here.

These findings were, once again, broadly supported by the YLS. This survey provided further evidence that drug use is linked to unemployment and other forms of marginalisation from the labour market. Young adults who were currently unemployed or had previously been so for a significant amount of time tended to report higher levels of use than those who had had little, if any, experience of unemployment. Abstinence was most evident among those who had least experience of unemployment, though beyond this general observation the pattern varied between substances. The multivariate models helped to clarify the nature of the relationship between unemployment and drug use (see Table 4.6). In all but its most limited form, unemployment increased the probability of recent cannabis use though these effects ceased to be significant once lifestyle indicators were taken into account. It follows from this that the link between unemployment and cannabis use can be explained by broader lifestyle differences. More persistent effects were evident in relation to the hallucinants and cocaine: unemployment continued to increase the probability of recent and past use of these substances even when lifestyle factors were taken into account.

Besides unemployment, drug use was also linked to other forms of marginalisation from the labour market. The heightened rates of use

**Table 4.6 Probability of drug use by unemployment – YLS (multivariate analysis, young adults)**

| | *Cannabis* | | | *Hallucinants* | | | *Cocaine* | | |
|---|---|---|---|---|---|---|---|---|---|
| | *Never* | *Past* | *Recent* | *Never* | *Past* | *Recent* | *Never* | *Past* | *Recent* |
| *Life-course model* | | | | | | | | | |
| Currently unemployed | | | | | | | | | |
| – one year or more | 0.46 | 0.17 | **0.36** | 0.56 | 0.21 | **0.23** | 0.80 | **0.12** | 0.08 |
| – less than one year | 0.46 | 0.18 | **0.36** | 0.58 | 0.20 | **0.22** | 0.91 | 0.04 | 0.05 |
| Not currently unemployed | | | | | | | | | |
| – previously one year or more | 0.45 | 0.20 | **0.35** | 0.54 | **0.25** | **0.21** | 0.83 | 0.06 | **0.11** |
| – previously six months or more | 0.46 | **0.24** | 0.29 | 0.59 | **0.26** | 0.15 | 0.86 | 0.06 | **0.09** |
| – never for six months or more† | 0.55 | 0.19 | 0.26 | 0.70 | 0.19 | 0.12 | 0.91 | 0.04 | 0.05 |
| *Lifestyle model* | | | | | | | | | |
| Currently unemployed | | | | | | | | | |
| – one year or more | 0.55 | 0.19 | 0.26 | 0.53 | 0.24 | **0.23** | 0.77 | **0.12** | **0.12** |
| – less than one year | 0.55 | 0.19 | 0.26 | 0.60 | 0.22 | **0.19** | 0.92 | 0.04 | 0.04 |
| Not currently unemployed | | | | | | | | | |
| – previously one year or more | 0.55 | 0.26 | 0.26 | 0.56 | **0.23** | **0.21** | 0.86 | 0.05 | **0.09** |
| – previously six months or more | 0.45 | **0.24** | 0.31 | 0.56 | **0.27** | **0.17** | | | |
| – never for six months or more† | 0.55 | 0.19 | 0.26 | 0.70 | 0.19 | 0.12 | 0.92 | 0.04 | 0.04 |

*Source*: YLS (1998/9) †reference category

*Notes:*

1. Statistically significant effects are highlighted in bold.
2. Effects on past or recent use were estimated vis-à-vis the probability of never having used.
3. Categories that had no significant effect on recent use or past use were excluded from the model and formed part of the reference category.
4. YLS cocaine model – not currently unemployed but had been previously for one year or more and not currently unemployed but had been previously for six months or more were combined into a single category (see Technical Appendix for details).

that were evident among those who were currently unemployed were more or less matched by those who were not formally unemployed but appeared to have a transient or tenuous relationship with the labour market. The latter stages of the multivariate analysis confirmed that these other forms of marginalisation from the labour market increased the probability of past and recent cannabis use and past and recent hallucinant use, though no such effects were evident in relation to cocaine (see Technical Appendix for details).

Although the YLS provided further evidence of a link between drug use and financial difficulty the nature of this relationship was, as indicated by the BCS, highly ambiguous. Young adults who had little disposable income tended to use drugs at a lower rate than those who were financially better off, but their rates of use varied quite markedly according to their level of financial difficulty. Those who had little disposable income and were in most financial difficulty reported higher rates of drug use than those who had a higher disposable income. By contrast, those who had little disposable income but appeared to be in little or no difficulty reported lower rates of drug use than those who had a higher disposable income. As noted earlier, a possible explanation for this pattern is that drug use provides a marker for a relatively expensive lifestyle which puts strain on those with low income. The multivariate models reinforced the conclusion that there is little by way of a direct relationship between financial difficulty and drug use: few significant effects were evident from the life-course and lifestyle models on the basis of such difficulties and those that were evident did not form a clear or consistent pattern (see Technical Appendix for details).

The YLS confirmed that educational failure has little, if any, impact on young adults' use of the drugs considered here. Prevalence rates for cannabis use, hallucinant use and cocaine use did not vary significantly according to whether or not respondents had left school with any qualifications. The multivariate models pointed in a similar direction, indicating that absence of qualifications had very little effect and those effects that were evident were of marginal importance (see Technical Appendix for details). The YLS also revealed little by way of a relationship between drug use and parental unemployment. Young adults who had grown up in families where one or both parents had experienced long-term unemployment reported very similar rates of cannabis use to those who had grown up in families with little, if any, history of unemployment. Although significant differences were evident in relation to the hallucinants and cocaine they were fairly modest and highly ambiguous. Recent hallucinant use was most common among young adults who had grown up in families where one parent had been long-term unemployed and one had not, while past use was most common among those who had grown up in families where both parents had been long-term unemployed (or, in the case of lone parents, where one had been). Cocaine use, both recent and past, was most common among young adults who had grown up in families where one parent had been long-term unemployed and one had not. A similar ambiguity was evident from the multivariate analysis (see Technical Appendix for details).

## Conclusion

The analysis presented in this, and the previous, chapter supports some elements of the new orthodoxy, but also raises important questions about their broader interpretation. Recreational drug use has become fairly widespread and extends well beyond the limits of what we might expect on the basis of 'positivist' psychology or subcultural strain theory. Social class, income and indicators of deprivation tend to be poor predictors of the more common forms of drug use considered here and apparently conventional young adults from privileged backgrounds are well represented among those who engage in such behaviour. In this sense, then, we can talk meaningfully of the 'normalised' drug user.

What is less clear is that this represents a significant departure, requiring a new explanatory framework. Put simply, drug use among young people from relatively privileged backgrounds is not a particularly recent development. Middle class youth were actively involved in the drug using scenes of the 1960s and generational comparisons suggest they have continued to be so ever since. Early involvement of middle class 'bohemian' youth was widely acknowledged at the time and was considered to be a manifestation of their privileged status as something of a leisure class (Young, 1971; see next chapter). The notion that 'traditional' differences between users and non-users have all but disintegrated is no less problematic. Although drug use has become much more widespread, it has not become so pervasive that 'traditional' differences between socio-demographic groups have been eliminated. Young women continue to use drugs at a lower rate than young men and there is little evidence that the gender gap is closing; young adults from black and minority ethnic groups use drugs at a lower rate than whites; and those who are actively religious do so at a lower rate than those who are not. Although the relationship between deprivation and recreational drug use is generally weak, moreover, unemployment and other forms of marginalisation from the labour market are associated with heightened rates of use, as are indicators of vulnerability, such as truancy, homelessness and the like.

There is, finally, nothing particularly new about the rejection of 'positivist' psychology or subcultural strain theory. Sociologists have repeatedly challenged the idea that drug users are the product of individual pathology or social dysfunction since first showing an interest in this area. Early studies displayed an antipathy to what Young (1999: 133) subsequently referred to as the 'fixed locus of the offender', sharing in the 'new' deviancy theories' rejection of correctionalist criminology and the assumption that criminals are somehow different from the rest of the population, being created out of dire and unusual circumstances. Among the many arguments used to reject this view, Young (1971) observed, in his early work, that large numbers of young people in areas like London's Notting Hill were involved in deviant activities such as drug-taking and that it was simply implausible to suggest all of them were psychologically inadequate or living in socially disorganised communities.

Evidence of continuity, whether it relates to the realities or drug use or their representation, creates real difficulties for the new orthodoxy. The claim that drug use was formerly an 'atypical' pursuit of the mainly 'delinquent and disordered' not only misrepresents the profile of those involved, but also fails to acknowledge that this characterisation was wholeheartedly rejected by sociologists at the time. As such, recent developments might be said to rely on a distorted image of the way things were and the way they were understood to be. This, as we shall see in the next chapter, is a criticism that extends to other aspects of the new orthodoxy.

# 5
# Consumption and Subterranean Play

> That humanity at large will ever be able to dispense with Artificial Paradises seems very unlikely. Most men and women lead lives at the worst so painful, at the best so monotonous, poor, and limited that the urge to escape, the longing to transcend themselves if only for a few moments, is and has always been one of the principal appetites of the soul...All the vegetable sedatives and narcotics, all the euphorics that grow on trees, the hallucinogens that ripen in berries or can be squeezed from roots – all, without exception, have been known and systematically used by human beings from time immemorial. And to these natural modifiers of consciousness modern science has added its quota of synthetics (Huxley, 1959: 51–2).

> Every man having tasted the paradise of play in his own childhood holds in his mind as an implicit utopia a world where economic necessity does not hold sway and where he is capable of free expression of his desires. This is the psychological basis of the subterranean values, and it is in one's leisure time that a watered-down expression of 'free time' and play holds sway (Young, 1971: 131).

In the search for new perspectives the sociology of drug use has come to focus on the related notions of lifestyle and consumption. The normalisation thesis and recent feminist accounts have both interpreted drug use in such terms, viewing it as lifestyle choice involving a particular commitment to hedonistic consumption. It is often implied that there is something distinctive or wholly new about this orientation, the rise of which has been linked to the restructuring of modernity.

With class affiliations, family ties and traditional expectations having weakened, consumption and lifestyles are said to have become central to the construction of individual identity. Apparently routine decisions about what to wear or what to eat etc have become decisions about 'who to be' and the more 'post traditional' the setting the more lifestyle concerns lay at 'the very core of self-identity, its making and remaking' (Giddens, 1991: 81). The following analysis considers how the notions of lifestyle and consumption might be applied to illicit drug use and, in keeping with the central theme of the book, identifies elements of both continuity and change. While the surveys are used to explore how drug use relates to various lifestyle indicators, the empirical analysis is framed within a broader discussion of the development of British youth culture and the role that consumption played in earlier attempts to understand the sociology of drug use.

## The rise of British youth culture

The end of the second world war is often identified as a turning point in British youth culture. A series of spectacular youth subcultures emerged in the years that followed, prompting many commentators to point to the birth of the modern teenager. Whilst capturing something of the time, such suggestions exaggerate the novelty of the post-war experience and underestimate the degree of continuity involved. The origins of British youth culture can be traced back to the profound social and economic changes of the Victorian and Edwardian era. When Queen Victoria came to the throne in 1837 Britain was in the midst of being transformed into the world's first modern industrial society, with huge increases in manufacturing activity being accompanied by rapid urbanisation, rising living standards and a restructuring of the labour market; all of which combined to create new opportunities for mass consumption and commercialised leisure (Evans, 1983). Although initially concentrated among the middle classes, the economic benefits associated with industrialisation began to filter down to ordinary industrial workers during the second half of the nineteenth century as real wage increases were accompanied by legally prescribed hours of work, statutory holidays and half day working on a Saturday. Against this background, a nascent entertainment industry began to develop in urban working class neighbourhoods and a distinct youth leisure market began to take shape. With new found economic independence young urban workers began to take advantage of the growing leisure opportunities that were becoming available to them and formed what some have considered to be the first modern youth subcultures (Davis, 1990; Newburn, 2002). Providing a template for much of what was to follow such developments gave rise to 'respectable fears' about hooliganism, delinquency and youthful affluence (Pearson, 1983; Osgerby, 1998).

Economic conditions continued to fuel the development of British youth culture for much of the twentieth century. The greater involvement of young people in the labour market following both world wars provided a ready market for an expanding commercial leisure industry (Fowler, 1995). Although the traditional industrial heartlands were hit hard by the Great Depression of the 1930s this experience was not typical of the country as a whole. Nationally the inter war years were a time of economic growth and relative affluence for many young wage earners who enjoyed high levels of disposable income. As leisure entrepreneurs began to tap into this market a plethora of magazines appeared that were targeted at young people and a distinct youth culture coalesced around the cinema, the dance hall and jazz music. With the outbreak of the second world war demand for youth labour increased, reawakening long-standing concerns about the detrimental influence of 'easy money'. Young people's employment opportunities and earning capacity continued to improve following the end of the war, due largely to the growth of production line technology, providing the basis for the continued expansion of youth-oriented leisure consumption.

The cultural significance of these trends was first identified by Mark Abrams (1959), a market researcher whose groundbreaking analysis of young people's spending patterns drew attention to the teenage consumer: a phenomenon he attributed to falling youth unemployment and improving wages. Although aspects of Abrams' analysis have been questioned his central thesis remains: young people's earnings rose steadily following the end of the second world war and commercial developments helped to provide British youth with an unprecedented 'social visibility' (Osgerby, 1998). This trend was augmented by a series of policy initiatives, which brought about the 'institutionalisation' of youth: compulsory education was extended, the school leaving age was raised to 15 years, youth service provision was formalised and National Service was introduced. Taken together these initiatives helped to restructure the nature of age-relations and reinforced the idea that young people were somehow different from adults.

The new found visibility of young people was evident in the spectacular youth subcultures of the period. From the Teddy Boys of the late 1950s, through the Mods and Rockers of the early-to-mid 1960s, to the Skinheads of the late 1960s, white working class subcultures provided an enduring focus for adult anxieties about youthful affluence, moral decline and juvenile delinquency. Although the vast majority of post-war youth styles were of working class origin, middle class youth also came to prominence through the rise of the counter culture. Until the mid-1960s, middle class youngsters had been relatively marginal to the development of British youth culture, not least because they had less disposable income than their working class peers and were, therefore, less commercially significant. As higher education expanded, however, a growing section of middle class youth experienced the relative freedom of living away from home on a student grant, which provided the foundations for a growing counter culture that was, for the most part, middle class in both composition and orientation.

Opinions about the counter culture tend to polarise into moral condemnation on the one hand and romanticised nostalgia on the other, but what is generally agreed is that the sixties represent something of a watershed. This era has recently been described as a 'totem', the historical equivalent of a brand identity which symbolises a particular orientation and provides a series of images that continue to pervade contemporary culture and are revisited repeatedly (Donnelly, 2005). In one of the most detailed historical reviews of the period, Arthur Marwick (1998) concludes that the sixties can reasonably be characterised in terms of a 'cultural revolution'. Whereas the fifties were defined by rigid social hierarchy; subordination of children to parents; repressed attitudes to sex; unquestioning respect for authority and strict formalism in language etiquette and dress codes; the sixties were defined by new subcultures and movements that were critical of mainstream society; the growing influence of youth subculture on the rest of society; massive improvements in material life and an expansion of the consumer society; the rise of 'permissiveness' and a general sexual liberation, involving striking changes in public and private morals; new modes of self-presentation; a participatory and uninhibited popular culture; and new concerns for civil and personal rights.

## Drugs, consumption and subterranean play

The development of post-war British youth culture and, in particular, the rise of the counter culture, dramatically altered the position of illicit drugs. It was, after all, during the sixties that society's defences against drug use were 'decisively breached' (Marwick, 1998: 4) and a new sensibility emerged. Official policy began to take the form of an extended 'moral panic', which was increasingly counter-posed by an alternative set of drug-friendly reference points. The hippies extolled the mind-expanding and enlightening qualities of psychedelic experiences, which they felt offered a route to a better society and celebratory images of drugs and drug use began to enter mainstream youth culture, due largely to the influence of popular music (Shapiro, 1990, 1999). The likes of The Velvet Underground, Jimi Hendrix and the Rolling Stones became well known for their drug-fuelled hedonism and explicit lyrical references to drug use. Even the Beatles, the most marketable musical commodity of the decade, went through a marihuana phase and an LSD phase, both of which were reflected in their work (Marwick, 1998). When Mick Jagger, and fellow Rolling Stone Keith Richards, were prosecuted for drugs offences in 1967 the case became 'symbolic of a wider contest between traditionalism and a new hedonism, the focal point of which was society's attitude towards recreational drugs' (Donnelly, 2005: 153). Several thousand demonstrators held a 'Legalise Pot Rally' in London's Hyde Park and an advert appeared in the *Times* newspaper calling for reform of the cannabis laws, which was paid for by Paul McCartney and signed by various luminaries, including Labour MP Brian Walden, artist David Hockney, journalists David Dimbleby and Jonathan Aitken, theatre director Peter Brook, writer Graham Greene and scientist Francis Crick.

The hedonistic sensibility of the time was reflected in contemporary developments in the sociology of drug use, particularly Young's emphasis on subterranean play. In developing this emphasis Young drew on the work of Matza and Sykes (1961) who, having previously considered how juveniles accommodate delinquent acts, went on to examine what it is that makes delinquency attractive in the first place. Echoing their earlier claim that delinquents typically adhere to conventional norms and codes of conduct, Matza and Sykes suggested that delinquency is considered attractive, not because of a deep-seated commitment to an oppositional morality, but because of an exaggerated adherence to 'subterranean' values. As such, they argued, the values behind much juvenile delinquency are far less deviant than is commonly supposed and this faulty picture is due to a gross oversimplification of the middle class value system. As well as pointing to significant variations in values across social divisions, including those based on class and race, Matza and Sykes highlighted contradictions and ambiguities within the dominant value system. Although the search for adventure is generally held in abeyance, for example, this does not mean it is completely rejected by society as a whole or never appears in the motivational structure of the law-abiding. Rather, the realisation of such desires is compartmentalised and allowed to take precedence at certain prescribed times in the form of sports, recreation and holidays. Accordingly (Matza and Sykes, 1961: 716):

> The search for adventure, excitement, and thrills, then, is a subterranean value that now often exists side by side with the values of security, routinization, and the rest. It is not a deviant value, in any full sense, but it must be held in abeyance until the proper moment and circumstances for its expression arrive.

Subterranean values then are those that are in competition with other deeply held values yet are recognised and supported by many. These competing values are not necessarily the opposing viewpoints of two different groups, moreover, but may co-exist within a single individual, giving rise to profound feelings of ambivalence. It follows, therefore, that delinquency does not exist outside of the conventional value system and may be readily understood in terms of widely accepted views. By accentuating subterranean values – the emphasis on daring and adventure, the rejection of the discipline of work, the taste for luxury and conspicuous consumption and the respect of masculinity – the juvenile delinquent is reminiscent of Veblen's (1899) 'gentlemen of leisure' and remains tied to the dominant order (Matza and Sykes, 1961: 717):

> In short, we are arguing that the delinquent may not stand as an alien in the body of society but may represent instead a disturbing reflection or a caricature. His vocabulary is different, to be sure, but kicks, big-time spending, and rep have immediate counterparts in the value system of the law-abiding. The delinquent has picked up and emphasized one part of the dominant value system, namely, the subterranean values that co-exist with other, publicly proclaimed values possessing a more respectable air. These subterranean values...bind the delinquent to the society whose laws he violates.

One of the main advantages of such a perspective is that it is better able to explain the distribution of delinquency than the dominant deficit based theories of the time (Downes and Rock, 2007). Explanations rooted in ideas such as status deprivation, social disorganisation and the like struggle to account for the occurrence of delinquency among the middle and upper classes. Matza and Sykes, by contrast, argued that, regardless of social class, all young adults are, to some extent, members of a leisure class because they move in a 'limbo' between earlier parental domination and future integration in the social structure through work and marriage.

Once all adolescents are viewed in this way it becomes much easier to explain the ubiquity of deviance and its presence at all levels of society.

Building on these insights, Young (1971) maintained that drug use represents a form of subterranean play. What was particularly distinctive about his analysis was the way it linked subterranean values to the political economy of 'late' or 'post' industrial societies. Young endorsed the idea that there is a basic bifurcation of values in such societies, but rejected the suggestion that formal values and subterranean values form isolated moral regions. Rather, he emphasised that these two value systems are mutually dependent upon one another, albeit with subterranean values being subsumed under the ethos of productivity (Young, 1971: 128):

> Leisure is concerned with consumption and work with production; a keynote of our bifurcated society, therefore, is that individuals within it must constantly consume in order to keep pace with the productive capacity of the economy. They must produce in order to consume, and consume in order to produce. The interrelationship between formal and subterranean values is therefore seen in a new light: hedonism, for instance, is closely tied to productivity.

Formal values were said to be consistent with the structure of modern industry because they serve to maintain diligent, consistent work and assist the realisation of long-term productive goals, while subterranean values were held to be identical to the customary definition of play. Alcohol and other 'psychotropic' drugs were considered to play a key role in this regard because they act as a '*vehicle* which enhances the ease of transition from the world of formal values to the world of subterranean values' (1971: 135). In the hands of those who live outside the ethos of productivity, moreover, such substances could be used to access more radical accentuations of subterranean reality. Young people, for example, were said to be in the privileged position of not having to justify their play through productivity, though they were expected to invest in their future through education and training. The hippies, in particular, as largely middle-class young people, discovered they could disdain work and demand authentic play in what was considered to be 'a common response to the problems of work and leisure which have arisen in post-industrial societies' (1971: 148). Similar sentiments were expressed by Fred Davis (1970: 330) in his essay, *Focus on the Flower Children: Why All of Us May Be Hippies Someday* when he suggested there was an 'elective affinity' between 'prominent styles and themes in the hippie subculture' and 'certain incipient problems of identity, work, and leisure' in an age of 'over-production', 'staggering material abundance' and unprecedented opportunities for 'creative leisure':

> ... the hippies, in their collective, yet radical, break with the constraints of our present society, are – whether they know it or not (some clearly do intuit a connection) – already rehearsing *in vivo* a number of possible cultural solutions to central life problems posed by the emerging society of the future.

## Youth lifestyles

Looking back with the benefit of hindsight, there can be little doubting the prescience of this analysis. Young's emphasis on subterranean play foreshadowed much that has recently been written about drug use as a form of consumption and anticipated the direction of some important dynamics of social change. Post-industrial societies have continued to experience a general increase in leisure, which has acquired greater importance, both as a form of consumption and source of economic growth (Gershuny, 2000). This trend has prompted Young (1999: 10) to suggest, in his more recent work, that late modern sensibilities have been profoundly shaped by a culture of individualism; so that the 'Keynesian balance between hard work and hard play' has become 'tipped towards the subterranean world of leisure'. In Britain, at least, the elevation of leisure is evident in the growth of the night-time economy (Hobbs et al., 2003). Deindustrialisation, it is argued, has created a void in numerous towns and cities, which government agencies and private entrepreneurs have sought to fill by establishing sites of consumption and leisure in the place of what were once thriving centres of production. Repeated regeneration initiatives have resulted in a massively expanding night-time economy that is geared towards young people, experiential consumption and the weekend ritual. Between 1980 and 2004 the number of on-license premises in England and Wales grew by a quarter and this growth was heavily concentrated in urban centres such as Manchester, where licensed capacity more than doubled in just four years and currently stands at around 200,000 (Institute of Alcohol Studies, 2007). With this growth, the annual turnover of the pub and club industry reached £23 billion or the equivalent of three per cent of gross domestic product and the sector employs around a million people, creating one in five of all new jobs

(Home Office, 2000). For those seeking release from 'the slate grey glare of daylight', the night-time economy offers a place of 'dangerous adventure'; one that is replete with suggestions of the illicit and is increasingly 'the amphitheatre of drug, alcohol and sexual experimentation' (Hobbs et al., 2003: 46).

## Drinking and the night-time economy

The expansion of the night-time economy has left its mark on patterns of alcohol consumption, particularly among young adults, but there are, nonetheless, important continuities at work here stretching back over several centuries. Drinking for pleasure and related fears about drunkenness and disorder were all familiar features of life in pre-industrial 'Merrie England', forming an integral part of the cycle of feasts and festivals that marked the passing of the seasons and in which youths and apprentices were centrally involved (Pearson, 1983; see also Glatt, 1977). A 'notorious example of alcoholic excess on a large scale' was provided by massive increases in gin consumption during the first half of the eighteenth century (Orford, 1985: 15) and the menace of gin was, once again, implicated in the unruliness of the Victorian era, which has been described as the 'most drunken age in British history' (Evans, 1983: 280). Despite the best efforts of the temperance movement, the pub remained central to working class leisure throughout the nineteenth century and alcohol consumption did not fall on any significant scale until the first world war, when supplies were limited and stricter licensing regulations were introduced alongside increases in taxation (Glatt, 1977). Unlike many other countries, Britain kept these stricter controls in place after the end of the war and by the 1950s the 'alcohol problem' was widely considered to be a thing of the past. Over the course of the next half a century, however, per capita alcohol consumption increased sharply, returning to something like the level of 1900, and Britain was firmly established as one of the world's heaviest consumers of alcohol amid widespread concerns about the rise of 'binge' drinking (Institute of Alcohol Studies, 2008).[1]

Although sharply increasing levels of alcohol consumption are not typical of late industrial societies, binge drinking has become something of a global phenomenon (WHO, 2004; see also Schmid et al., 2003; Martinic and Measham, 2008). In a trend some commentators have attributed to the spread of 'Anglo-Irish' style pubs, young people have become more hedonistic in their attitudes to alcohol and drinking in order to get drunk has become a common feature of youth lifestyles in many countries. Once closely associated with northern Europe, binge drinking is now being recorded in countries, such as France and Spain, where drunkenness has traditionally been alien to the drinking culture and where overall levels of alcohol consumption are declining fairly steeply. Despite these signs of convergence, regional differences remain and binge drinking continues to be especially common in Britain, alongside other north European countries, with an estimated two-fifths of male drinking sessions conforming to this style of consumption (Alcohol Concern, 2003; see also NIAAA, 2003). Mirroring recent trends in drug use, the proportion of young Britons who drink beyond recommended weekly limits increased throughout the 1990s, peaking around the turn of the century before returning to lower levels thereafter (Goddard, 2006).

Alcohol has become a particularly prominent feature of youth lifestyles in Britain due largely to the repositioning of the pub and the expansion of the night-time economy. Having previously made little effort to court the youth market, the drinks industry began to target young people from the early 1960s, with the result that 'pub culture' and alcohol were quickly installed as 'central pillars' of youth oriented leisure (Osgerby, 1998). Many city centre pubs had already become the preserve of 18 to 24 year olds by the 1980s and the further expansion of the night-time economy created greater competition between outlets, leading to heavy discounting and the proliferation of marketing strategies that actively encourage the transgression of traditional drinking norms. Such strategies, combined with increases in disposable income, mean that alcohol has become much more affordable – 54 per cent more so in 2003 than 1980 (Institute of Alcohol Studies, 2007). In commercial terms, alcohol has become the primary commodity that draws people into city centres after dark, sustaining other complimentary markets, but its cultural meaning is closely tied up with the promise of transgression and release. As such, alcohol provides 'the vital lubricant that aids the propulsion of young people into' the 'carnivalesque and consumer-oriented world' that is the night-time economy (Hobbs et al., 2003: 36).

The BCS and YLS confirm that many, though by no means all, young adults spend a considerable amount of leisure time away from home and that pubs and clubs provide an important focus for their 'time out' activities. Approximately three-quarters of those who responded to the BCS had been out in the evening at least once during the previous week and slightly more than a fifth had been out most evenings; slightly more than two-fifths had been to the pub at least one evening a week in the last month and a similar proportion had been to a club or a disco during this time; approximately one-in-five had been to the pub on three evenings a week or more, while one-in-eight had been to a club or disco on a weekly basis or more. Similarly, the YLS found that three-quarters of young adults go out in the evening at least once a week and two-fifths go out three evenings a week or more, while three-quarters had been to a pub in the last month, two-thirds had been to a party, dance, nightclub or disco and three-fifths had been to both a pub and party etc.

Both surveys found young adults commonly drink up to four days a week, consuming an average of four units a day on the days they drink and ten units a week during the weeks they drink.[2] Although tending to drink beyond sensible daily limits, most have regular alcohol free days which keep them within recommended weekly limits.[3] According to the BCS three-in-five young adults typically consume more than the sensible daily limit on the occasions they drink, but projected figures suggest no more than one-in-five exceeded the sensible weekly limit.[4] A similar degree of excess was suggested by the YLS, which found that one-in-five young adults had consumed more than the sensible weekly limit during the previous week. A more detailed classification of drinking styles, which combined measures of frequency and quantity, confirmed that most young adults drink regularly but in moderation, while a sizeable minority drink to excess (see Figures 5.1a and 5.1b). Further evidence of heavy drinking was evident in relation to episodes of drunkenness, with the YLS indicating that one-in-three young adults had been very drunk at least once a month during the previous year and almost one-in-ten had been so on a weekly basis.

## Smoking

Originating in the Americas, tobacco has been widely consumed throughout Europe since the seventeenth century and is currently smoked by more than one billion people worldwide (Jha and Chaloupka, 1999). The global distribution of tobacco consumption has changed markedly over the last half a century or so, as reductions in high-income countries have been accompanied by increases in less well off countries. A marked economic divide is also evident within high-income countries as the traditional pattern, whereby smokers were more likely to be affluent than poor, has been reversed. Consequently, smoking is concentrated among the poor and less educated worldwide.

Britain has shared in the general reduction in smoking that is typical of high-income countries. From a situation where nearly four-in-five men smoked in the late 1950s, just over one-in-five currently do so, while the proportion of women who smoke has fallen to a similar level,

*Figure 5.1a* Young adults' drinking styles – BCS (percentages)

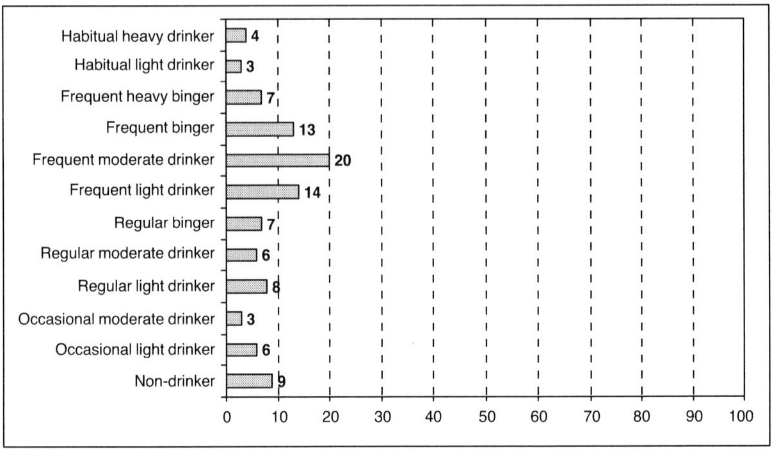


*Source*: BCS (1998) n = 2,850

| **Key – drinking styles** | **Frequency of drinking** | **Amount consumed on days that drink – average number of drinks shown in brackets** |
|---|---|---|
| Habitual heavy drinker | Five or more days a week | More than sensible daily limit (5) |
| Habitual light drinker | Five or more days a week | Within sensible daily limit (2) |
| Frequent heavy binger | One to four days a week | At least four times sensible daily limit (12) |
| Frequent binger | One to four days a week | More than twice sensible daily limit (8) |
| Frequent moderate drinker | One to four days a week | One to two times sensible daily limit (4) |
| Frequent light drinker | One to four days a week | Within sensible daily limit (2) |
| Regular binger | One to three times a month | More than twice sensible daily limit (7) |
| Regular moderate drinker | One to three times a month | One to two times sensible daily limit (4) |
| Regular light drinker | One to three times a month | Within sensible daily limit (2) |
| Occasional moderate drinker | Less than once a month | More than sensible daily limit but only moderately so (4) |
| Occasional light drinker | Less than once a month | Within sensible daily limit (1) |
| Non-drinker | Never | Does not apply |

albeit from a more modest peak of just over two-in-five during the 1960s (Marsh and McKay, 1994; Goddard, 2006). As in most other high-income countries, Britain's decline in smoking has been concentrated among higher income groups to the point that such behaviour has become strongly associated with poverty and social exclusion. While reductions in smoking have been evident across all age groups, older smokers have given up in such large numbers that this behaviour is now most prevalent

*Figure 5.1b* Young adults' drinking styles – YLS (percentages)

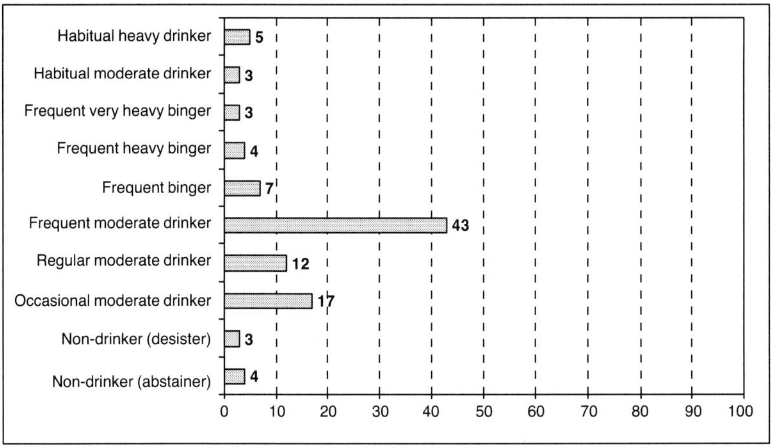


*Source*: YLS (1998/9) n = 3,473

| **Key – drinking styles** | **Frequency of drinking** | **Amount consumed in last week – average number of drinks shown in brackets** |
|---|---|---|
| Habitual heavy drinker | Five or more days a week | More than sensible weekly limit (32) |
| Habitual moderate drinker | Five or more days a week | Within sensible weekly limit (12) |
| Frequent very heavy binger | One to four days a week | More than twice sensible weekly limit (46) |
| Frequent heavy binger | One to four days a week | More than one-and-a-half times sensible weekly limit (31) |
| Frequent binger | One to four days a week | More than sensible weekly limit (21) |
| Frequent moderate drinker | One to four days a week | Within sensible weekly limit (8) |
| Regular moderate drinker | Once or twice a month | Almost all within sensible weekly limit (5) |
| Occasional moderate drinker | Less than once a month | Almost all within sensible weekly limit (3) |
| Non-drinker (desister) | Not in last year | Does not apply |
| Non-drinker (abstainer) | Never had a drink | Does not apply |

among 20 to 24 year olds (Rickards et al., 2004). Most young adults do not go on to become long-term smokers, but the majority do have some experience of smoking. According to the YLS two-fifths (39 per cent) are regular smokers, doing so every day or consuming more than ten cigarettes a week, while less than a fifth (16 per cent) have never smoked. The remainder have smoked on a few occasions but never regularly (27 per cent), smoked regularly but no longer do so (11 per cent) or smoke between one and ten cigarettes a week (four per cent).

Britain's decline in smoking is all the more striking given that it has taken place in the context of rising alcohol consumption and illicit drug use. This decline also suggests that contemporary youth lifestyles cannot be fully understood in terms of increasingly hedonistic consumption and highlights a competing set of influences based around heath promotion and 'healthy' living, which have been considered symptomatic of a broader cultural shift (Bunton et al., 1995). As well as playing a central role in the political transformation of health care, health promotion has entered ever more deeply into the domain of consumer culture. Not only is this domain replete with images of youthful vitality, but the number of 'health-related' commodities has increased sharply so that they now cover an array of goods and services including food, drink, clothing, insurance policies, gym-membership, sports equipment, dietary supplements and so on. The consumption of such goods offers a potentially important source of identity, but is not necessarily organised into a coherent lifestyle based around a single organising principle. As such, extravagance and hedonism may co-exist with a culture of health and body maintenance.

## Drug use as lifestyle

Studies covering a range of countries have repeatedly found that young people's propensity to use illicit drugs is strongly linked to their drinking and smoking habits (Kandel and Faust, 1975; Yamaguchi and Kandel, 1984; Torabi et al., 1993; Bailey, 1992; Blaze-Temple and Lo, 1992; Duncan et al., 1998; Galanti et al., 1998; Johnson et al., 2000; McVie and Bradshaw, 2005; see also http://www.aic.gov.au/research/drugs/pathway). Adding to this body of work, the BCS and YLS indicated that cannabis use, hallucinant use and cocaine use tended to form part of a distinct leisure style in which the search for pleasure and excitement feature prominently. Whilst prevalence rates varied with each of the lifestyle indicators included in the analysis, the multivariate models helped to clarify the nature of the relationships involved, highlighting the particular significance of drinking and smoking as concurrent predictors of illicit drug use.

### Drinking

Ecstasy culture seemed fleetingly to threaten the vested interests of the drinks industry, but, like many previous youth styles, was both facilitated by, and ultimately incorporated into, the world of corporate youth entertainment. What started out as an 'underground' of unlicensed outdoor events and warehouse parties, where alcohol was consciously rejected in favour of ecstasy, was co-opted and repackaged by established commercial interests (Collin with Godfrey, 1997). As part of this process distinctions between pubs and bars, night clubs and dance clubs, 'raves' and festivals have been blurred and a pattern of 'serious' recreational drug use emerged, whereby alcohol is commonly used alongside cannabis, ecstasy, amphetamines and cocaine (Measham et al., 2001). Such patterns were evident from the BCS and YLS which confirmed that illicit drug use is most prevalent among young adults who drink most heavily. In broad terms, the BCS indicated that habitual drinkers and frequent bingers reported the highest rates of drug use, while non-drinkers and occasional or regular light drinkers reported the lowest rates of use, with moderate drinkers tending to be located somewhere in between. More than one-in-three habitual heavy drinkers and frequent heavy bingers had recently used cannabis, almost one-in-five had recently used the hallucinants and almost one-in-ten had recently used cocaine, which compared with no more than one-in-seven, one-in-15 and one-in-100 of those who drank occasionally, if at all.

This general pattern was broadly replicated by the YLS, which confirmed that the highest rates of drug use are to be found among habitual drinkers and (very) heavy bingers, followed by more modest drinkers and non-drinkers. More than half the habitual heavy drinkers and very heavy bingers had recently used cannabis, more than one-in-three had recently used the hallucinants and up to one-in-four had recently used cocaine, which compared with one-in-five, less than one-in-ten and one-in-100 of those who drank occasionally and in moderation. Notable differences were also evident among non-drinkers depending on whether or not they had ever drunk alcohol. Among those who never had, negligible rates of drug use suggested a broader commitment to abstinence: one-in-33, one-in-50 and one-in-100 had recently used cannabis, the hallucinants and cocaine respectively. Among ex-drinkers, moderate rates of use suggested a greater affinity with the more modest drinkers.

The concentration of recent drug use among the heaviest drinkers points to a particular orientation towards excess and intoxication. Further evidence of this orientation was provided by the clear link between drug use and drunkenness. The prevalence of drug use increased sharply with the frequency that young adults had been very drunk during the last year: more than half of those who had been drunk on a weekly basis had recently used cannabis, more than one-in-three had recently used the hallucinants and almost one-in-five had recently used cocaine, which compared with one-in-eight, one-in-20 and one-in-100 of those who had not been drunk in the last year.[5]

The multivariate models indicated that the link between drinking and drug use is a robust one. Even allowing for the influence of other variables, the BCS models showed that heavy drinking increased the probability of cannabis use, hallucinant use and cocaine use (see Table 5.1). The more modest drinking styles were rather more varied in their effects depending on the substance. Being an occasional or light drinker, as opposed to a non drinker, had most effect in relation to cannabis, which suggests that this type of drug use is particularly sensitive to slight differences in drinking habits. The effects of the more modest drinking styles also tended to be most evident in relation to past use rather than recent use, suggesting a particular propensity towards desistance. All things being equal, habitual drinkers and frequent (heavy) bingers were more likely to be recent cannabis users than past users, while modest drinkers were more likely to be past users than recent users. It follows, therefore, that modest drinking styles are suggestive of particularly tentative forms of cannabis use and/or may form part of a broader process of 'calming down', whereby young adults moderate their drinking habits and their drug use.

The effects that were evident in relation to the hallucinants and cocaine were less finely graded. Drinking modestly had relatively little impact on the use of these substances, resulting in more polarised patterns of use: not drinking or drinking modestly was associated with a high probability of abstinence, while more frequent and/or heavier drinking increased the probability of use. That said, there was some evidence of a middle ground in relation to the hallucinants as both frequent light drinking and regular moderate drinking increased the probability of past use, though they had no discernible effect on recent use. As noted above this pattern suggests a particular propensity towards desistance and is consistent with a more general process of 'calming down'.

The YLS models provided further evidence of a direct link between drinking and drug use, though the situation was complicated by the inclusion of separate indicators relating to drinking style and frequency of drunkenness (see Table 5.2).[6] In general, frequency of drunkenness was a more influential predictor of drug use than was drinking style, though the extent to which this was the case varied depending on the type of drug use. For cannabis, both variables were associated with a range of significant effects that produced a cumulative pattern whereby its use became increasingly likely the more that young adults drank and the more often they got drunk. For the hallucinants and cocaine,

**Table 5.1 Probability of drug use by drinking style – BCS (multivariate analysis, young adults)**

| | *Cannabis* | | | *Hallucinants* | | | *Cocaine* | | |
|---|---|---|---|---|---|---|---|---|---|
| | *Never* | *Past* | *Recent* | *Never* | *Past* | *Recent* | *Never* | *Past* | *Recent* |
| Habitual drinker | | | | | | | | | |
| – heavy | 0.46 | **0.21** | **0.33** | 0.64 | **0.23** | **0.13** | 0.88 | **0.07** | **0.05** |
| – light | 0.46 | **0.21** | **0.33** | 0.80 | 0.12 | 0.08 | 0.88 | 0.03 | **0.09** |
| Frequent drinker | | | | | | | | | |
| – heavy binger | 0.39 | **0.28** | **0.33** | 0.55 | **0.31** | **0.14** | 0.86 | **0.07** | **0.07** |
| – binger | 0.49 | **0.21** | **0.30** | 0.68 | **0.21** | **0.11** | 0.92 | 0.03 | **0.05** |
| – moderate | 0.52 | **0.23** | **0.25** | 0.68 | **0.21** | **0.11** | 0.92 | 0.03 | **0.05** |
| – light | 0.53 | **0.26** | **0.21** | 0.74 | **0.18** | 0.08 | 0.95 | 0.03 | 0.02 |
| Regular drinker | | | | | | | | | |
| – binger | 0.52 | **0.26** | **0.22** | 0.63 | **0.25** | **0.12** | 0.95 | 0.03 | 0.02 |
| – moderate | 0.63 | **0.18** | **0.19** | 0.73 | **0.20** | 0.07 | 0.92 | 0.03 | **0.05** |
| – light | 0.69 | **0.19** | 0.12 | 0.80 | 0.12 | 0.08 | 0.95 | 0.03 | 0.02 |
| Occasional drinker | | | | | | | | | |
| – moderate | 0.62 | **0.20** | 0.18 | 0.80 | 0.12 | 0.08 | 0.95 | 0.03 | 0.02 |
| – light | 0.69 | **0.19** | 0.12 | 0.80 | 0.12 | 0.08 | 0.95 | 0.03 | 0.02 |
| Non-drinker† | 0.78 | 0.12 | 0.12 | 0.80 | 0.12 | 0.08 | 0.95 | 0.03 | 0.02 |

*Source*: BCS (1998) †reference category *Model*: Lifestyle model

*Notes*:

1. Statistically significant effects are highlighted in bold.
2. Effects on past or recent use were estimated vis-à-vis the probability of never having used.
3. Categories that had no significant effect on recent use or past use were excluded from the model and formed part of the reference category.

frequency of drunkenness tended to override the effects of drinking style. There were, nonetheless, some general patterns across the various categories of drug use: heavy drinking and/or frequent drunkenness were consistently associated with a heightened probability of recent drug use; moderate drinking habits were associated with desistance (i.e. the probability of past use relative to recent use was high); and having never drunk alcohol or having stopped doing so increased the probability of abstinence (this was the case in relation to cannabis and the hallucinants, though not cocaine).

**Table 5.2 Probability of drug use by frequency of drunkenness and drinking style – YLS (multivariate analysis, young adults)**

| *Drunkenness in last year* | *Cannabis* | | | *Hallucinants* | | | *Cocaine* | | |
|---|---|---|---|---|---|---|---|---|---|
| | *Never* | *Past* | *Recent* | *Never* | *Past* | *Recent* | *Never* | *Past* | *Recent* |
| At least once a week | 0.38 | **0.21** | **0.41** | 0.51 | **0.20** | **0.29** | 0.78 | **0.06** | **0.16** |
| Several times a month | 0.36 | **0.19** | **0.45** | 0.42 | **0.35** | **0.23** | 0.80 | **0.07** | **0.13** |
| Once or twice a month | 0.34 | **0.24** | **0.43** | 0.51 | **0.26** | **0.24** | 0.82 | **0.07** | **0.11** |
| Every couple of months | 0.45 | **0.22** | **0.33** | 0.63 | **0.22** | **0.15** | 0.88 | 0.05 | **0.08** |
| Less often | 0.48 | **0.22** | **0.30** | 0.68 | 0.20 | **0.12** | 0.94 | 0.03 | 0.03 |
| Not in last year† | 0.68 | 0.17 | 0.16 | 0.76 | 0.16 | 0.08 | 0.95 | 0.03 | 0.02 |
| Non-drinker | 0.91 | **0.01** | 0.08 | 0.88 | **0.05** | 0.08 | 0.95 | 0.02 | 0.03 |

*Source*: YLS (1998/9) †reference category *Model*: Lifestyle model

*Notes*:
1. Differences in drinking style were taken into account by weighting the relevant effects according to the drinking profile associated with the given rate of drunkenness. Non drinkers were those who had abstained from ever having drunk alcohol and were assumed to have never been drunk.
2. Statistical significance was assessed primarily in relation to drunkenness. 'Not been drunk in the last year' provided the reference category and all significant effects associated with the drunkenness variable have been marked in bold. Where the effect of being a 'non-drinker (abstainer)' was significant compared to being a 'habitual heavy drinker' (the reference category for drinking style) this has also been marked in bold. See Technical Appendix for details.
3. Effects on past or recent use were estimated vis-à-vis the probability of never having used.
4. Categories that had no significant effect on recent use or past use were excluded from the model and formed part of the reference category.

## Smoking

Reflecting the convergence of trends in illicit drug use and tobacco smoking, there is now a considerable overlap between these forms of consumption. Current smokers tend to be the most active users of illicit drugs, with more than half the heaviest smokers having recently used cannabis, slightly more than one-in-four having recently used the hallucinants and one-in-eight having recently used cocaine. Those who had never smoked, by contrast, were the least likely to have used illicit drugs, with fewer than one-in-ten having ever used cannabis, the hallucinants or cocaine. Ex-smokers and, to a lesser extent, experimental smokers were different again because they tended to report considerably higher rates of past drug use than recent use, suggesting a particular propensity towards desistence.[7]

The multivariate models confirmed the link between smoking and drug use. Striking effects were evident across all three categories of drug use, which broadly followed the pattern described above. An average young adult who had never smoked tobacco was unlikely to have used cannabis, the hallucinants or cocaine and the probability of such use was greatly increased if they had smoked, particularly if they had done so on more than an experimental basis (see Table 5.3). Whether or not they continued to smoke also had important implications for their involvement in drug use. Being a current smoker, in all its various guises, increased the probability of recent drug use to a much greater degree than being an ex-smoker, though its effect on the probability of past use tended to be more limited. Giving up smoking, by contrast, tended to have a greater effect on the probability of past use than recent use, which markedly increased the odds of desistance. All things being equal,

**Table 5.3 Probability of drug use by smoking habits – YLS (multivariate analysis, young adults)**

| | *Cannabis* | | | *Hallucinants* | | | *Cocaine* | | |
|---|---|---|---|---|---|---|---|---|---|
| *Smoking habits* | *Never* | *Past* | *Recent* | *Never* | *Past* | *Recent* | *Never* | *Past* | *Recent* |
| Moderate to heavy | 0.23 | **0.19** | **0.58** | 0.46 | **0.28** | **0.27** | 0.79 | **0.09** | **0.12** |
| Light | 0.26 | **0.22** | **0.52** | 0.47 | **0.31** | **0.22** | 0.86 | 0.05 | **0.09** |
| Occasional | 0.31 | **0.21** | **0.47** | 0.56 | **0.27** | **0.18** | 0.82 | **0.09** | **0.09** |
| Ex-smoker | 0.36 | **0.35** | **0.29** | 0.60 | **0.29** | **0.11** | 0.89 | **0.08** | 0.03 |
| Experimenter | 0.65 | **0.16** | **0.20** | 0.87 | 0.09 | 0.05 | 0.97 | 0.01 | 0.02 |
| Non-smoker† | 0.92 | 0.05 | 0.03 | 0.87 | 0.09 | 0.05 | 0.97 | 0.01 | 0.02 |

*Source*: YLS (1998/9) †reference category *Model*: Lifestyle model

*Notes*:

1. Statistically significant effects are highlighted in bold.
2. Effects on past or recent use were estimated vis-à-vis the probability of never having used.
3. Categories that had no significant effect on recent use or past use were excluded from the model and formed part of the reference category.

ex-smokers were much more likely to have used illicit drugs than non-smokers, but were much more likely to have stopped doing so than current smokers.

## Onset of drinking and smoking

By the time they use illicit drugs the vast majority of young people have already started to drink and smoke. For the most part, therefore, drug use represents an extension of existing patterns of behaviour. Recent surveys have repeatedly identified the 11 to 15 year age range as a key period of experimentation, during which many young people start to use alcohol, tobacco and/or illicit drugs. Surveys have also shown that such early experiences tend to follow a particular order, with alcohol and tobacco typically being used before illicit drugs. This gap in onset is conceptually significant because it underpins the suggestion that drinking and smoking may be considered predictors of illicit drug use. Empirical analysis indicates that this is indeed the case, having shown that early experiences of drinking and smoking are associated with heightened rates of drug use (Golub and Johnson, 2001; Boreham and McManus, 2003; Fuller, 2005; Wagner et al., 2005).

The YLS confirmed that young adults typically first use illicit drugs some time after they have started to drink and/or smoke (no such judgements could be made on the basis of the BCS because it did not provide the relevant information).[8] Young adults reported having had their first 'proper' alcoholic drink at an average of 14 years of age and of having first tried smoking at around the same time.[9] Those who had used illicit drugs reported slightly earlier experiences of drinking and smoking than those who had not, extending the gap between these different forms of consumption a little further. On average, therefore, young adults reported having first tried illicit drugs three years after having had their first proper alcoholic drink and/or first trying smoking.

Early experiences of drinking and smoking were also associated with heightened rates of drug use. Young adults who had their first alcoholic drink and/or tried smoking before their tenth birthday consistently reported the highest rates of recent drug use: one-in-two had recently used cannabis, one-in-three had recently used the hallucinants and one-in-ten had recently used cocaine. These prevalence rates were more than twice those reported by young adults who did not drink or smoke until they were 14 or 15 years old and were more than three-and-a-half times those reported by young adults who did not drink or smoke until after their 15$^{th}$ birthday. Similar, albeit slightly reduced, differences were evident from the multivariate models, which showed that early onset drinking and/or smoking sharply increased the probability of recent use across all three drug-types and that later onset increased the odds of desistance, suggesting particularly tentative forms of drug use (see Table 5.4).

## Combined effects of drinking and smoking

The analysis presented so far has concentrated on separating out the effects of various lifestyle indicators. Such an approach helps to specify the effect of each of the indicators, but takes little account of the links between them. This is particularly important in relation to drinking and smoking habits because they are fairly closely related to one another: young adults are more likely to smoke the more they drink and the more often they get drunk and vice versa; and those who smoke and drink most heavily are most likely to have had their first alcoholic drink and/or tried smoking at a relatively young age.[10] In relation to drug use, therefore, the effects of drinking and smoking tend to be cumulative (see Table 5.5). Young adults who had little or no experience of these forms of consumption had a very low probability of any kind of illicit drug use, be it recent or past. Even fairly unremarkable drinking and smoking profiles (e.g. Type C) greatly increased the probability of drug use, though much of their effect was evident in relation

**Table 5.4 Probability of drug use by age that first drank and/or smoked – YLS (multivariate analysis, young adults)**

| *Age first drank or smoked* | *Cannabis* | | | *Hallucinants* | | | *Cocaine* | | |
|---|---|---|---|---|---|---|---|---|---|
| | *Never* | *Past* | *Recent* | *Never* | *Past* | *Recent* | *Never* | *Past* | *Recent* |
| < 10 years† | 0.28 | 0.25 | 0.47 | 0.53 | 0.26 | 0.21 | 0.86 | 0.06 | 0.09 |
| 10–13 years | 0.39 | 0.22 | **0.39** | 0.53 | 0.26 | 0.21 | 0.86 | 0.06 | 0.09 |
| 14–15 years | 0.55 | **0.20** | **0.25** | 0.68 | **0.20** | **0.12** | 0.91 | 0.05 | **0.04** |
| 16 years or older | 0.67 | **0.16** | **0.17** | 0.82 | **0.12** | **0.06** | 0.96 | **0.02** | **0.02** |

*Source*: YLS (1998/9) †reference category *Model*: Lifestyle model

*Notes*:

1. Statistically significant effects are highlighted in bold.
2. Effects on past or recent use were estimated vis-à-vis the probability of never having used.
3. Categories that had no significant effect on recent use or past use were excluded from the model and formed part of the reference category.

to past use, which suggests a particular propensity towards desistance and moderation. Heavier drinking and smoking profiles (e.g. Type D) had a rather different set of effects, dramatically increasing the probability of recent use, while having a marked, but less striking, effect on past use. Such a pattern clearly suggests that heavier drinking and smoking profiles are linked to relatively active patterns of drug use.

## Participation in the night-time economy

Various club based surveys have found those in attendance to be considerably more drug experienced than the general youthful population (Release, 1997; Petridis, 1996; Measham et al., 2001). The significance of this link was confirmed by the BCS and YLS, both of which found recent drug use to be most prevalent among the most active participants in the night-time economy (see Table 5.6). According to the BCS, young adults who went to the pub most often reported the highest rates of recent drug use and the lowest rates of abstinence across all three drug-types. Conversely, those who had been to the pub least often consistently reported the lowest rates of recent use and the highest rates of abstinence. A similar pattern was evident in relation to time spent in clubs. The YLS also found that young adults who

**Table 5.5 Probability of drug use by drinking and smoking habits – YLS (multivariate analysis, young adults)**

| | *Cannabis* | | | *Hallucinants* | | | *Cocaine* | | |
|---|---|---|---|---|---|---|---|---|---|
| | *Never* | *Past* | *Recent* | *Never* | *Past* | *Recent* | *Never* | *Past* | *Recent* |
| Type A | 0.99 | <0.01 | 0.01 | 0.95 | 0.02 | 0.03 | 0.98 | 0.01 | 0.01 |
| Type B | 0.97 | 0.03 | 0.01 | 0.93 | 0.05 | 0.02 | 0.99 | 0.01 | <0.01 |
| Type C | 0.26 | 0.41 | 0.33 | 0.50 | 0.35 | 0.15 | 0.81 | 0.14 | 0.05 |
| Type D | 0.10 | 0.15 | 0.76 | 0.21 | 0.23 | 0.56 | 0.46 | 0.11 | 0.43 |

*Source*: YLS (1998/9) *Model*: Lifestyle model

Key – drinking and smoking habits

Type A: Never had a proper alcoholic drink and never tried smoking.

Type B: Does drink, but not been drunk in last year, never smoked, had first drink when 16 years or older.

Type C: Been drunk once or twice a month in last year, ex-smoker, first drank and/or smoked at 14 or 15 years.

Type D: Been drunk at least once a week in last year, regular moderate to heavy smoker, first drank and/or smoked when 10–13 years old.

*Note*: the effects of drinking style were taken into account by weighting them according to the profile associated with the given rate of drunkenness.

**Table 5.6 Prevalence of drug use by participation in the night-time economy (percentages, young adults)**

| | *Cannabis* | | | *Hallucinants* | | | *Cocaine* | | |
|---|---|---|---|---|---|---|---|---|---|
| | *Never* | *Past* | *Recent* | *Never* | *Past* | *Recent* | *Never* | *Past* | *Recent* |
| *BCS* | | | | | | | | | |
| *Evenings visited pub in last month* | | ** | | | ** | | | ** | |
| Almost every day | 31 | 24 | 45 | 50 | 25 | 25 | 83 | 7 | 11 |
| About three times a week | 40 | 22 | 38 | 57 | 27 | 16 | 91 | 3 | 6 |
| Once or twice a week | 51 | 23 | 27 | 72 | 16 | 13 | 95 | 2 | 3 |
| Less often | 60 | 23 | 17 | 76 | 18 | 6 | 95 | 3 | 2 |
| None | 74 | 15 | 11 | 84 | 12 | 4 | 96 | 3 | 1 |
| *Visits to a club or disco in last month* | | ** | | | ** | | | ** | |
| At least once a week | 43 | 18 | 39 | 58 | 19 | 23 | 89 | 4 | 7 |
| Less often | 50 | 22 | 28 | 68 | 21 | 11 | 94 | 3 | 3 |
| None | 63 | 21 | 16 | 78 | 15 | 6 | 96 | 3 | 2 |
| *YLS* | | | | | | | | | |
| *Visits to pub and/or club etc in last month* | | ** | | | ** | | | ** | |
| Pub and club | 44 | 19 | 36 | 59 | 22 | 19 | 87 | 5 | 8 |
| Club but not pub | 64 | 12 | 24 | 80 | 11 | 10 | 94 | 4 | 3 |
| Pub but not club | 51 | 26 | 23 | 68 | 25 | 7 | 92 | 4 | 4 |
| Neither pub nor club | 68 | 15 | 17 | 78 | 16 | 7 | 95 | 4 | 1 |

*Source*: BCS (1998) and YLS (1998/9) ** $p < 0.01$ * $p < 0.05$ ns $p < 0.05$

*Notes*:

1. BCS, pub: Kendall's tau-c = 0.24 (cannabis); 0.17 (hallucinants); and 0.04 (cocaine).
2. BCS, club: Kendall's tau-c = 0.18 (cannabis); 0.16 (hallucinants); and 0.08 (cocaine).
3. YLS, pub and/or club: Kendall's tau-c = 0.15 (cannabis); 0.13 (hallucinants); and 0.05 (cocaine).

had been to a pub and club in the last month consistently reported the highest rates of recent drug use and the lowest rates of abstinence. By contrast, those who had not been to a pub or club during this period reported the lowest rates of recent use and some of the highest rates of abstinence.

The results of the multivariate analysis were less clear-cut. All things being equal, the BCS models indicated that spending regular evenings in the pub increased the probability of recent cannabis use, hallucinant use and cocaine use: for an average young adult, having spent almost every evening in the pub in the last month roughly doubled the probability of recent use across all three drug types. Regular clubbing was also found to have a similar effect on the use of hallucinants and cocaine, though no such effect on the use of cannabis. The YLS models, by contrast, indicated that the relationship between drug use and the use of pubs and clubs was largely mediated by the other variables included in the analysis. Evidence of a direct link was limited to the hallucinants and was fairly modest even here: having been to a pub and a club in the last month, rather than having been to neither, increased the probability of recent use by slightly less than half, but having been to one or the other had no discernible effect. No such effects were evident in relation to either cannabis or cocaine.

Given the differences between the surveys it remains unclear whether the use of pubs and clubs is directly linked to drug use or whether these links are mediated by other variables, particularly those relating to the consumption of alcohol and tobacco. The YLS contained more detailed information than the BCS about drinking and smoking habits and this extra level of detail may have over-ridden the effects that would otherwise have been associated with the use of pubs and clubs. That said, the YLS also contained less detailed information than the BCS about the use of pubs and clubs, which may have meant that some significant effects remained hidden.

**Time spent with friends and participation in street networks**

Social networks have been identified as an important influence on young people's relationship with illicit drugs. It is well established that drug use provides a basis for peer clustering, with users and non-users tending to form distinct networks, but there is some disagreement over the precise interpretation of these patterns. In particular, accounts that emphasise the role of peer pressure have been challenged on the basis that peer selection provides a more realistic explanation (Coggans and McKellar, 1994; but see Santor et al., 2000). What remains clear, however, is that some social networks are more involved with illicit drugs than others and differences in this regard may be related to broader socio-environmental factors. Several commentators have pointed to a link with social exclusion, for example, arguing that where young people are involved in street-centred networks this is likely to increase their knowledge about, and access to, illicit drugs (Johnston et al., 2000; Shildrick, 2002).

The role of social networks could only be assessed in a fairly rudimentary fashion in this study because the surveys provided little detailed information on such matters. Nonetheless, the YLS did indicate that drug use is linked to sociability and participation in street networks. Rates of recent use increased quite sharply according to the frequency with which young adults spent time with a close friend: those who were in such company most often reported rates of recent use that were at least four times the rate reported by those who were never in such company.[11] Even when other variables were taken into account, the multivariate models indicated that spending little or no time with a close friend reduced the probability of recent use across all three drug-types (see Technical Appendix for details).

Participation in street networks was also associated with heightened rates of drug use, though this relationship was largely mediated by other factors. The rates of recent drug use reported by young adults who had 'hung around' on the street in the last month were approximately one-and-a-half times greater than the rates reported by those who had not spent time in this way.[12] The multivariate models confirmed that participation in street networks increased the probability of recent drug use, but these effects were modest when compared to differences in rates of use. For an average young adult, 'hanging around' on the street increased the probability of recent cannabis use from 0.26 to 0.30, of recent hallucinant use from 0.13 to 0.17 and of recent cocaine use from 0.05 to 0.08. To a large extent, therefore, the link between participation in street networks and drug use appears to be mediated by other variables included in the models. Age plays a particularly important role in this regard because 'hanging around' on the street was largely limited to young adults in their late teens and early twenties, which also happens to be the peak period for illicit drug use (see Chapter 6).

## Conclusion

The analysis presented in this chapter reaffirms the meaningful, goal oriented nature of illicit drug use. Such behaviour is strongly linked to other leisure-related activities and tends to form part of a distinct package based around pubs, clubs, binge drinking, drunkenness and smoking, which suggests a particular commitment to hedonistic consumption and intoxication. Alcohol and tobacco play a particularly important role in this regard because they tend to serve as a gateway to illicit drug use (Parker et al., 1998). Very few young people use illicit drugs without first gaining some experience of drinking and/or smoking and the earlier they start to drink and/or smoke the more likely they are to go on to use illicit drugs. Desistence from drug use, on the other hand, often forms part of a broader process of 'calming down', while, for some at least, non-use is symptomatic of a more general emphasis on abstinence.

The use of illicit drugs alongside alcohol and tobacco does not represent the radical departure that is sometimes suggested, but is rather the latest expression of an age old pursuit. As a more or less permanent feature of human history, the search for intoxication has been described by American psychopharmacologist, Robert K. Siegel (2005), as the 'fourth drive'; as deep-rooted and instinctual as our cravings for food, water and sex. Nor is the commercial exploitation of this drive a particularly recent phenomenon. What Courtwright (2001: 2) refers to as the 'psychoactive revolution' was, by his own account, a protracted process that combined the discoveries and innovations of the early modern period with new, nineteenth century, techniques of industrial production and distribution to 'refine and mass market an impressive array of psychoactive pleasures', including alcohol, caffeine, cannabis, coca, cocaine, opium, morphine and tobacco; so that 'millions of ordinary people throughout the world could lead, in neurochemical terms, a life-style unimaginable for even the wealthiest five hundred years earlier'.

Whilst stimulating supply, through improved productivity, industrialisation also fuelled consumer demand by yielding improved living standards, increased disposable income and more clearly delineated free-time. This combined set of circumstances created the conditions for a mass market in what were previously considered to be luxury items and laid the foundations for the growing commodification of leisure. With time on their hands and money to spend, young working class wage-earners provided an obvious target for early forms of commercialised leisure and were identified as a key segment of the consumer market during the post-war boom. From the early 1960s young people were increasingly targeted by the drinks industry and the emergence of widespread drug use was accompanied by a sharp increase in alcohol consumption and the growth of binge drinking. Anticipating the emphasis that has come to be placed on lifestyle and consumption, Young (1971) considered alcohol and illicit drugs to serve a similar function, providing a route into the world of subterranean values, and viewed the hippies' calls for authentic play as an attempt to resolve the central problems of work and leisure that were (already) being generated by late industrial societies. In the wake of deindustrialisation and the post-industrial transformation, these problems have become all the more acute and leisure has continued to acquire greater importance, both as a form of consumption and source of economic growth. With an explicit emphasis on adventure, intoxication and release the night-time economy has become the primary site of subterranean play and its expansion has encouraged the growth of a distinctly hedonistic leisure style, which has, in turn, helped to create a platform for accelerating rates of illicit drug use. In Britain, at the least, the emergence of widespread drug use cannot be understood separately from increases in alcohol consumption and the related activities of the drinks industry.

# 6
# Just a Phase?

> Young people certainly do seek to inhabit worlds (the pub, the club, the disco floor) in which they are in control. But so do adults, who also indulge in leisure, use it as a source of fantasy, a place to act out 'subterranean values'. The distinctive nature of youth culture must be explained, then, not by reference to leisure itself, but to young people's position in work and family, to the 'reality' from which leisure is, on occasion, an escape (Frith, 1985: 360).

What Young (1971) described as the ambivalent position of youth was largely a product of the changing patterns of employment associated with industrialisation. Child labour was essential to the early phase of the industrial revolution, as it had been to the preceding family based economy, but became less important as the factory reform movement gained ground and technological innovations yielded more efficient forms of production (Evans, 1983). By the time compulsory education was introduced towards the end of the nineteenth century, children were no longer so central to the working of the economy and demand for their labour had already declined (Musgrove, 1964). The expansion of the education and apprenticeship system absorbed the potential labour surplus and regulated entry into the labour market, hiving young people off from the rest of society and committing them to a state of 'limbo' between childhood and adulthood (Young, 1971: 141). Subsequent developments, rooted in changing patterns of production and employment, have further magnified the ambivalent position of youth and have resulted in longer, more fragmented journeys into adulthood. What implications this has had for drug use will be considered below. Whereas the previous chapter concentrated on the agential processes associated with leisure and consumption, the analysis presented here examines how the choices young adults make about drug use vary with age, work status and domestic circumstances. The results are discussed in light of recent developments in life-course criminology, which, it will be shown, not only help to explain why drug use is distributed in the way that it is, but also serve to clarify the social meaning of such behaviour.

## Life-course criminology

The observation that crime is mostly committed by young people has prompted suggestions that any theory of criminal offending should seek to explain how such behaviour fits with the course of individual development from infancy to old age (Smith, 2002). That offending behaviour is closely related to the course of individual development is not in doubt, but the nature of this relationship is a matter of debate. Hirschi and Gottfredson (1983) famously claimed that the age distribution of crime – its onset and desistance – is invariant across time, space and historical context. They subsequently went onto argue that age has a direct effect on crime, so that desistance is something that 'just happens' due to 'the inexorable aging of the organism' (Gottfredson and Hirschi, 1990: 141). Critics have rejected the claim that the relationship between age and crime is invariant and have challenged the notion that age causes desistance (see Farrall and Bowling, 1999; Laub and Sampson, 2003). Age, they note, is not a personal characteristic, but an index of the likely stage of development that someone has reached and of their social standing. Such objections have been reinforced by evidence that desistance is related to changes in a range of sociological and psychological variables, including life-course events such as marriage, employment and education.

In what is arguably the most significant contribution to life-course criminology in recent years, Robert Sampson and John Laub (1993, 2005; see also Laub and Sampson, 2003) developed an 'age-graded theory of informal social control'. As this description implies, their approach rests on a sympathetic critique of control theory. Rather than trying to explain deviant impulses, control theory assumes that individuals are subject to many temptations to engage in rewarding criminal behaviour and will do so unless they are held in check (Reiss, 1951; Reckless, 1967). As one of the leading advocates of this perspective, Hirschi (1969) argued that the key to delinquency control is provided by the social bond, which is made up of the emotional connections that individuals feel towards others and includes sensitivity to their opinions, feelings and expectations (attachment); the accumulated investment that individuals have in relationships, activities and objects and is, in effect, their stake in conformity (commitment); participation in legitimate activities and the extent to which individuals are tied to appointments, deadlines, hours and plans (involvement); and the extent to which they feel they should obey the rules of society (belief).

Laub and Sampson (2003) identify various weaknesses in traditional control theory, the most important of which is the failure to address the role of human agency and motivation. Despite these misgivings, they initially viewed informal social control as providing the primary explanation of crime and desistance over the life-course and have continued to favour a modified version of this position. In their later work, Laub and Sampson highlight several components, including human agency, situational choice, routine activities, ageing and historical context, which they feel should be incorporated into control theory in order to provide a fuller explanation of criminal behaviour. Rather than representing a simple weakening of the social bond, they argue crime provides a vehicle for demonstrating freedom and choice. Drawing on insights provided by the likes of Matza and Becker, as well as the more recent work of Jack Katz (1988), Laub and Sampson acknowledge the 'seductions' of crime, which they argue is purposeful, systematic and meaningful; attractive because it offers a source of excitement. At the same time, in a move that echoes Giddens' (1984) theory of structuration, they maintain that such 'agential processes' are reciprocally linked to situations and larger structures: that is, situations and structures are said to be partly determined by the choices individuals make, yet simultaneously constrain, modify and limit the choices that are available to them. Because situations vary in the extent to which they constrain behavioural choices, crime is considered to represent a form of 'situated choice'.

What Laub and Sampson consider important, then, is the interplay of agency, action and structure through time. Based on this interplay, they maintain that persistence in, and desistance from, crime can be meaningfully understood within the same theoretical framework. Persistence is said to be explained by a lack of social controls, few structured routine activities and purposeful human agency, while desistence is attributed to a confluence of social controls, structured routine activities and purposeful human agency. Viewing persistence and desistance as ongoing processes, Laub and Sampson emphasise the important role that social ties play across all stages of the life-course. Informal and formal social controls are said to become more salient with age, however, and the influence of social bonds is said to interact with age and life experiences. During adolescence the bonds that tie children to family and school tend to weaken and are yet to be replaced by a new set of adult relationships and associated commitments. As a result young people are generally less constrained during adolescence than at any other time of their lives and are freer to engage in acts of delinquency and deviance. With the transition into adulthood new bonds are acquired through spouses, children, employers and friends, which have the potential to act as catalysts for change.

Laub and Sampson go on to argue that desistance from crime is facilitated by 'turning points' or changes in situational and structural life circumstances like a 'good' marriage or a stable job. These turning points are not considered to be deterministic; nor is desistance said to depend on cognitive transformation or identity shifts. Rather, it is said to occur by default (2003: 278–9):

> Desistance for our subjects was not necessarily a conscious or deliberate process but rather a consequence of what Howard Becker calls 'side bets' (1960: 38). Many men made a commitment to go straight without even realizing it. Before they knew it they had invested so much in the marriage or job that they did not want to risk losing their investment.

The main turning points identified by Laub and Sampson are marriage, employment and military service, which are said to have the potential to reshape life-course trajectories by reordering short-term situational inducements to crime and redirecting long-term commitments to conformity. Social ties created through marriage are considered to be important in so far as they create interdependent systems of obligation and restraint that impose significant costs on criminal activity. Marriage may also facilitate desistance through direct monitoring and social control by spouses and consequent changes in everyday routines, including potential separation from delinquent peer groups. Parenting responsibilities bring further changes to routine activities as more time is spent in family-centred activities rather than unstructured time with peers. Finally, marriage and parenthood may encourage desistance through a reorganisation of self-identity as people come to think of themselves as 'getting serious' or 'settling down'.

Laub and Sampson acknowledge that desistance may occur in response to enduring attachments rather than marriage per se, but emphasise the special qualities of marital bonds. In so doing, they support the view that marriage differs from cohabitation and has a more significant role in crime prevention. While some, such as Gottfredson and Hirschi (1990), consider the marriage-crime relationship to be spurious on the grounds that marital bonds do not 'just happen' and are created by individual choice, Laub and Sampson maintain that the impact of marriage cannot simply be dismissed as a selection-effect. In particular they argue that selection into marriage is less systematic than many people assume, often originating in fortuitous contacts made through routine activities; that the personality and interactional styles individuals bring to the marriage are malleable and can be altered by the emergent qualities of the marriage itself; and that the individual differences which are presumed to influence the marriage process do not explain desistance, much less the marriage effect.

The processes by which work and military service are held to encourage desistance are very similar to those described in relation to marriage. Work, perhaps even more than marriage, changes routine activities and provides social ties, monitoring, direct supervision as well as an alternative source of identity. These changes are felt particularly sharply in relation to the military, which introduces a major source of discontinuity in the life-course. A prominent feature of military service is said to be the 'knifing off' of past experiences and its potential for reorganising social roles and life opportunities. Similar to marriage and work, but more consciously by design, the military changes routine activities, provides direct supervision and social support, and allows for the possibility of identity change. While highlighting the importance of marriage, work and military service, Laub and Sampson acknowledge that the turning points they describe are historically embedded, yet are equally clear that their theory has relevance beyond the immediate context in which it was developed: 'the patterns of persistence and desistance from crime that we have uncovered are more general than specific with respect to place, historical time, gender and race' (Laub and Sampson, 2003: 283).

## Understanding early adult transitions

The transition from childhood to adulthood is widely considered to constitute a key phase of the life-course, but is not one that is easily defined, in part at least, because of differences in emphasis and interpretation (Coleman and Hendry, 1999; Furlong and Cartmel, 2007). Psychologists tend to refer to this phase as 'adolescence', by which they mean a period of physical, sexual and emotional development that occurs roughly between 12 and 18 years of age. Adolescence is generally said to start with the onset of puberty, though this now occurs at a younger age than previously due to improvements in nutrition. The point at which adolescence ends and adulthood begins is less clear-cut and depends on the way that individuals come to terms with physiological changes and establish adult identities. Sociologists tend to reject the term adolescence in favour of the term 'youth', which draws attention to the socially constructed nature of the transition into adulthood. Youth is an 'elastic' concept which means different things at different times and in different places (Newburn, 2002); partly, no doubt, because the boundary between youth and adulthood is blurred and, legal definitions aside, can not be identified in anything other than a fairly general way. Although obviously linked to age, the transition into adulthood cannot be fully understood in such terms because it also involves changing roles and responsibilities. These changes do not occur simultaneously, moreover, but are staggered over time and take effect at different ages for different people, so that youth 'has neither a clear chronological beginning nor end' (Coles, 1995: 7).

Despite their disciplinary differences, most psychologists and sociologists agree that the transition into adulthood has changed significantly in recent times, becoming longer and more complex. This 'transformation', moreover, is said to have taken place in 'all highly industrialized countries' (Chisholm and Hurrelmann, 1995: 133). Whereas in the 1950s and 1960s youth was widely held to be synonymous with the teenage years, it is now generally considered to extend from the mid-teens to the mid-twenties. Such developments have reinforced existing doubts about whether youth can be realistically considered a single phase, prompting claims that it should be conceptualised as a series of transitions, each of which should be viewed as a separate event. Coles (1995), for example, identifies three main 'youth transitions' that denote entry into adulthood: the transition from full-time education and training to a full-time job in the labour market (the school to work transition); the transition from family of origin to family of destination (the domestic transition); and the transition from living with (surrogate) parents to living away from them (the housing transition).

Although distinct, these transitions are closely related to one another and delays in one may well impact upon the others. Thus it is that the extended nature of youth is often linked to economic changes and to what some commentators have characterised as a shift from a Fordist to post-Fordist system of production. During the 1950s and 1960s a buoyant manufacturing sector generated considerable demand for low skilled labour, creating jobs for large numbers of unqualified school-leavers, who were thus able to transfer directly from school to work. With the end of the post-war consumer boom, which followed in the wake of the 1973 oil crisis, and growing competition from foreign markets, late industrial societies experienced a sharp decline in manufacturing activity and the related collapse of the youth labour market. Subsequent economic development came to focus on an increasingly dominant service sector and employment opportunities were restructured within a policy framework that prioritises training, flexible specialisation and reduced labour costs.

Deindustrialisation and associated policy responses have channelled young people away from full-time paid work into post-compulsory education. In Britain, as in most late industrial societies, direct entry into the labour market has become the exception rather than the rule and many more young people are going into further and higher education, though the origins of these trends predate the shift to post-Fordist production. Entry into further education has increased fairly steadily since the mid 1950s, while entry into higher education has increased largely on the basis of two periods of rapid growth – one in the mid 1960s and another in the early 1990s (McVicar and Rice, 2001; Machin and Vignoles, 2005). Given these trends, young people across all social classes are spending greater amounts of time in education, though residual forms of disadvantage persist. A sizeable minority of young people remain outside of any education, training or work, some of whom, having experienced unemployment after completing their education or training, may withdraw from the labour market (Furlong and Cartmel, 2007).

As young people have been channelled away from the labour market and into post-compulsory education it has taken them longer to achieve financial independence. This, in turn, has had significant implications for their ability to set up home for themselves and start their own family (Furlong and Cartmel, 2007). During the 1950s and 1960s, full employment and relative prosperity facilitated rapid housing and domestic transitions, which tended to involve an ordered sequence of events , whereby young people left school, then had their first sexual encounter, moved out of the parental home and married sometime later. This was particularly the case for young people from working class families, who generally went directly from school into full-time paid work and left the parental home, got married and had children in fairly quick succession. By virtue of their greater involvement in post-compulsory education, the children of the middle classes tended to remain dependent on their parents for longer, often into their early twenties. In Britain, as elsewhere, the subsequent collapse of the youth labour market, reinforced by the withdrawal of welfare benefits, has seen the state effectively relinquish economic responsibility for young people, making parents financially responsible for their children for longer and extending the period of dependency to the age of 18 years and of semi-dependency to the age of 25 years (Jones, 1995). With these developments youth transitions have become less obviously demarcated by social class, though significant areas of inequality remain. As direct entry into the labour market has all but disappeared, working class transitions have come to approximate more closely to what was previously the quintessential middle class experience of delayed transitions and an extended period of (semi-)dependence.

As well as taking longer to complete, housing and domestic transitions have fragmented and the previous sequence of events has been disrupted. The gaps between leaving home, getting married and becoming a parent have widened as young people are tending to leave home earlier than they used to, yet marrying and having children later. One of the most striking aspects of this revised pattern is the greater separation of housing and domestic transitions. Despite being dependent on their families for longer, the average age at which young people first move away from the parental home has declined, though the number returning at a later date has increased, giving rise to the distinction between 'living away' and 'leaving home'. This trend is due, in no small part, to the expansion of higher education, particularly for young people from middle class families, though it also reflects the growing importance of 'intermediary households' more generally. Although precise arrangements vary, it has become increasingly common for young people to live away from their parents, often alone or with peers, before getting married or cohabiting. The growth of intermediary or transitional households has been evident across much of the late industrial world, with the majority of young people in Europe, Australia and north America experiencing some form of communal living (Heath and Cleaver, 2003) and the desire to establish an independent lifestyle featuring more prominently in decisions to leave home (Furlong and Cartmel, 2007). In some such societies, however, particularly those in the Mediterranean region of southern Europe, intermediary households remain unusual and more traditional arrangements continue to dominate due to a combination of economic constraints, government policy and cultural tradition.

With the fragmentation of housing and domestic transitions, marriage and parenthood may be considered the 'definitive step to adulthood'

(Kiernan, 1986: 11), albeit one that has been reconfigured. In *The End of Marriage?*, Jane Lewis (2001) argues that the 'facts' of family change are real and hard to exaggerate: in just one generation, she notes, the numbers marrying have halved, the numbers divorcing have trebled and the proportion of babies born outside marriage has quadrupled. For people born in the first half of the twentieth century marriage was almost universal and provided the main reason for leaving the parental home, but this ceased to be the case for subsequent cohorts. In Britain, as in much of the late industrial world, young people have postponed and forsaken marriage in increasing numbers since the early 1970s (Sigle-Rushton, 2008; Self and Zealey, 2008). Cohabiting and living alone have become much more common, though, ultimately, the majority of adults do still get married. For some, cohabitation offers a temporary arrangement that comes to an end with the break-up of the relationship, while for others it acts as a prelude or alternative to marriage. With more couples cohabiting, there has been a move towards later marriage: between 1971 and 2004 the average age at first marriage increased from 25 years to 31 years for males and from 23 years to 29 years for females. A similar pattern of postponement has been evident in relation to parenting, with the average age of mothers at first birth increasing from around 24 years in the 1960s to 28 years in 2006. Delayed childbirth does not necessarily mean young adults are waiting to get married before starting a family, however, and the relationship between marriage and parenthood has weakened in recent decades. Not only has the proportion of births outside marriage increased sharply, from nine per cent in 1975 to 44 per cent in 2006, but married couples across all social classes are waiting longer before having their first child. Although lone parenthood has become more common, the vast majority of non-marital births are to cohabiting couples, who are just as likely to have dependent children as married couples (Smallwood and Wilson, 2007). In terms of the stability of the relationship, moreover, the distinction between married and cohabiting partnerships with children appears to have become less important (Sigle-Rushton, 2008).

## Surveying early adult transitions

The BCS and YLS contained a range of indicators relating to the three main youth transitions and covered such issues as work, housing and family formation. Respondents' circumstances varied considerably and included positions of (semi-)dependence and independence. Around three-in-five were single, one-in-two were working full-time, one-in-four were buying their own home, one-in-five were married, one-in-four had dependent children and somewhere in the region of one-in-six were studying full-time. The circumstances young adults were in varied sharply depending on their age. Those aged 16 or 17 years were, by some dis-

*Figure 6.1* Young adults' domestic circumstances by age (percentages)

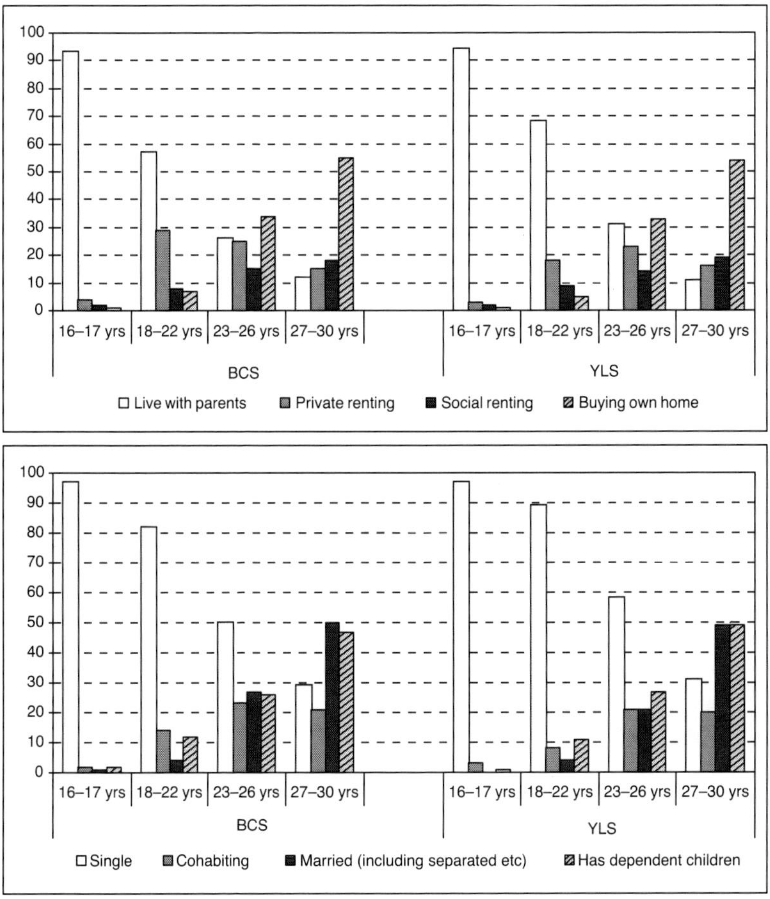


*Source*: BCS (1998) and YLS (1998) n =2,855 (BCS) and 3,548 (YLS)

*Notes*:
- BCS: Kendall's tau-c = 0.41 (marital status by age); 0.50 (housing status by age); and 0.36 (parental status by age). P < .01 in all cases.
- YLS: Kendall's tau-c = 0.41 (marital status by age); 0.52 (housing status by age); and 0.39 (parental status by age). P < .01 in all cases.

tance, the most likely to be studying full-time and the least likely to be engaged in full-time work, while the reverse was the case for 27 to 30 year olds. Striking differences were also evident in relation to housing, marital status and parenthood (see Figure 6.1).

Although the transition into adulthood has fragmented, young adults' work, housing and domestic circumstances continue to be closely related to one another.[1] The proportion of young adults who had dependent children was greatest among those who were or had been married, followed by those who were cohabiting and then those who were single. Similar patterns were evident in relation to housing, with the highest rates of owner occupation being evident among those who were or had been married, followed by those who were cohabiting and then those who were single. This, in turn,

**Table 6.1 Young adults' domestic circumstances**

| | *BCS* | | *YLS* | |
|---|---|---|---|---|
| | *Percentage* | *Confidence interval* | *Percentage* | *Confidence interval* |
| Single | | | | |
| – no children, live with parents | 36 | 34–39 | 43 | 40–45 |
| – no children, private renting | 12 | 10–13 | 10 | 9–12 |
| – no children, social renting | 2 | 1–2 | 2 | 1–3 |
| – no children, buying own home | 4 | 3–5 | 5 | 4–6 |
| – with children | 5 | 4–7 | 5 | 4–6 |
| Cohabiting | | | | |
| – no children, not buying own home | 5 | 4–6 | 3 | 2–4 |
| – no children, buying own home | 7 | 6–8 | 5 | 4–6 |
| – with children | 5 | 4–6 | 6 | 5–7 |
| Divorced, separated or widowed | | | | |
| – no children | 1 | 1–1 | 1 | 0–1 |
| – with children | 2 | 1–3 | 2 | 1–3 |
| Married | | | | |
| – no children | 7 | 6–9 | 7 | 6–8 |
| – with children | 14 | 12–16 | 12 | 10–13 |

*Source*: BCS (1998) and YLS (1998) n = 2,831 and 3,548

*Note*: when combining domestic and housing circumstances priority was given to marital status and parental status because of their particular importance in the transition to adulthood (see above). Housing status has been taken into account for young adults who did not have dependent children and were either cohabiting or single. The nature of the distinctions that were made in this regard depended on the number of cases in each category.

meant that young adults who had dependent children were concentrated in the more stable forms of accommodation: four-in-five were either buying their own home or were renting some kind of social housing. Overall then, approximately one-in-eight young adults were married with dependent children; around one-in-six were cohabiting, mainly without dependent children; while two-in-five were single, childless and yet to (permanently) leave the family home (see Table 6.1).

## Drug use and early adult transitions

The changing nature of youth transitions has created some doubt about whether young people are growing out of drug use, as well as other forms of criminal behaviour, in the way they used to. A few years into the North West Cohort Study, the authors of the normalisation thesis questioned whether 'recreational drug use will be left behind by 1990s adolescents as they reach young adulthood' (Parker et al., 1998: 20). When participants in the study were approximately 18 years old and there were no signs that their drug use was slowing down, it was suggested that such behaviour is neither 'transitory nor closely tied to the period of adolescence' (1998: 91). Similar claims were repeated following the next sweep of the survey, which was administered some four years later. By this time there were signs of more moderate and strategic substance use, which were attributed to the requirements of the working week, but overall there was said to be a 'remarkable consistency in on-going drug taking' (Williams and Parker, 2001: 405). Thus, it was concluded that recreational drug use is extending beyond 'traditional markers' (Parker et al., 2002: 960) and that the 'drug-wise children of the nineties are indeed bringing their psycho-active substance use with them into young adulthood' (Williams and Parker, 2001: 410).

This conclusion may be considered a little premature, not least because participants in the study had, at the time, only been surveyed up to the age of 22 years, which was really to early to assess the extent to which they may or may not 'grow out' of drug use. In addition, no attempt was made to distinguish between respondents on the basis of their work and/or domestic circumstances, so, by implication, the transition into adulthood was treated as though it were simply a matter of age. The following analysis, by contrast, examines drug use among young adults up to the age of 30 years and considers the role of various life-course indicators as well as age.

## Age

Drug use is heavily concentrated among young adults, not just in Britain, but across the late industrial world (United Nations, 2008; EMCDDA, 2007; Adlaf et al., 2005; Flight, 2005; Ross, 2007; SAMHSA, 2007; Schulenberg et al., 1997; Stefanogiannis et al., 2007). The international evidence, covering a range of countries from various regions, points to a 'fundamental uniformity of onset patterns by age' in contrast to 'wide variations in lifetime prevalences' (Vega et al., 2002: 285). Initiation typically occurs in late adolescence and, though there is some suggestion that the period of 'risk' may be extending further into adulthood (Degenhardt et al., 2008), the age distribution of drug use remains fairly stable, broadly conforming to the widely observed age-crime curve. British surveys dating back to the mid 1980s have repeatedly found that drug use is relatively unusual among young people in their early teens, but increases sharply in the last few years of compulsory education, before reaching a peak among those in their late teens or early twenties and then falling away quite markedly (see, for example, ISDD, 1993; Graham and Bowling, 1995; Mott and Mirrlees-Black, 1995; Flood-Page et al., 2000). The BCS has consistently found that recent drug use peaks among young adults in their late teens or early twenties and then declines quite sharply among those in their mid-to-late twenties: the 1994, 1998, 2003/4 and 2006/7 sweeps indicate that the average (mean) age of recent users remained stable at 21 or 22 years. These surveys also provide little support for the suggestion that young adults are 'growing out' of drug use in smaller numbers or are taking longer to do so: the desistence rate increased from 43 per cent to 53 per cent between 1994 and 2006/7, while the average (mean) age of desisters remained stable at 24 years.

More detailed findings from the 1998 BCS and 1998/9 YLS confirmed the general pattern. Both surveys found recent drug use to be most prevalent among young adults in their late teens or early twenties, in part, at least, because those in older groups had desisted from such behaviour in greater numbers (see Table 6.2). Among 18 to 22 year olds recent cannabis users outnumbered past users by one-and-a-half or two-and-a-half to one, depending on the survey, but among those in their late twenties past users outnumbered recent users. A broadly similar pattern was evident in relation to the hallucinants: among 18 to 22 year olds there were similar numbers of recent users and past users, but among those in their late twenties past users outnumbered recent users by almost three to one. The situation was less clear-cut in relation to cocaine, though the YLS did indicate that the ratio of past to recent users was

**Table 6.2 Prevalence of drug use by age (percentages, young adults)**

| | *Cannabis* | | | *Hallucinants* | | | *Cocaine* | | |
|---|---|---|---|---|---|---|---|---|---|
| | *Never* | *Past* | *Recent* | *Never* | *Past* | *Recent* | *Never* | *Past* | *Recent* |
| *BCS* | | ** | | | ** | | | ** | |
| 16–17 years | 59 | 14 | 27 | 80 | 9 | 10 | 99 | 1 | 1 |
| 18–22 years | 51 | 19 | 31 | 67 | 19 | 15 | 93 | 4 | 4 |
| 23–26 years | 55 | 23 | 22 | 69 | 22 | 9 | 91 | 5 | 4 |
| 27–30 years | 63 | 24 | 13 | 79 | 16 | 6 | 96 | 2 | 2 |
| *YLS* | | ** | | | ** | | | ** | |
| 16–17 years | 58 | 10 | 32 | 79 | 9 | 12 | 97 | 2 | 2 |
| 18–22 years | 44 | 16 | 40 | 58 | 20 | 23 | 87 | 4 | 9 |
| 23–26 years | 47 | 23 | 30 | 59 | 27 | 14 | 86 | 6 | 8 |
| 27–30 years | 57 | 24 | 18 | 70 | 23 | 8 | 91 | 5 | 4 |

*Source*: BCS (1998) and YLS (1998/9) ** $p < 0.01$ * $p < 0.05$ ns $p < 0.05$

*Notes*:
1. BCS: Cramer's V=0.13 (cannabis); 0.11 (hallucinants); and 0.07 (cocaine).
2. YLS: Cramer's V=0.16 (cannabis); 0.16 (hallucinants); and 0.10 (cocaine).

greater among those in their late twenties than those in their late teens to mid twenties. Across all three categories of drug use, therefore, older young adults displayed a particular propensity towards desistance.

Notable differences were also evident in relation to abstinence. A relatively large proportion of young adults in their late twenties had never used cannabis, the hallucinants or cocaine and this can best be explained in terms of a cohort effect. Compared to their slightly younger counterparts, fewer of those in this age group had used illicit drugs because they had gone through late adolescence at a time when such behaviour was less common. The most marked differences were evident in relation to the hallucinants and cocaine, which is to be expected given that the use of these substances increased most markedly during the subsequent period.

The multivariate models confirmed the link between age and drug use. Both surveys highlighted a series of direct age effects, which persisted when other demographic, life-course and lifestyle variables had been taken into account (see Table 6.3). Although the precise nature of these effects varied between the surveys,[2] there was a clearly discernible pattern, whereby desistance became more likely with age. According to the final lifestyle models, young adults in their late twenties were, by virtue of their age, approximately two to three times more likely to have stopped

**Table 6.3 Probability of drug use by age (multivariate analysis, young adults)**

| | *Cannabis* | | | *Hallucinants* | | | *Cocaine* | | |
|---|---|---|---|---|---|---|---|---|---|
| | *Never* | *Past* | *Recent* | *Never* | *Past* | *Recent* | *Never* | *Past* | *Recent* |
| *BCS* | | | | | | | | | |
| 16–17 years | 0.39 | 0.19 | **0.42** | 0.69 | 0.14 | **0.17** | 0.95 | 0.03 | 0.02 |
| 18–22 years | 0.49 | **0.23** | **0.28** | 0.68 | **0.21** | **0.11** | 0.95 | 0.03 | 0.02 |
| 23–26 years | 0.58 | 0.20 | **0.22** | 0.71 | 0.20 | **0.09** | 0.92 | **0.04** | 0.05 |
| 27–30 years† | 0.64 | 0.21 | 0.15 | 0.78 | 0.17 | 0.06 | 0.95 | 0.03 | 0.02 |
| *YLS* | | | | | | | | | |
| 16–17 years | 0.64 | **0.12** | 0.24 | 0.81 | **0.09** | **0.10** | 0.97 | **0.01** | **0.02** |
| 18–22 years | 0.48 | 0.18 | **0.34** | 0.60 | **0.21** | **0.19** | 0.90 | **0.04** | 0.07 |
| 23–26 years | 0.48 | 0.22 | **0.30** | 0.60 | 0.26 | **0.14** | 0.88 | 0.07 | 0.05 |
| 27–30 years† | 0.55 | 0.22 | 0.23 | 0.69 | 0.21 | 0.10 | 0.88 | 0.07 | 0.05 |

*Source*: BCS (1998) and YLS (1998/9) †reference category *Model*: Lifestyle model

*Notes*:

1. Statistically significant effects are highlighted in bold (including interaction effects).
2. Effects on past or recent use were estimated vis-à-vis the probability of never having used.
3. Categories that had no significant effect on recent use or past use were excluded from the model and formed part of the reference category.
4. Analysis of the YLS indicated that the effect of being 18 to 22 years old on recent hallucinant use was very close to the cut-off denoting statistical significance (p = .06) and, for the purposes of the analysis shown here, this has been treated as a significant effect.

using cannabis than those aged 16 or 17 years (see Figure 6.2). Similar effects were evident in relation to the hallucinants, with young adults in their late twenties again being approximately two to three times more likely to have stopped using these substances than those aged 16 or 17 years. The situation regarding cocaine use was less clear-cut as the BCS indicated little by way of a direct relationship with age, while the YLS revealed a series of direct age-effects that were broadly consistent with the pattern that was evident in relation to cannabis and the hallucinants.

The effects described here can be attributed directly to age in the sense that they are independent of all the other variables included in the models, but this does not necessarily mean the relationships are causal. After all, age is an ambiguous variable which is linked to various physical, psychological and emotional developments, so that apparent

*Figure 6.2* Odds of desistence by age (multivariate analysis, young adults)

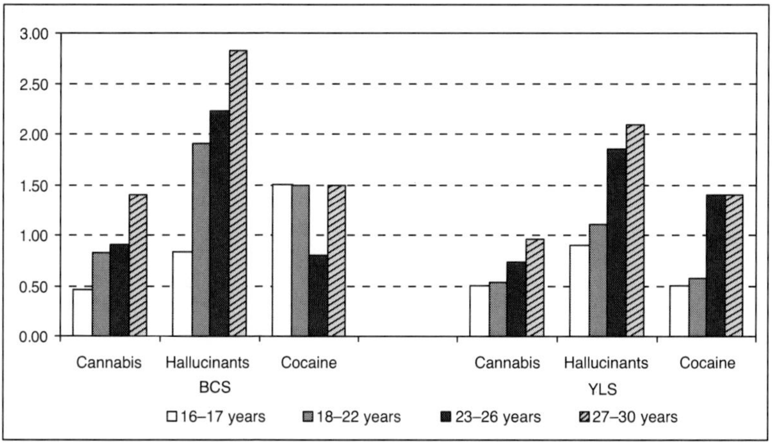


*Source*: BCS (1998) and YLS (1998/9)
*Model*: Lifestyle model

*Notes*:

1. Odds of desistance were calculated by dividing the estimated probability of past use by the estimated probability of recent use (see Table 6.3). A value of one indicates parity; a value of less than one indicates a tendency towards recent use; and a value of more than one indicates a tendency towards past use. The higher the value the greater the odds of desistance.
2. The final models were respecified with recent use set to the reference category and these revised models indicated that age had a significant effect on desistances (i.e. past use versus recent use).

age effects may actually reflect the process of maturation (Rutter et al., 1998; Laub and Sampson, 2003). Desistance is not simply the product of objective transformations, moreover, but involves a range of subjective phenomena (Gadd and Farrall, 2004) and, as such, links between drug use and age may be mediated by social and cultural influences, including judgements about the kind of behaviour that is appropriate to a certain age.

## Life-course

Drug use, like offending behaviour more generally, is bound up with the transition into adulthood, with domestic circumstances playing a particularly prominent role in this regard. There was little to suggest from either survey that the school-to-work transition constitutes much by way of a watershed in relation to illicit drug use (see Table 6.4). Young adults who were working full-time reported similar rates of recent use

**Table 6.4 Prevalence of drug use by work status (percentages, young adults)**

| | *Cannabis* | | | *Hallucinants* | | | *Cocaine* | | |
|---|---|---|---|---|---|---|---|---|---|
| | *Never* | *Past* | *Recent* | *Never* | *Past* | *Recent* | *Never* | *Past* | *Recent* |
| *BCS* | | ** | | | ** | | | * | |
| Work full-time | 54 | 24 | 21 | 71 | 19 | 10 | 93 | 3 | 3 |
| Work part-time | 62 | 17 | 21 | 77 | 14 | 10 | 97 | 1 | 2 |
| Student | 60 | 12 | 28 | 79 | 11 | 10 | 93 | 3 | 4 |
| Look after home | 68 | 22 | 10 | 82 | 15 | 4 | 97 | 3 | * |
| Unemployed | 42 | 19 | 39 | 55 | 27 | 18 | 92 | 3 | 5 |
| Other | 45 | 22 | 33 | 60 | 23 | 17 | 92 | 6 | 2 |
| *YLS* | | ** | | | ** | | | * | |
| Work full-time | 48 | 23 | 30 | 61 | 24 | 15 | 89 | 4 | 7 |
| Work part-time | 61 | 21 | 19 | 69 | 20 | 12 | 91 | 3 | 6 |
| Student | 56 | 10 | 34 | 76 | 11 | 13 | 92 | 4 | 4 |
| Look after home | 61 | 21 | 18 | 70 | 21 | 9 | 94 | 5 | 2 |
| Unemployed | | | | | | | | | |
| < one year | 41 | 16 | 43 | 49 | 32 | 19 | 77 | 16 | 7 |
| > one year | 42 | 15 | 42 | 54 | 18 | 28 | 85 | 7 | 8 |
| Other | 35 | 24 | 42 | 54 | 28 | 18 | 89 | 6 | 5 |

*Source*: BCS (1998) and YLS (1998/9) ** $p < 0.01$ * $p < 0.05$ ns $p < 0.05$

*Notes*:
1. BCS: Cramer's V = 0.13 (cannabis); 0.11 (hallucinants); and 0.07 (cocaine).
2. YLS: Cramer's V = 0.13 (cannabis); 0.12 (hallucinants); and 0.09 (cocaine).

to students and though they tended to report higher rates of past use these differences could be readily explained by the influence of other variables such as age.[3] Recent use tended to be more widespread among the unemployed and those who were otherwise marginalised from the labour market, however, and the significance of these differences was confirmed by the multivariate analysis. Life-course models, particularly those based on the YLS, indicated that unemployment and other forms of marginalisation from the labour market increased the probability of use, though many of these effects were explainable in terms of broader lifestyle choices (see Chapter 4 and Technical Appendix).

Based on the insights of the 'new' deviancy theories it is, perhaps, unsurprising that widespread drug use appears to transcend the transition into full-time work. After all, as Young (1971) noted, consumption and production are closely entwined in late industrial economies and the working week leaves regular spaces for the expression of subterranean values, primarily through the weekend ritual. Nonetheless, for young adults who work, or engage in some other routine activity, these spaces are compartmentalised in a way that they are not for those who are unemployed or otherwise marginalised from the labour market. Young adults who do not have commitments to work, study or to looking after the home are relatively untouched by some of the main constraints that make up the social bond, which leaves them freer to engage in drug use and other forms of subterranean play. Rather like the hippies of the 1960s, however, their ability to participate in consumer oriented activities is likely to be limited by economic constraints (see Furlong and Cartmel, 2007).

The influence of the social bond can clearly be seen in relation to the domestic sphere. Both surveys indicated that drug use was particularly widespread among young adults whose living arrangements conferred considerable independence, but implied little responsibility (see Table 6.5). The highest rates of recent use tended to be reported by those who were single or cohabiting, who did not have children and were living in rented accommodation. Cohabitation tends to be less stable than marriage, particularly where there are no children involved, and the assumption in much of the literature is that this arrangement is tipped towards independence, while marriage is tipped towards relatedness (Lewis, 2001; Sigle-Rushton, 2008). Such assumptions are reflected in the claim that marriage has a more important role than cohabitation in relation to crime prevention (Laub and Sampson, 2003). Given all this, it is perhaps unsurprising that young adults who were married reported low rates of recent drug use, regardless of whether or not they had children, and high rates of both abstinence and desistance. Whilst such findings are consistent with the international evidence (see, for example, Bachman et al., 1997; Schulenberg et al., 2005; Degenhardt et al., 2008), the distinction between marriage and cohabitation appears to be rather less clear cut than is often implied (see also Duncan et al., 2006). Where cohabitation was reinforced by other commitments, such as having children or, more equivocally, buying a home, then the ratio of past-to-recent users was relatively high, suggesting a particular propensity towards desistance. In relation to drug use, therefore, the distinction between marriage and cohabitation appears to be part of a broader distinction between relationships that are reinforced by external commitments and those that are not.

Where marriages had broken down or ended with the death of a spouse, the propensity towards desistance was less marked. Young adults who had been, but were no longer, married tended to report higher

**Table 6.5 Prevalence of drug use by domestic circumstances (percentages, young adults)**

| | *Cannabis* | | | *Hallucinants* | | | *Cocaine* | | |
|---|---|---|---|---|---|---|---|---|---|
| | *Never* | *Past* | *Recent* | *Never* | *Past* | *Recent* | *Never* | *Past* | *Recent* |
| *BCS* | | ** | | | ** | | | ** | |
| Single | | | | | | | | | |
| – no children, living with parents | 59 | 17 | 24 | 75 | 15 | 10 | 95 | 2 | 2 |
| – no children, renting | 43 | 15 | 42 | 63 | 21 | 16 | 88 | 5 | 8 |
| – no children, buying own home | 50 | 26 | 23 | 72 | 18 | 11 | 95 | 1 | 4 |
| – with children | 54 | 23 | 23 | 65 | 23 | 12 | 95 | 4 | 1 |
| Cohabiting | | | | | | | | | |
| – no children, not buying own home | 33 | 29 | 37 | 52 | 27 | 21 | 91 | 6 | 3 |
| – no children, buying own home | 51 | 31 | 18 | 72 | 20 | 8 | 93 | 4 | 4 |
| – with children | 55 | 32 | 13 | 71 | 22 | 7 | 96 | 4 | 0 |
| Divorced, separated or widowed | 64 | 20 | 16 | 81 | 9 | 10 | 96 | 3 | 1 |
| Married | | | | | | | | | |
| – no children | 70 | 21 | 9 | 88 | 10 | 2 | 99 | 1 | * |
| – with children | 71 | 23 | 6 | 81 | 17 | 2 | 97 | 2 | * |

**Table 6.5 Prevalence of drug use by domestic circumstances (percentages, young adults)** – *continued*

| | *Cannabis* | | | *Hallucinants* | | | *Cocaine* | | |
|---|---|---|---|---|---|---|---|---|---|
| | *Never* | *Past* | *Recent* | *Never* | *Past* | *Recent* | *Never* | *Past* | *Recent* |
| *YLS* | | ** | | | ** | | | * | |
| Single | | | | | | | | | |
| – no children, living with parents | 53 | 13 | 34 | 69 | 14 | 17 | 91 | 3 | 6 |
| – no children, renting | 35 | 19 | 46 | 53 | 23 | 24 | 80 | 7 | 13 |
| – no children, buying | 42 | 31 | 28 | 61 | 30 | 9 | 86 | 8 | 7 |
| – with children | 44 | 19 | 37 | 52 | 29 | 19 | 85 | 11 | 4 |
| Cohabiting | | | | | | | | | |
| – no children, not buying own home | 32 | 17 | 52 | 44 | 33 | 23 | 79 | 10 | 10 |
| – no children, buying own home | 42 | 27 | 31 | 59 | 24 | 17 | 88 | 3 | 9 |
| – with children | 49 | 31 | 20 | 63 | 29 | 8 | 92 | 6 | 2 |
| Divorced, separated or widowed | 60 | 25 | 16 | 64 | 28 | 8 | 93 | 5 | 2 |
| Married | | | | | | | | | |
| – no children | 65 | 28 | 8 | 78 | 20 | 3 | 95 | 3 | 3 |
| – with children | 69 | 22 | 9 | 73 | 24 | 3 | 97 | 3 | 1 |

*Source*: BCS (1998) and YLS (1998/9) ** $p < 0.01$ * $p < 0.05$ ns $p < 0.05$

*Notes*:

1. BCS: Cramer's V = 0.21 (cannabis); 0.15 (halluinants); 0.11 (cocaine).
2. YLS: Cramer's V = 0.22 (cannabis); 0.18 (halluinants); 0.14 (cocaine).
3. Most of the young adults who were separated, divorced or widowed had children (approximately three-in-four according to both the BCS and YLS) and the number who did not was small (n = 40 and n = 22 respectively). The multivariate analysis also indicated that effects of being separated, divorced or widowed were similar regardless of whether or not children were involved and thus these circumstances were treated as a single category. The categories 'single, no children, private renting' and 'single, no children, social renting' were also combined into a single category because they were associated with a similar set of effects.

rates of recent drug use and a lower ratio of past-to-recent users than those who were still married, suggesting something of a return to a single way of life. Single young adults who had never been married reported some of the highest rates of recent use, though notable variations were evident here: those who were living with parents or independently in rented accommodation tended to report higher rates of recent use and/or a lower ratio of past-to-recent users than those who had children or were buying their own home.

The relationship between drug use and domestic circumstances was clearly linked to differences in age and lifestyle, but could not be fully explained in this way. Even allowing for the influence of these, and other, variables, being married continued to be associated with a relatively low probability of recent use across all three drug-types (see Table 6.6). Being single, on the other hand, substantially increased the probability of recent use regardless of whether or not children were involved and regardless of housing status. Although single parents and single home owners tended to report lower rates of recent use than single people living independently in rented accommodation, the multivariate models revealed that these categories tended to have similar effects on recent use. All things being equal, the probability of recent use did not vary greatly among single young people who were living independently. As such, the different rates of recent use that were evident among these young adults cannot be attributed directly to their differing domestic circumstances.[4]

Cohabitation was rather more mixed in its effects. In the absence of children, both surveys indicated that, compared to being married, cohabiting increased the probability of recent use across all three drug-types and these effects tended to be most marked where respondents were not buying their own home. Where children were involved, the BCS also indicated that cohabiting increased the probability of recent cannabis use and hallucinant use. The YLS revealed no such pattern, however, indicating instead that this arrangement was similar in its effect to being married. These discrepancies between the surveys can be largely explained by the role of lifestyle indicators. Until such indicators were included in the models, both surveys pointed to a similar set of effects whereby cohabiting with children increased the probability of recent cannabis use and hallucinant use, but not cocaine use (see Technical Appendix for details). Differences emerged subsequently because the YLS models included more detailed information about broader lifestyle choices, which explained the effects of cohabiting with children in a way that the more limited information contained in

**Table 6.6 Probability of drug use by domestic circumstances (multivariate analysis, young adults)**

| | *Cannabis* | | | *Hallucinants* | | | *Cocaine* | | |
|---|---|---|---|---|---|---|---|---|---|
| | *Never* | *Past* | *Recent* | *Never* | *Past* | *Recent* | *Never* | *Past* | *Recent* |
| *BCS* | | | | | | | | | |
| Single | | | | | | | | | |
| – no children, living with parents | 0.65 | 0.13 | **0.23** | 0.79 | **0.13** | 0.08 | 0.91 | 0.02 | **0.06** |
| – no children, renting | 0.57 | 0.16 | **0.27** | 0.67 | 0.18 | **0.15** | 0.86 | 0.04 | **0.11** |
| – no children, buying | 0.53 | 0.23 | **0.24** | 0.69 | 0.18 | **0.13** | 0.86 | 0.04 | **0.11** |
| – with children | 0.32 | **0.30** | **0.37** | 0.56 | **0.31** | **0.14** | 0.90 | 0.05 | **0.05** |
| Cohabiting | | | | | | | | | |
| – no children, not buying own home | 0.40 | 0.25 | **0.35** | 0.58 | 0.24 | **0.18** | 0.91 | 0.05 | **0.04** |
| – no children, buying own home | 0.50 | 0.28 | **0.22** | 0.66 | 0.25 | **0.09** | 0.91 | 0.05 | **0.04** |
| – with children | 0.47 | **0.33** | **0.20** | 0.66 | 0.25 | **0.09** | 0.96 | 0.03 | 0.01 |
| Divorced, separated or widowed | 0.48 | 0.24 | **0.27** | 0.73 | **0.11** | **0.15** | 0.96 | 0.03 | 0.01 |
| Married | | | | | | | | | |
| – no children | 0.65 | 0.24 | 0.11 | 0.80 | **0.12** | 0.07 | 0.96 | 0.03 | 0.01 |
| – with children† | 0.65 | 0.24 | 0.11 | 0.73 | 0.22 | 0.05 | 0.96 | 0.03 | 0.01 |

**Table 6.6 Probability of drug use by domestic circumstances (multivariate analysis, young adults)** – *continued*

| | *Cannabis* | | | *Hallucinants* | | | *Cocaine* | | |
|---|---|---|---|---|---|---|---|---|---|
| | *Never* | *Past* | *Recent* | *Never* | *Past* | *Recent* | *Never* | *Past* | *Recent* |
| *YLS* | | | | | | | | | |
| Single | | | | | | | | | |
| – no children, living with parents | 0.53 | 0.15 | **0.32** | 0.70 | **0.16** | **0.15** | 0.89 | 0.04 | **0.07** |
| – no children, renting | 0.44 | 0.18 | **0.39** | 0.62 | 0.19 | **0.19** | 0.87 | 0.04 | **0.09** |
| – no children, buying | 0.47 | 0.23 | **0.30** | 0.62 | 0.21 | **0.17** | 0.86 | 0.06 | **0.08** |
| – with children | 0.47 | 0.21 | **0.33** | 0.54 | 0.23 | **0.24** | 0.88 | **0.07** | **0.05** |
| Cohabiting | | | | | | | | | |
| – no children, not buying own home | 0.36 | 0.15 | **0.49** | 0.47 | 0.29 | **0.25** | 0.87 | 0.05 | **0.08** |
| – no children, buying own home | 0.40 | 0.25 | **0.35** | 0.61 | 0.22 | **0.17** | 0.89 | 0.03 | **0.09** |
| – with children | 0.60 | 0.24 | 0.16 | 0.68 | 0.25 | 0.07 | 0.95 | 0.03 | 0.02 |
| Divorced, separated or widowed | 0.60 | 0.24 | 0.16 | 0.68 | 0.25 | 0.07 | 0.95 | 0.03 | 0.02 |
| Married | | | | | | | | | |
| – no children | 0.60 | 0.24 | 0.16 | 0.68 | 0.25 | 0.07 | 0.95 | 0.03 | 0.02 |
| – with children† | 0.60 | 0.24 | 0.16 | 0.68 | 0.25 | 0.07 | 0.95 | 0.03 | 0.02 |

*Source*: BCS (1998) and YLS (1998/9) †reference category *Model*: Lifestyle model

*Notes*:

1. Statistically significant effects are highlighted in bold (including interaction effects).
2. Divorced, separated or widowed, with children and divorced, separated or widowed, no children were combined into a single category because they had similarly marked effects that were not necessarily statistically significant. Single, no children, private renting and single, no children, social renting were also combined into a single category because they represent comparable situations and had very similar effects. Other categories were combined as necessary (see Technical Appendix for details).

the BCS models did not. On balance, therefore, it seems that the effects of cohabiting with children, compared to being married, are mediated by other lifestyle factors. A similar pattern was evident in relation to separation, divorce and widowhood, indicating that the effects associated with marriage break-up are also mediated by broader lifestyle choices.

The multivariate models confirmed that domestic circumstances are significantly linked to the probability of desistance. Even allowing for the influence of other variables, including those related to broader lifestyle choices, being married or cohabiting with children was associated with a heightened probability of desistance (see Figure 6.3).

*Figure 6.3* Odds of desistence by domestic circumstances (multivariate analysis, select categories only, young adults)

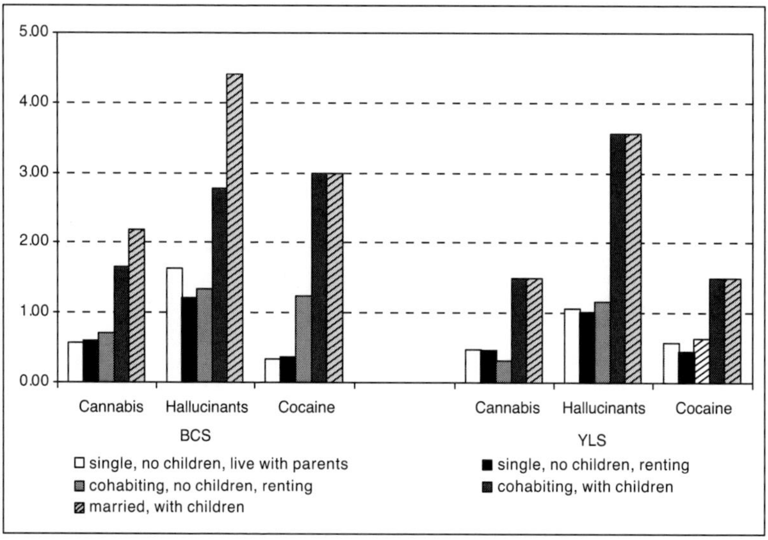


*Source*: BCS (1998) and YLS (1998/9)
*Model*: Lifestyle model

*Notes*:
1. Odds of desistance were calculated by dividing the estimated probability of past use by the estimated probability of recent use (see Table 6.6). A value of one indicates parity; a value of less than one indicates a tendency towards recent use; and a value of more than one indicates a tendency towards past use. The higher the value the greater the odds of desistance.
2. The final models were respecified with recent use set to the reference category and these revised models indicated that domestic circumstances had a significant effect on desistance (past use versus recent use).

Quite what it is about certain domestic circumstances that facilitates or inhibits drug use is not entirely clear from the type of analysis presented here. As noted elsewhere, the meaning of these all important social relations cannot simply be 'read off' from evidence of their presence and thus the underlying processes remain obscure (Gadd and Farrall, 2004: 126). Nonetheless the effects described here are consistent with established criminological perspectives, which show how changing domestic circumstances can provide structural turning points and/or stimulate cognitive transformations that help to explain fluctuations in offending (Laub and Sampson, 2003; Maruna, 2001). Whatever the precise explanation, the influence of domestic arrangements can be usefully linked to the notion of subterranean play. Arrangements that confer considerable independence but entail little responsibility facilitate drug use by providing plenty of opportunities for the expression of subterranean values. 'Settling down', by contrast, implies a practical and symbolic reorganisation which includes a shift towards the formal values that Young (1971) considered to be characteristic of the work sphere. Traditional ties of obligation and permanence may have loosened (Beck, 1997; Giddens, 1998), but connectedness, commitment, caring and the subordination of self-interest continue to play a key role in contemporary family life (Crow, 2002; Williams, 2004). This is particularly so where domestic partnerships are reinforced by investments in the possibility of permanence through marriage and/or parenthood as such arrangements tend to involve acceptance of a greater loss of potential freedom (Burgoyne, 1991; Lewis, 2001). With the acquisition of domestic responsibilities, life away from work tends to be tipped away from spontaneity, ego-expressivity and short-term hedonism and towards deferred gratification, planning, routine and predictability. All of which militates against the expression of subterranean values and helps to explain the sharp increase in desistance.

## Age and life-course effects

The analysis presented so far has shown that age and domestic circumstances effect drug use independently of one another, but to fully appreciate the value of a life-course perspective it is necessary to consider the cumulative nature of these effects. Getting older and 'settling down' both tend to reduce the probability of recent drug use and increase the probability of desistance. When taken together, these effects reinforce the conclusion that illicit drug use is quintessentially a youthful form of behaviour. All things being equal,

**Table 6.7 Probability of drug use by age and domestic circumstances (multivariate analysis)**

| | *Cannabis* | | | *Hallucinants* | | | *Cocaine* | | |
|---|---|---|---|---|---|---|---|---|---|
| | *Never* | *Past* | *Recent* | *Never* | *Past* | *Recent* | *Never* | *Past* | *Recent* |
| *BCS* | | | | | | | | | |
| 16–17 years, single, no children, living with parents | 0.48 | 0.11 | 0.41 | 0.74 | 0.10 | 0.16 | 0.94 | 0.02 | 0.04 |
| 18–22 years, single, no children, renting | 0.48 | 0.17 | 0.35 | 0.62 | 0.20 | 0.18 | 0.90 | 0.04 | 0.07 |
| 23–26 years, cohabiting, no children, not buying own home | 0.41 | 0.24 | 0.35 | 0.56 | 0.26 | 0.18 | 0.88 | 0.05 | 0.07 |
| 23–26 years, cohabiting, with children | 0.48 | 0.32 | 0.21 | 0.65 | 0.26 | 0.09 | 0.96 | 0.03 | 0.01 |
| 27–30 years, married, with children | 0.70 | 0.22 | 0.08 | 0.77 | 0.20 | 0.03 | 0.97 | 0.03 | 0.01 |
| *YLS* | | | | | | | | | |
| 16–17 years, single, no children, living with parents | 0.63 | 0.10 | 0.28 | 0.82 | 0.07 | 0.11 | 0.97 | 0.01 | 0.03 |
| 18–22 years, single, no children, renting | 0.39 | 0.16 | 0.45 | 0.55 | 0.19 | 0.26 | 0.85 | 0.03 | 0.12 |
| 23–26 years, cohabiting, no children, not buying own home | 0.31 | 0.17 | 0.52 | 0.39 | 0.36 | 0.25 | 0.83 | 0.09 | 0.08 |
| 23–26 years, cohabiting, with children | 0.55 | 0.28 | 0.18 | 0.60 | 0.33 | 0.07 | 0.92 | 0.06 | 0.02 |
| 27–30 years, married, with children | 0.60 | 0.27 | 0.13 | 0.69 | 0.26 | 0.06 | 0.92 | 0.06 | 0.02 |

*Source*: BCS (1998) and YLS (1998/9) *Model*: Lifestyle model

a single 18 to 22 year old who did not have children and was living in rented accommodation was more than three times as likely as a married 27 to 30 year old who had children to have recently used cannabis; was more than four times as likely to have recently used a hallucinant; and was at least six times as likely to have recently used cocaine (see Table 6.7). Similar effects were evident in relation to desistance (see Figure 6.4). Simply by virtue of their age and domestic circumstances, for example, a married 27 to 30 year old who had children was at least five times as likely to have stopped using cannabis, the hallucinants and cocaine as a single 18 to 22 year old who did not have children and was living independently in rented accommodation.

*Figure 6.4* Odds of desistence by age and domestic circumstances (multivariate analysis, select categories only, young adults)

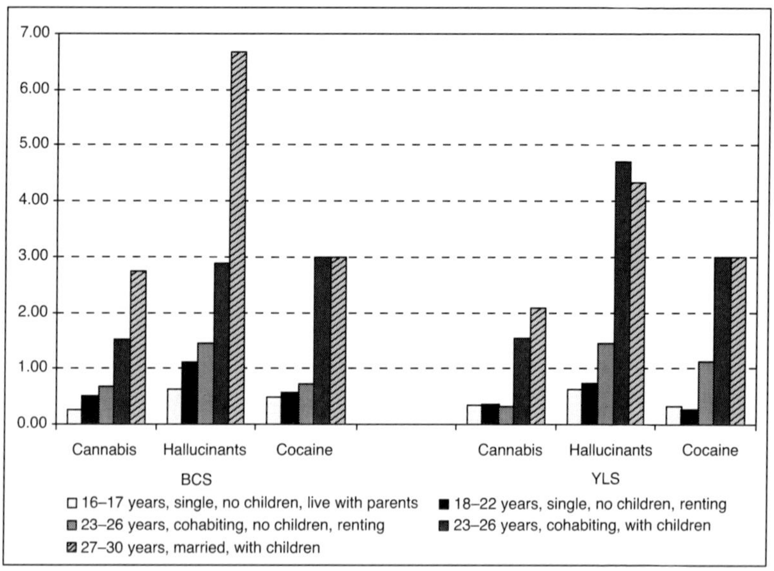


*Source*: BCS (1998) and YLS (1998/9) *Model*: Lifestyle model

*Note*: odds of desistance were calculated by dividing the estimated probability of past use by the estimated probability of recent use (see Table 6.7). A value of one indicates parity; a value of less than one indicates a tendency towards recent use; and a value of more than one indicates a tendency towards past use. The higher the value the greater the odds of desistance.

## The gendered nature of early adult transitions

Early adult transitions vary between males and females in ways that have important implications for their use of illicit drugs. Females are generally considered to mature earlier than males and are quicker to adopt explicitly adult roles, particularly within the domestic sphere (Coleman and Hendry, 1999; Rutter et al., 1998). The BCS and YLS confirmed that women tend to leave the parental home and form families of their own at a younger age than men. One in ten women in the 18 to 22 year age group had married or were cohabiting with children compared with one in 30 men or fewer depending on the survey. Many men do start to 'settle down' during the course of their mid-to-late twenties, so differences between the sexes become much less marked. Both surveys indicated that almost half the men aged 27 to 30 years were married or cohabiting with children, which was only marginally less than the proportion of women. A further one in four were cohabiting without children and/or buying their own home.

Given their particularly lengthy transitions, it is perhaps to be expected that men 'grow out' of crime more slowly than women. The peak age of offending for males is generally higher than for females (Newburn, 2002) and this difference has been linked to the influence of early adult transitions. Based on the 1992 YLS, Graham and Bowling (1995) showed that the proportion of females who were actively involved in offending began to decline from the late teens onwards and that this downward trend was closely related to leaving home and school, forming partnerships and new families and becoming economically independent. The situation among males was less clear-cut. On the one hand, men in their early twenties had committed fewer and less serious offences than their teenage counterparts, but relatively few had stopped offending altogether. The proportion of males that were actively involved in offending remained fairly stable across the 14 to 25 year age range and appeared to be unaffected by the vicissitudes of early adulthood: 'Thus, it appears to be the case that not only do many young men fail to successfully make the transition to adulthood by their mid twenties', but 'those who do appear to be no more likely to desist than those who do not' (Graham and Bowling, 1995: 64–5). Similar analyses were conducted on the basis of the 1998/9 YLS, which had the advantage of a larger sample covering a wider age range. These analyses reinforced the conclusion that women 'grow out' of crime at an earlier age than men, though they also indicated that the proportion of men who are actively involved in offending declines from the age of 22 years onwards (Flood-Page et al., 2000).

Drug use was excluded from these earlier analyses, though certain similarities were noted between it and other forms of offending. The 1992 YLS indicated that the proportion of females who used illicit drugs peaked among 17 year olds, but then fell away quite sharply, while the proportion of males who engaged in such behaviour continued to increase up to the age of 20, before falling away at a more modest rate (Graham and Bowling, 1995). Consequently, male users were found to outnumber female users from the age of 18 onwards, though not before. Similar patterns were noted on the basis of the 1992 BCS, which extended the usual adult sample to include 12 to 15 year olds (Mott and Mirrlees-Black, 1995), and the 1998/9 YLS, prompting the conclusion that females 'grow

*Figure 6.5* Prevalence of recent drug use by age and sex (percentages, young people)

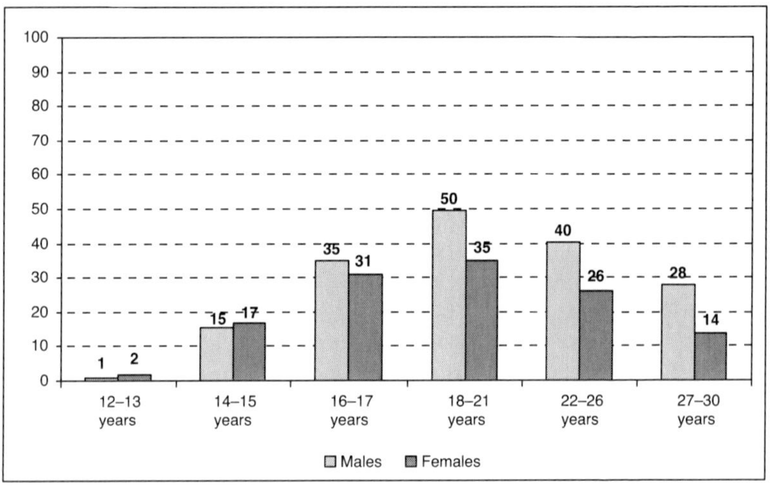


*Source*: YLS (1998/9)

*Notes*:
1. The prevalence rates shown here are based on the use of cannabis, the hallucinants and/or cocaine.
2. No statistically significant differences were evident between the sexes among 12 to 17 year olds (p > .05 for each group), but significantly more men than women in the 18 to 30 year age range had recently used these drugs. Cramer's V = 0.15 (18 to 22 year olds), 0.15 (23 to 26 year olds) and 0.18 (27 to 30 year olds). P < .01 for each group.
3. Similar, statistically significant, differences were evident among the 18 to 30 year olds included in the 1998 BCS. Once again, no significant differences were evident among 16 and 17 year olds.

out' of drug use, as well as other forms of 'anti-social behaviour', at an earlier age than males (see Figure 6.5; see also Flood-Page et al., 2000 and DeWit et al., 1997). These findings are particularly notable because they reinforce the suggestion that the gender gap constitutes a persistent feature of early adulthood.[5]

The emergence of a gender gap during the late teens and early twenties can be readily understood in the context of early adult transitions (see Shiner, 2006). As most men do not get married or have children until their late twenties or beyond they tend to experience an extended period of youth, which leaves considerable room for illicit drug use. Women's lifestyle choices, on the other hand, appear to be rather more limited because they tend to 'settle down' more quickly, thereby establishing a domestic context which is less conducive to such behaviour. It may be that females also experience the constraining influences of adulthood more sharply than males. After all, women consistently spend more time than men doing housework, particularly if they are married or have children, and generally assume greater responsibility for domestic tasks as an extension of their ascribed roles as mothers and primary caregivers (Fox, 1997; Cheal, 2002). As a result, it has been suggested, they face a 'contradictory double life' of work and family, which creates 'conflictual crises and continuing incompatible demands' (Beck, 1992: 132).

The possibility that women experience the constraining influence of early adult transitions more sharply than men was formally assessed on the basis of the multivariate analysis. Interaction terms were included in each of the models to test whether the effects of age and domestic circumstances vary by sex. What was most striking about the results of the analysis was how similar these effects were for males and females (see Technical Appendix for details). Some variations were evident, though there were discrepancies between the surveys. According to the BCS models, it was the effects of domestic circumstances, rather than age, that varied most between the sexes, while the YLS models suggested the opposite. Despite this, the interaction effects highlighted by both sets of models conformed to the general pattern noted above, whereby the gender gap was relatively narrow during the early stages of the transition into adulthood, but then opened up more widely. Crucially, the effects associated with marriage, cohabiting and having children were very similar for men and women.

## Early adult transitions and patterns of consumption

Variations in drug use across early adulthood are symptomatic of broader patterns of lifestyle consumption (Jones and Martin, 1997; see also

Gershuny, 2000). Young people who live with parents or in 'transitional' households spend a relatively large amount of their income on leisure products, including alcohol, that are consumed away from home. Among those living with their parents, this pattern of consumption is said to provide the basis for gaining greater independence, whereas among those in transitional households it has been attributed to a combination of push and pull factors. Such households often lack 'home comforts', which encourages those living in them to spend much of their time elsewhere, particularly as they tend to be at a stage in their lives when participating in leisure away from the home is important for meeting potential partners. Whatever the precise reason, the formation of more permanent households is generally accompanied by a greater emphasis on home-centred consumption.

Evidence from the BCS and YLS supports the observation that lifestyle consumption becomes increasingly home-centred with the transition into adulthood. Young adults in their late teens or early twenties displayed a particular commitment to the night-time economy and associated forms of consumption, so that, as well as being the most active users of illicit drugs, they made most use of pubs and clubs, drank most heavily and got 'very drunk' most often (see Table 6.8). Sixteen and 17 year olds revealed a similar orientation, albeit one that reflected their partial exclusion from the night-time economy.[6] The

**Table 6.8 Drinking habits and participation in the night-time economy by age (young adults)**

| *Age in years* | *Usually drink once a week or more (%)* | *Usual intake as multiple of sensible daily limits (median)* | *Very drunk once a month or more in last 12-months (%)* | *Been to pub once a week or more in last month (%)* | *Been to club once a week or more in last month (%)* |
|---|---|---|---|---|---|
| | ** | ** | ** | ** | ** |
| 16–17 | 44 | 1.0 | 34 | 26 | 13 |
| 18–22 | 68 | 2.0 | 43 | 57 | 26 |
| 23–26 | 63 | 1.5 | 30 | 44 | 9 |
| 27–30 | 62 | 1.3 | 17 | 34 | 4 |

*Source*: BCS (1998) and YLS (1998/9 ** $p < 0.01$ * $p < 0.0$ ns $p < 0.05$

*Notes*:
1. BCS: Cramer's V = 0.13 (frequency that usually drink alcohol); 0.15 (frequency of visits to the pub); and 0.23 (frequency of visits to clubs); and Eta = 0.09 (usual alcohol intake).
2. YLS: Kendall's tau = 0.15 (frequency of drunkenness in last 12 months).

vast majority of young people in this age group were living with their parents and spent a considerable amount of leisure time away from home. A sizeable proportion were also getting 'very drunk' on a regular basis, though they drank less often than their slightly older counterparts, consuming less alcohol on the days they drank and making less use of pubs and clubs.

The patterns that were evident among 23 to 30 year olds, by contrast, suggested a partial withdrawal from the night-time economy and the adoption of a more home-centred leisure style. Young adults in this age range spent relatively few evenings away from home and went to pubs and clubs less often than their slightly younger counterparts. Approximately three-quarters had been to a pub in the previous month and close to a third had been to a club, but relatively few had visited such venues on a weekly basis. Despite their partial withdrawal from the night-time economy, most 23 to 30 year olds continued to drink on a regular basis and this reflected a greater emphasis on home-centred consumption. Responding to the YLS, almost two-thirds of the 27 to 30 year olds and half the 23 to 26 year olds who had drunk alcohol in the last year indicated that they usually did so at home, which compared with a third or so of 18 to 22 year olds and 16 to 17 year olds. This apparent shift towards home-based consumption was accompanied by greater evidence of moderation. Young adults in their mid-to-late twenties tended to stick more closely to recommended sensible drinking levels than their younger counterparts and fewer of them got 'very drunk' on a regular basis.

Further lifestyle differences were evident on the basis of young adults' domestic circumstances.[7] Such differences were most marked in relation to pubs, clubs and home-based drinking, reinforcing the suggestion that transitions into adulthood often involve partial withdrawal from the night-time economy. Single young adults who did not have children tended to go to pubs and clubs most often, while those who were married or cohabiting and who had children tended to make the least use of such venues (see Figure 6.6). Once again, apparent withdrawal from the night-time economy was accompanied by greater emphasis on home-centred consumption and moderation. Of those who had drunk alcohol in the last year, the proportion that usually did so at home was considerably larger among groups that made relatively little use of pubs and clubs: two-in-three young adults who had children and were married or cohabiting usually drank at home, as did a similar proportion of those who did not have children but were either married or were cohabiting and buying their own home. These figures

*Figure 6.6* Participation in the night-time economy by domestic circumstances (young adults)

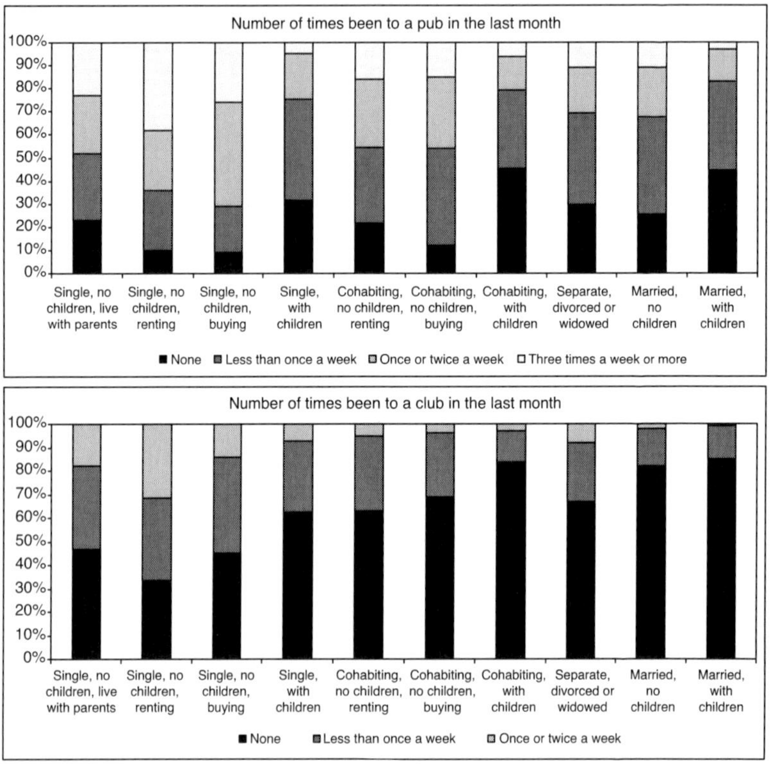


*Source*: BCS (1998)

*Note*: Cramer's V = 0.21 (pub) and 0.29 (club). P < .01 in both cases.

compared with less than one-in-three of those who were single, childless and living with their parents and less than half of those who were similarly positioned but living independently in rented accommodation.

As well as being among the most frequent users of pubs and clubs, single young adults who did not have children tended to drink most often and most heavily: those who were living independently in rented accommodation, for example, usually drank three or four days a week, consuming twice the recommended sensible daily limit. At the other end of the scale, young adults who were married or were cohabiting with children tended to drink no more than once a week and stuck closely to recommended limits, with the result that they got drunk much less often. Two-in-five young adults who were single, childless and either living with their parents or living independently in rented accommodation had been 'very drunk' on a monthly basis or more during the previous year, which compared with approximately one-in-ten of those who were married or were cohabiting with children.

Finally, lone parents and young adults who were separated, widowed or divorced (most of whom had children) revealed a distinct set of drinking habits that reflected their equivocal status in relation to early adult transitions and were also consistent with their intermediate rates of recent drug use (see earlier). On the one hand, these young adults tended to drink fairly infrequently, doing so, on average, two or three times a month, which was similar to those who were married or cohabiting with children. In other respects, however, their drinking habits differed quite markedly from those who were living as part of a couple and who had children. Lone parents and those who were separated, widowed or divorced were much less home-centred in their drinking, for example, with less than half those who had drunk alcohol in the last year usually doing so at home. They were also more actively involved in the night-time economy, particularly clubs (see Figure 6.6) and tended to get 'very drunk' more often, with approximately one-in-five having done so on a monthly basis or more during the last year. For those who had previously been married, such habits reinforce the earlier suggestion of a partial return to a single way of life.

## Conclusion

Illicit drug use, like criminal behaviour more generally, cannot be fully understood outside of a life-course perspective. Young adults are the primary users of illicit drugs and the acquisition of adult roles, particularly through marriage and family formation, is strongly associated with desistance and abstinence. Such patterns have been noted across a range of jurisdictions going back some considerable time (see above and Bachman et al., 1984 and 2002; Yamaguchi and Kandel, 1985; Hammer and Vaglum, 1990; Turner et al., 2003; Leonard and Homish, 2005), once again, illustrating the central theme of continuity within change. The concentration of recent drug use among young people in their late teens and early twenties who have little by way of domestic responsibilities attests to what Young (1971) referred to as the ambivalent position of youth and provides further insights into the privileged nature of their relationship with the world of subterranean play. It is not just that young people are less constrained by the immediate dictates of the ethos of productivity, but that their domestic arrangements provide greater space for hedonistic pursuits. Once stable relationships are formed and reinforced by external commitments, such as marriage and parenthood, then these spaces are squeezed and the domestic sphere becomes characterised less by the subterranean values of independence, spontaneity and ego-expressivity and more by connectedness and responsibility. Consequently, life outside work becomes more closely aligned with the formal values of routine, planning and deferred gratification. Or, to echo Laub and Sampson (2003), short-term situational inducements to drug use are reordered as long-term commitments are redirected towards conformity. Thus, illicit drug use, alongside active participation in the night-time economy, regular binge-drinking and frequent drunkenness, remains a quintessentially youthful activity; one that encapsulates and celebrates freedom from adult roles and responsibilities, enabling young people to act out their ambivalent position in the social structure.

Locating drug use within a life-course perspective also helps to explain the emergence of a gender gap during early adulthood. For all that has been said about similarities between the sexes, young women tend to 'grow out' of drug use, as well as other forms of offending, at an earlier age than young men and this reflects notable differences in the timing of some key transitions. Most men do not get married or have children until after their mid-twenties, which provides the basis for an extended period of youth, leaving considerable room for illicit drug use and other hedonistic pursuits. Young women's lifestyle choices, on the other hand, are rather more limited because they tend to 'settle down' more quickly, thereby establishing a domestic context which is less conducive to such behaviour.

What has changed, or has rather been magnified, is the ambivalent position of youth. Driven by the restructuring of the labour market and the expansion of post-compulsory education, the journey into adulthood has become increasingly protracted and fragmented during the last four decades or so. Young people are not only taking longer to complete the transition from school to work, but are also delaying their first partnership, spending greater amounts of time outside of relationships and postponing having children (Sigle-Rushton, 2008). Whilst partly a response to structural constraints, it has been noted that young adults are entering live-in relationships and having children later because they want to enjoy the freedoms contained in the space between conventional childhood and full adulthood (Arnett, 2004; Furlong and Cartmel, 2007). Despite the associated uncertainty and anxiety, therefore, late modernity is said to have created space where young people can explore possibilities and enjoy freedoms that were closed to most members of previous generations. Such changes have not only resulted in greater opportunities for drug use, but have also promoted a degree of democratisation. As delayed transitions have become commonplace across classes, recreational drug use has gone from being a largely middle class bohemian phenomenon to one that appears to transcend class distinctions (see Chapter 4).

# 7
# Drug Use and Social Change

> Drugs have lost their history. A few antique episodes remain in popular consciousness: opiate use among Romantic poets, Freud's unwise dalliance with cocaine, Britain's Opium Wars against China, the drug fever of pre-Hays Code Hollywood. But there is little sense of how certain drugs came to assume their special role, corrosive and Dionysiac, in twentieth century culture (Kohn, 1992: 1).

If, as Phillip Larkin (1990) declared, sexual intercourse began in 1963, between the end of the Chatterley ban and the Beatles first LP, then one might be forgiven for thinking that drug use began in 1988, between the arrival of acid house and the introduction of the Criminal Justice Bill. The reality, of course, in both cases, is rather more prosaic. Larkin's was a satirical, rather than literal, truth, which signified the changing sensibility of the time, whilst also, perhaps, parodying the exaggerated sense of self-importance that seems to imbue each new generation. Drug use did not begin in 1988 any more than sexual intercourse began in 1963 and the realities of the past should put us on guard against the construction of overly simplistic theoretical models. All too often, particularly in the wake of postmodern theory, social change is assessed on the basis of depthless, prefabricated versions of the past, giving rise to millenarian visions of a world turned upside down. By glossing over the complexities and nuances of earlier times, much that is now written and said about illicit drug use not only exaggerates the extent and pace of change, but also loses sight of some important lessons from the past.

As a counterpoint to the new orthodoxy, I have sought to locate the emergence of widespread illicit drug use within the historical development of late industrial societies and, in so doing, have drawn on earlier contributions to the sociology of drug use. The central argument running throughout the book is based on three main claims: firstly, drug use is subject to much greater continuity than is generally recognised; secondly, this continuity is evident in the on-going value of established perspectives; and thirdly, recent theoretical developments do not represent the radical departure that is often supposed, but repeat some of the key themes of earlier work. To draw the argument to a close, this final chapter discusses whether, and in what ways, the emergence of widespread illicit drug may be considered symptomatic of broader processes of social change; evaluates how we should interpret evidence of continuity and change; examines whether new perspectives are really required; and assesses the implications for policy.

## Drug use in late industrial societies

The proliferation of illicit drug use, like the upsurge in crime more generally, may be considered an altogether predictable, though unintended, consequence of the broad processes of social change that characterise late industrial societies. Globalisation, the sixties 'cultural revolution' and deindustrialisation have combined to accentuate the motives behind drug use, to provide the means and opportunity for realising them and to relax the controls that might otherwise have held them in check (see Reiner, 2007).[1] The rise of individualism, increases in free-time and the commodification of leisure have all helped to create a platform for widespread illicit drug use by encouraging the development of a distinctly hedonistic leisure style which appeals to the heightened subterranean sensibility of the time. Whether or not this style involves drug use depends, in part, on means and opportunity, which are largely a function of availability and supply. Globalisation has played a key role in this regard, facilitating the movement of people, goods and cultural practices across national borders and providing transnational crime organisations with opportunities to open up new markets (Seddon, 2005). With greater availability and increases in disposable income, illicit drugs have become a relatively accessible and affordable commodity. Just as motives, means and opportunity have increased, informal social controls have weakened. Alongside the greater questioning of traditional authorities and the rise of 'permissiveness', life-course influences have been reconfigured, and young people are spending longer outside the disciplines of family life and full-time work.

Whilst symptomatic of broader processes of social change, the rise of illicit drug use has been mediated by established patterns of organisation, which are geographically and socially bounded. Consequently, the particularities of time and place remain important. Globalisation has played a key role in widening availability, but its effects have been felt unevenly and international drug markets continue to reflect the influence of location and lineage. North America's enduring status as the world's largest cocaine market, for example, is partly a function of its proximity to the main producer countries to the south, with the primary trafficking route still running from Columbia, Peru and Bolivia, through Mexico, into the United States (United Nations, 2008). As established markets have approached saturation point and consumer demand in north America has stabilised, trafficking routes have diversified and western Europe has become the second most important destination for Andean produced cocaine, most of which is channelled through Spain and Portugal, reflecting their long history of involvement in the Americas. Similar influences have been implicated in the proliferation of the 'ganja complex', which has been linked to a particular pattern of migration that, in Britain at least, forms part of its colonial heritage (Hamid, 2002).

On the demand side, the role and regulation of alcohol has been crucial in mediating the rise of illicit drug use. Drinking, smoking and drug use provide the basis of a distinctly hedonistic leisure style which is concentrated among young adults and, in Britain at least, centres around the night-time economy. This style is most commonly found among white young adults, moreover, suggesting a greater emphasis on abstinence and moderation among black and minority ethnic groups, which is linked to the role of religion. The particular importance of alcohol and related forms of regulation becomes clear when trends in consumption are compared. Tobacco use, in Britain as in most other late industrial societies, declined sharply during the second half of the twentieth century as repeated governments pursued an explicit policy of demand reduction, based on price controls, advertising restrictions, smoking bans and health promotion campaigns (Jha and Chaloupka, 1999; see also Peto et al., 2000) and as the concept of 'healthy' living took root (Bunton et al., 1995). Whilst at odds with the long-term decline in smoking, the proliferation of illicit drug use has been matched by an increasingly hedonistic orientation towards alcohol, which cuts across national boundaries and is most evident among young people.

Recent trends in Britain and the United States suggest a close relationship between alcohol consumption and drug use, though there are notable differences in trajectory and patterns of consumption. In the United States, binge drinking and illicit drug use peaked among young people during the late 1970s (Johnston et al., 2007), while, in Britain, drinking and drug use did not peak for another 20 years or so (Goddard, 2006; Murphy and Roe, 2007). Although levels of illicit drug use have traditionally been higher in the United States than Britain, levels of alcohol consumption have tended to be more moderate (WHO, 2004; Grube, 2005), reflecting notable differences in cultural orientation and modes of regulation. Bars and clubs are central, perhaps uniquely so, to youth oriented leisure in Britain, but are largely peripheral to the experience of adolescence in the United States. Whilst describing the 'pub or public house' as a 'quintessentially British institution', Thornton (1995: 20) suggests the car has acquired a similar status in America, especially in the suburbs, where it offers a sense of freedom, mobility and independence. This reliance on the car, she goes on to note, provides the main reason behind the strict enforcement of the minimum drinking age of 21 years, which contrasts with the more relaxed approach in Britain, where the putative minimum age of 18 years is 'rarely' enforced. Binge drinking is fairly widespread among college students in the United States, particularly in the context of private 'frat' parties, and some cities have experimented with alternative models of nightlife regulation (Moloney et al., 2009), but alcohol policy remains a 'morality issue', with any moves towards liberalisation being sharply opposed by religious traditionalists (Wald and Calhoun-Brown, 2007). While reasonably strict controls have been maintained in the United States, including the minimum legal drinking age of 21 years, the drinks industry in Britain has been given a fairly free reign and has actively targeted the youth market (see Hobbs et al., 2003; Roberts et al., 2006). This more accommodating approach to the regulation of the night-time economy helps to explain why alcohol consumption and illicit drug use continued to increase in Britain, well after they had reached a peak in the United States. It also helps to explain why Britain has some of the highest rates of binge drinking and illicit drug use in Europe.

## Continuity within change

The theme of continuity within change is central to the book and is based partly on the observation that social change is mediated by established patterns of organisation. This formulation has been preferred to the more conventionally used 'continuity and change' to emphasise the point that these apparently opposing forces do not operate in isolation from one another, but are bound together in an interactive, dialectical relationship. The key point here is not simply that social change is mediated by established arrangements, but that there are invariably considerable continuities embedded within it. As an example consider how recent changes in the nature of adolescence, which have been billed by some as a 'qualitative transformation' (Chisholm and Hurrelmann, 1995), have magnified the already ambivalent position of youth. In this case, what is change (the extension and pluralisation of adolescence) is also continuity (the ambivalent position of youth).

While recent studies of drug use emphasise change, we must also recognise there are important continuities at work here, which are embedded in enduring patterns of social organisation. State governments continue to be heavily invested in prohibition, creating familiar, yet powerful, social controls which present practical and ideological barriers that users must negotiate. For all that has been said about normalisation, illicit drug use continues to occupy an ambiguous position, which is neatly encapsulated by the notion of primary deviance: many young adults have direct experience of drug use, but such behaviour typically remains hesitant, tentative and short-lived. Contrary to recent claims, moreover, drug use has not become so ubiquitous as to transcend traditional distinctions between users and non-users: persistent differences continue to be evident on the basis of sex, ethnicity and religiosity, to say nothing of age, life-course events and broader lifestyle orientation. The one area where traditional distinctions do seem to have blurred is social class, but even here the process has not taken the form that recent theories imply. Rather than spreading from 'delinquent' working class subcultures to the middle classes, all the indications are that drug use has gone from being a largely middle class phenomenon to one that cuts across class boundaries.

Extended youth transitions and the expansion of the night-time economy have created greater space for illicit drug use, but there are, nonetheless, notable continuities embedded within these processes of change. The concentration of drug use among young adults, alongside binge drinking and active participation in the night-time economy, continues to reflect their privileged access to the world of subterranean play. While deindustrialisation has magnified the incipient problems of work, identity and leisure that the hippies faced in the sixties, young people have continued to seek solutions through the expression of subterranean values. It is largely on the basis of such parallels that 'rave' has been said to have simply replayed and reworked the subcultural experiences of previous generations, signifying a gesture of avoidance and a shirking of adult responsibility in favour of a universe of pleasure and play (Smith, 1992; see also Osgerby, 1998 and Thompson, 1998).

The theme of continuity within change can be traced back further still, to the 'birth of the British drug underground'. Britain's history of drug use, notes Marek Kohn (1992), divides into two eras: the modern one which began around 1960 and an earlier one that developed around the Jazz Age during the aftermath of the first world war, when drug use was a minor metropolitan phenomenon based around London's west end. Whilst the 'styles' and 'issues' had changed, Kohn (1992: 182) was struck by the durability of the 'grand themes', which included disrupted social boundaries, racial tensions, drug-fuelled hedonism and moral panics:

> One moment the events seem antique, sealed beyond living memory, and the next they seem to be in the present tense. At these instants it appears almost as though everything to do with drugs was present in miniature, eighty odd years ago.

There are, then, clear threads of continuity running from the 'psychotropic revolution', which came to fruition in the early part of the last century (Courtwright, 2001), through the sixties counter culture, to 'rave' and its aftermath. In a more fundamental sense, moreover, the activities of the 'chemical generation' and those who have followed may be considered part of the universal, age-old, pursuit of intoxication (Siegel, 2005).

## The need for new perspectives?

Such are the continuities involved that established criminological perspectives have considerably more to offer the sociology of drug use than is often supposed. Although cannabis use has been most fully implicated in the normalisation thesis, the value of previous work is evident even here. Attitudes to cannabis have become more relaxed in recent decades and its use has lost the implications of social protest and opposition to the mainstream that it once carried (May et al., 2002). Nonetheless, opinion remains divided over issues such as harmfulness and legalisation, whilst, in the United States at least, regular marihuana use continues to be subject to high rates of disapproval among young people (Gould and Stratford, 2002; Pearson and Shiner, 2002; Johnston et al., 2007). Under these circumstances, and given the persistence of legal controls, normalisation cannot be assumed, but must be negotiated *in situ* and certain adaptations may be required to maintain the 'subculture of secrecy', whilst also conveying the 'dynamic expressiveness' involved (Johnson et al., 2006: 46). This is pretty much what Becker (1955, 1963) had in mind half a century ago and his observations about marihuana use provide 'the most obvious and lasting example of the relevance of labelling theory' (Downes and Rock, 2007: 319). In a recent 'update', Becker's account of using marihuana for pleasure was judged to have 'survived the test of time remarkably well' (Hallstone, 2002: 840), while others have used Becker's insights to make sense of the social processes surrounding ecstasy and its use (Gourley, 2004). Young's (1971) work has proved no less valuable, identifying much of what it is about late industrial societies that has given rise to widespread illicit drug use.

The prescience of the 'new' deviancy theories is further evident from the way they anticipated subsequent developments in sociology and related disciplines. These theories are said to have been 'born post-modern' in the sense that they were crucially concerned with the social construction of reality, the role of discourse and vocabularies of motive (Downes and Rock, 2007: 312). 'The irony', then, 'is that post-modernism arrived comparatively early on in the post-war development of criminology and that many of the recent converts to its cause do not seem to have realized that a rich and developed tradition pre-dates them' (Young, 1999: 33). In much the same way, recent contributions to the sociology of drug use have glossed over earlier work, whilst claiming many of its central themes as their own, including the rejection of traditional deficit based perspectives and the emphasis on consumption and pleasure-seeking.

This does not mean the 'new' deviancy theories are beyond criticism, nor that they represent the final word on the subject of drug use. Despite being presented as a radical alternative, these theories replicated some of the blind-spots of mainstream criminology, with feminist critics, in particular, pointing to the continued invisibility of women (Millman, 1982; Heidensohn, 1989). As a corrective to the gender-blindness of previous work, recent feminist perspectives have much to offer, though they, like the normalisation thesis, represent less of a radical departure than is often implied and could plausibly have been formulated within the framework provided by established perspectives (Shiner, 2006). Where 'new' deviancy theories really struggle is in explaining patterns of behaviour, in large part because they were not designed to provide causal explanations and paid little attention to the role of structural influences. The problem here, as with the interpretive paradigm more generally, is the tendency to explain all human conduct in terms of motives at the expense of causal conditions, making it very difficult to account for the regular and enduring nature of social life (Giddens, 1976). This is a problem that has been replicated in more recent theories of drug use, moreover, including the normalisation thesis, which have downplayed the role of structural influences in favour of a rational action model (see also Measham and Shiner, 2008).

Any adequate theory of illicit drug use must be able to explain why it is that such behaviour is concentrated among young adults who have little by way of domestic responsibilities. It must also be able to explain why drug use is more prevalent among the unemployed and those who are otherwise marginalised from the labour market, as well as among vulnerable young people, but is less common among black and minority ethnic groups and those who are actively religious. Many of these findings are consistent with control theory and, while neither disproving nor discrediting the 'new' deviancy theories, do suggest the need for greater synthesis. Despite differing, sometimes sharply, in their emphasis, the main criminological theories are 'not as mutually inconsistent as their proponents would have us believe' (Braithwaite, 1989: 16) and the boundaries between them are not as fixed or absolute as they may appear. The work of Matza and Sykes (1961: 218), for example, was explicitly rooted in the concerns of the 'new' deviancy theories, but contained clear traces of control theory, which are evident in the claim that: 'all adolescents at all class levels are to some extent members of a leisure class, for they move in a limbo between earlier parental domination and future integration with the social structure through the bonds of work and marriage'. Similarly, Young (1971: 91) emphasised the ambivalent position of youth, while also noting that the ability of social groups to invoke 'novel conceptions of drug use' varies depending on the extent to which they 'are supervised by the surrounding society'. The potential for synthesis has been realised recently by Laub and Sampson (2003), who explicitly combined the insights of 'new' deviancy theories with those of control theory and located them within a life-course perspective. Although presented as a general theory of crime, the results of this synthesis have a clear application to drug use and compliment Young's (1971) earlier work by providing further insights into the ambivalent position of youth. As well as helping to explain why drug use is distributed across the population in the way that it is, Laub and Sampson's age graded theory of informal social control clarifies the meaning of such behaviour. By viewing drug use as a form of 'situated choice', we can see how it provides young people with a means of celebrating freedom from adult roles and responsibilities.

Established criminological theories, then, have not been exhausted by the pace of change, but continue to enliven and animate our understanding of drug use and its place in the social world. It may be a truism to say that the past holds the key the future, but the implications are clear: established theories, possibly reworked and reframed, have a key role to play in helping us understand social change and the role of continuity within it; for as Ulrich Beck (1992: 12) noted:

> More urgently than ever, we need ideas and theories that will allow us to conceive the new which is rolling over us in a new way, and allow us to live and act within it. At the same time we must retain good relations with the treasures of tradition, without a misconceived and sorrowful turn to the new, which always remains old anyway.

Above all else, what this means for the sociology of drug use is reconnecting with its criminological past.

## Drug policy and the 'new' deviancy critique

The damaging and unwanted side-effects of prohibition have been 'exhaustively chronicled' and the case for 'alternative, and on the balance of the evidence, more efficient and harm-reducing regulation has been endlessly put' (Downes and Rock, 2007: 320). Rather than put the case yet again, the aim of this final section is to show how the policy implications of the 'new' deviancy critique and the contemporary politics of reform fit within the overall theme of continuity within change.

The first point to note is that drugs policy has not moved in the direction favoured by the 'new' deviancy theorists, but has become progressively more punitive. In 1971, the year *The Drugtakers* was published, Richard Nixon, then President of the United States, declared a 'total war on drugs', setting the tone for much of what was to follow. This war has been escalated by almost every subsequent presidential administration and has formed an integral part of America's more general war on crime, helping to push the prison population to around two million and to create the highest imprisonment rate in the world (Garland, 2001; Simon, 2007). Nixon's was not simply a domestic war, moreover, but was aimed squarely at producer countries and ushered in a new era in global drugs control. Working partly through the United Nations, the United States government exercised exceptional influence over international drugs policy, taking the lead in building support for higher levels of enforcement and 'deepening the culture of prohibition' (Elvins, 2003: 182). Even without the benefit of hindsight, these developments were noted with a sense of foreboding by liberal critics. Young (1971) warned that more punitive policies could only exacerbate the problem, while Schur (1969: 217) maintained: 'It is reasonable to predict that if the British do move significantly in the direction of American policy, the consequences of doing so will be unhappy ones.'

The second point to note is that the pursuit of more punitive polices failed to prevent the continued escalation of drug use. Despite a flurry of activity in the early 1970s, which aimed to strengthen international prohibition, the ensuing period witnessed an 'explosive world wide growth in the production and trafficking of virtually all types of illicit drugs' (Stares, 1996: 28). As part of this activity, Britain developed one of the harshest drug regimes in Europe, yet became host to one of the region's largest drug markets. More spectacularly still, the United States' 'war' on drugs has left it with a drug problem worse than that of any other wealthy nation and, even though reductions in use have been evident, this has largely been down to factors other than policy change (MacCoun and Reuter, 2001). The key lesson from the last four decades of punitive prohibition, then, is this: consumer demand cannot be legislated out of existence and 'it is only by treating citizens as responsible human beings that any sane and long-lasting control can be achieved' (Young 1971: 222). What chance, then, a 'sane' and 'just' policy?

Prohibition became the dominant paradigm for global drugs control despite very little available evidence as to its efficacy and has at least as much to do with politics and ideology as with practical social policy (Elvins, 2003). Nonetheless the proliferation of drug use has exposed the limitations of the criminal justice state and forms part of a broader 'criminological *predicament*' that constrains contemporary policy and practice (Garland, 2001). State authorities have responded to this predicament in contradictory ways, based on two major strategies: one that is pragmatic and adaptive and another that is primarily expressive and seeks to reassure the public, often by denying the problem and 'acting out' through impulsive, almost knee-jerk reactions. Adaptive solutions, have increasingly been eclipsed by more politicised alternatives such as the 'war' on drugs, which, Garland (2001: 132) maintains has 'all the hallmarks of a sovereign state dealing with its limitations by denying they exist'.

Behind the rhetoric, there are signs of adaptive responses, not least in the emphasis that has come to be placed on containment, whereby the 'manageability' of crime and drug problems replaces 'the more heroic but politically risky "war" stance' (Dorn and Lee, 1999: 97). Consider, for example, how the United Nations has come to define success. Having previously worked under the slogan, 'A Drug Free World – We Can Do It' (*United Nations Chronicle*, Summer 1998), the United Nations Office on Drugs and Crime recently claimed 'drug control is working and the world drug problem is being contained' (United Nations, 2007: 1), describing the situation in which less than five per cent of the adult population has used illicit drugs in the last year as an 'impressive achievement' and an 'undeniable success when compared to the consumption of tobacco or alcohol' (United Nations, 2008: 1). There is, perhaps, no greater sign of the futility of prohibition than one of the 'global leaders' in the 'fight against illicit drugs and international crime' (http://www.unodc.org) defining success in such limited terms. The over-riding point, surely, is that the drugs trade represents 'the largest and most successful form of criminal activity ever developed' (Bean, 2002: 99). Proclaiming success on the basis of comparisons with alcohol or tobacco, moreover, is not only nebulous – these are, lest we forget, legally available substances that have been relentlessly promoted by multinational corporations using global marketing techniques – but also serves to show how distant and remote a possibility prohibition really is.

The choice we face is not simply one of prohibition or the free market. Nor is it the claim of this book that regulation does not matter: we need only look to the examples of tobacco and alcohol to see that it does. The main point, and one that was well established by the 'new' deviancy theorists, is this: prohibition is an ineffective and counter-productive form of control, which forfeits the possibility of effective regulation by pushing drug use into illicit markets that operate outside the orbit of the state. There is nothing inherent in this critique that leads to a free-market solution and, indeed, the 'new' deviancy theorists advocated more effective forms of regulation. If the aim is to reduce harm, as they began to argue, then we require more effective controls than prohibition is able to provide, whether this be through 'maintaining cultures', 'positive propaganda' or what is now routinely referred to as harm reduction or state regulated supply (see Rolles et al., 2004). The immediate prospects for such an approach are to be found in adaptive responses, including legal reclassification, medically authorised supply, drug consumption rooms, the distribution of injecting paraphernalia and the promotion of drug testing kits. Beyond these responses, there are signs of a more fundamental shift in political thinking as the consensus underpinning prohibition appears to be fragmenting. Drugs possession has been decriminalised in parts of Europe and South America (Rolles et al., 2004), while, in Britain, the Select Committee on Home Affairs (2002) recommended that harm reduction, not retribution, should provide the primary focus of policy towards drug users. So it is that we find ourselves at a cross-roads in our relationship with illicit drugs, caught between the apparent certainty of prohibition and a growing awareness that existing arrangements do not, and cannot, deliver on their promises. If history really repeats itself, first as tragedy, second as farce (Marx, 1864), then the tragedy of our current predicament is that it was all too predictable and it is only by learning from the past that we can now hope to avoid straying into the realms of farce.

# Technical Appendix

This appendix augments the brief discussion of the methodology included in the introduction and provides further details about the analysis. In so doing it concentrates almost exclusively on the multivariate procedures, explaining the underlying rationale, the procedures used and how the results should be interpreted. For each survey, the variables are described and the results presented in summary form.

Before discussing the multivariate analysis, some brief comments are required regarding the sampling and weighting of the data. Both the BCS and YLS were based on hierarchical stratified samples, with random selection at three levels – postcode sector, household and individual – and oversampling in inner city neighbourhoods. Weights were provided with the data and were used to correct for sampling bias and to improve the representativeness of the sample. Percentages, averages and bivariate measures of association were all estimated on the basis of weighted data because the aim was to generalise such figures to the wider population. Probability values, by contrast, were estimated using unweighted data because they are affected by the actual numbers of cases included in the analysis (and the weights altered this number). Unless otherwise stated all the bivariate relationships discussed in the main body of the book were statistically significant at the 0.05 level or below. Multivariate analyses were also based on unweighted data although the potential effects of weighting were taken into account by including those variables that were involved in the weighting in the analysis as potential predictor variables (Skinner, 1994).

## The rationale for multivariate analysis

Bivariate statistical techniques highlight potentially important variations in the prevalence of drug use: that is, they show the percentage of people in a given category who have engaged in a certain type of drug use during a specified period of time. Multivariate techniques help to deepen our understanding by isolating the 'effect' that each independent variable has on the probability of drug use. By controlling for, or holding constant, all of the other independent variables included in the model, such techniques are able to specify which variables are most important in explaining variations in drug use.

The analysis presented here is the most technically sophisticated of its type yet to be published on the basis of British drug use data. Multivariate techniques have only rarely been applied to such data and, where they have been, have been based on a logistic regression procedure that is limited to analysing binary dependent variables (see Ramsay and Percy, 1996; MacDonald, 1999; Roe and Man, 2006). The models presented below were developed using a related, but more advanced procedure, known as multinomial logit regression (Futing Liao, 1994). The main advantage of this procedure is that it can be used to analyse dependent variables with more than two categories, which meant it was possible to distinguish between recent drug use, past use and abstinence. This was important because it meant that consideration could be given to abstinence and desistance as well as recent use.

## The modelling procedure

Multinomial logistic regression is a form of probability modelling and is based on an extension of classic linear regression (Futing Liao, 1994). It is appropriate when the dependent variable is made up of three or more categories. Like other forms of regression, probability models estimate the effects of various independent variables on a single dependent variable, which in this case was provided by a specific drug or group of drugs – separate models were developed for cannabis use, hallucinant use and cocaine use. In each case distinctions were drawn between abstinence (never used), past use (used but not in the last 12 months) and recent use (used in the last 12 months).

Multinomial logit model are based on a transformation of the dependent variable known as the log odds. Odds express the probability of two possible outcomes in relation to one another – such as the probability of never having used cannabis versus the probability of having used it in the last 12 months – and log odds are produced by taking natural logarithms of the odds. This transformation is required because it ensures that the model does not generate estimated probabilities outside the range zero to one (Altman, 1991). All the models required that one category of the dependent variable was selected as a reference, against which the likelihood of being in the remaining categories was compared. Never used was chosen to be the reference category, so that the effects associated with the independent variables were estimated in relation to the two remaining categories. The first set of effects was based on the odds of past use versus never used and the second set of effects was based on the odds of recent use versus never used.

Most of the independent variables included in the models also had a categorical structure and were entered into the models as a series of dummy variables, where one indicated the presence of a given characteristic and zero indicated its absence. For such variables a reference category is required, against which the effects associated with the other categories are compared. Thus, for example, the variable sex shows the effect of being female rather than male because male was set to the reference.

### Building the models

The multivariate models were developed in a series of stages. A preliminary stage was established during which variables were entered into the model if they were involved in the weighting of the data or indicated something about the process of the survey interview (e.g. who else, if anybody, was present during the interview). This was followed by the main body of the analysis, which was divided into four stages. Demographic variables were entered into the model during the first stage, followed by variables relating to deprivation and area of residence, then the lifecourse and then lifestyle. The lifestyle stage was further subdivided so that variables not directly related to the consumption of alcohol and tobacco were entered first, followed by those that were directly related to these forms of consumption.

At each stage, the most parsimonious model was developed. All the variables that were relevant to a given stage were initially included in the model, alongside any that had been retained from previous stages, and non-significant variables were then excluded one by one. Decisions to include or exclude variables were based on probability values, which were multiplied by the appropriate design factor to take account of the error associated with the survey design (see Hales and Stratford, 1999; Stratford and Roth, 1999). Variables were excluded if they did not meet the criteria for significance (i.e. $p < .05$) on either set of effects. Initially, at each step, the variable with the largest single probability value was excluded, providing that the value on both sets of effects was greater than 0.1. Once this process had been exhausted, variables with probability values between 0.05 and 0.1 on both sets of effects were then excluded, starting with that which had the largest single probability value.

Although non-significant variables were generally excluded from the models, this was not always the case. Where one category of a given variable did not meet the criteria for inclusion it was combined with another category of the same variable providing that it was conceptually meaningful to do so and one of the following criteria was met: the non-significant category was associated with a sizeable effect (the absolute value of the regression co-efficient was greater than 0.4); the non-significant category was closer in its effect to the other (significant) category than it was to the reference; or the 95 per cent confidence interval for the non-significant category included the effect associated with the other (significant) category or vice versa.

Once the most parsimonious model had been developed at each stage, the variables that had been excluded in previous stages were re-entered individually to assess whether they now met the criteria for inclusion. Analyses proceeded iteratively in this way until all significant variables were included in the model.

## Interpreting the models

While probability values indicate whether the effects associated with a given variable are statistically significant they provide little information about the nature of the effect. In multinomial logit models, as in other forms of generalised linear model, the size and direction of an effect are summarised by the regression coefficient. The direction of an effect is evident from the sign in front of the coefficient: a negative coefficient indicates an inverse relationship, whereby an increase in the independent variable is associated with a decrease in the dependent variable, whereas a positive coefficient (where no sign is given) indicates that an increase in the independent variable is associated with an increase in the dependent variable. Regression coefficients provide very specific information about the size of the effect, indicating the change in the dependent variable associated with a one unit increase in the independent variable. Where the independent variable is a categorical variable a one unit increase means moving from the reference category to the category of interest. Though conventionally described as an 'effect', the change in the dependent variable associated with a one unit increase in the independent variable does not necessarily signify a causal relationship.

Interpreting regression coefficients in a multinomial logit model is complicated by the fact that the dependent variable is defined in terms of log odds, which are not immediately meaningful. To provide greater clarity, both sides of a model can be exponentiated (that is, the antilogarithm can be taken to the base *e*) so that the regression coefficient indicates the effect of a given variable on the odds. More complex calculations can be carried out which allow the effects of each variable to be expressed in terms of probabilities, which has the advantage of being easily understood (see Futing Liao, 1994). In logit models probabilities are estimated from regression scores, which are, in turn, generated from regression coefficients. A particular profile is selected, based on the independent variables included in the model, and regression coefficients are multiplied by the set of values which reflect this profile. By varying the multipliers, the effect of any given variable may be isolated, providing that the effects of all other independent variables are held constant (this can be achieved by using the mean score for each variable as the multiplier). Suppose, for example, we are interested in the effect of sex, where male is coded as zero and female as one. The effects of all other variables are held constant by multiplying the coefficient by the mean of the independent variable and two sets of scores are calculated: one for males, where the effect of sex is multiplied by zero, and one for females, where the effect of sex is multiplied by one. Scores are generated for each set of effects (i.e. past use versus abstinence and recent use versus abstinence) and these scores are then exponentiated and converted into probabilities using the established formula (see Futing Liao, 1994; STATA, 1999).

For the models to be meaningful, they must first fit the data. That is, the independent variables included in the model must predict the response variable more accurately than the model that includes only the intercept. The difference between these models may be assessed on the basis of the likelihood ratio statistic, which has an approximately chi-square distribution. Judged on these criteria, all the models fitted the data significantly better than the model with just the intercept ($p < 0.01$ at each stage of each model). Another statistic, known as Psuedo $R^2$, summarises the goodness of fit of the model and, though not entirely satisfactory, this statistic has been cited in the summaries given below. The adequacy of the models may also be assessed by estimating the probability of the various outcomes based on a statistically average set of characteristics and comparing the resulting estimates with the observed probabilities. Such comparisons indicated that the models tended to under-predict the probability of recent drug use. In illustrating the results of the multivariate analysis adjustments have been made to take account of this apparent bias.

## BCS models

Variables were included in the multivariate models in the following format:

*Preliminary stage*

Inner city

- Lives in inner city area (reference)
- Does not live in inner city area

Number of adults in household (continuous variables)

Completed

- Respondent completed questionnaire on own (reference)
- Respondent discussed questionnaire with someone else
- Interviewer completed questionnaire

Others present during the self-completion exercise

- Nobody else present (reference)
- Spouse or partner present
- Other adult household member present
- Child household member present
- Non-household member present

*Stage one: Demographics*

Age

- 16–17 years
- 18–22 years
- 23–26 years
- 27–30 years (reference)

Sex

- Male (reference)
- Female

Age * Sex (interaction terms between age and sex)

Ethnicity

- White (reference)
- Black Caribbean
- Black African
- Indian
- Pakistani or Bangladeshi
- Other

*Note*: Pakistani and Bangladeshi were combined because they contained a small number of cases and because they share a similar religious and socio-economic profile (Modood et al., 1997).

Social class

- Professional
- Managerial/technical
- Skilled non-manual
- Skilled manual
- Partly skilled
- Unskilled (reference)
- Unclassified

*Note*: respondents were classified according to their current or most recent job.

Parents' social class

- Professional or managerial/technical (reference)
- Skilled non-manual
- Skilled manual
- Partly skilled or unskilled
- Unclassified

*Note*: respondents were classified according to the current or last job of the head of the household. The BCS did not include direct questions about parental occupation and this information could only be retrieved for respondents who were living in a household headed by one of their parents. Respondents who were living independently were included in the unclassified category. Some categories had to be combined because the number of cases was insufficient to support meaningful analysis: the BCS contained only 24 cases where the head of the household was professional and 36 cases where he/she was unskilled.

Household income

- Less than £10,000 (reference)
- £10,000 to £14,999
- £15,000 to £19,999
- £20,000 to £29,999
- £30,000 or more
- Unknown

*Note*: these variables were entered into the model in a way that distinguished between those who lived with their parents and those who did not.

Health status (self-assessed)

- Very good (reference)
- Good
- Fair to very bad

*Note*: the categories fair to very bad were combined because very few respondents felt their health was bad or very bad.

Disability status

- Not disabled (reference)
- Disabled but not limiting
- Disabled, limiting

*Stage two: Deprivation/area of residence*

To make this stage more manageable variables were entered into the model in two groups. Those that measured individual or household characteristics were entered first, followed by those that measured neighbourhood or area characteristics.

Unemployment

- Unemployed
- Otherwise marginalised from the labour market
- Neither of the above (reference)

*Note*: respondents were considered to be unemployed if they had not done any paid work in the previous week but had been looking for work. Those who had not done any paid work and had not been looking for work were considered to be otherwise marginalised from the labour market providing that they were not studying full-time or looking after the home or family. This category included those who were permanently sick, waiting to take up a job, intending to work but were temporarily sick, on a government scheme, doing unpaid work or doing something else.

Qualifications

- Has formal qualifications (reference)
- Not have formal qualifications

*Note*: respondents who were 16 years of age may not have reached the official school leaving age and were included in the no qualifications category only if they had no qualifications and appeared to have left school.

Financial difficulty

- Not living in a low-income household (reference)
- Living in a low-income household experiencing little financial difficulty
- Living in a low-income household experiencing moderate financial difficulty
- Living in a low-income household experiencing extreme financial difficulty

*Note*: low-income households were those with an annual income below £10,000 per year. This figure approximated to 50 per cent of the average household income (after housing costs) which is a commonly used measure of the poverty line. For low-income households, financial difficulty was assessed on the basis of their ability to pay an unexpected bill of a specified amount: those that would find it impossible to pay a bill of £100 or would find it impossible or problematic to pay a bill of £20 were considered to be in considerable financial difficulty; those that did not meet these criteria but would find it problematic to pay a bill of £100 were considered to be in some financial difficulty; and those that would not have a problem paying a bill of £100 were considered to be in little financial difficulty.

Region

- North (reference)
- Yorkshire/Humberside
- North West
- East Midlands
- West Midlands
- Wales

- East Anglia
- South East
- South West
- Greater London

Type of neighbourhood

- Thriving (reference)
- Expanding
- Rising
- Settling
- Aspiring
- Striving

*Note*: neighbourhoods were rated according to A Classification of Regional Neighbourhoods or ACORN for short. This system was developed by CACI Ltd as a marketing tool and provides a geographical and demographic classification of local areas (see: www.caci.co.uk). Each postcode is allocated to one of 54 neighbourhood types, which can then be grouped into 17 distinct categories or the six major categories shown above. The striving category is made up almost exclusively of deprived neighbourhoods (www.odpm.gov.uk).

Inner city (already entered in the preliminary stage).

Community cohesiveness

- People go their own way (reference)
- Mixed
- People help each other

*Note*: respondents were asked: In general what type of neighbourhood would you say you live in? Would you say it is a neighbourhood in which people do things together and try to help each other or one in which people mostly go their own way?

Incivility

- None (reference)
- Low
- Moderate
- High

*Note*: respondents were asked to rate their local area in relation to a range of possible problems: noisy neighbours or loud parties; teenagers hanging around on the streets; drunks or tramps on the streets; rubbish and litter lying about; vandalism, graffiti and deliberate damage to property; racially motivated attacks; and people using or dealing in drugs. The number of issues that were considered to be a very big problem or a fairly big problem were added together to create a single index of neighbourhood incivility and this index was then divided into the four categories shown above: none (no incivilities); low (one or two issues were considered problematic); moderate (three or four issues were considered problematic); and high (five or more issues were considered problematic).

*Stage 3: Life-course*

Work status (reference)

- Working full-time
- Working part-time
- Studying
- Looking after the home
- Unemployed
- Other

Domestic circumstances

- Married with children (reference)
- Married, no children
- Separated, divorced or widowed (with or without children)
- Cohabiting with children
- Cohabiting, no children, buying own home
- Cohabiting, no children, not buying own home
- Single with children
- Single, no children, buying own home
- Single, no children, renting
- Single, no children, living with parents

*Note*: the number of separated, divorced or widowed respondents who did not have children was fairly small (n = 40) and the multivariate models indicated that this position was very similar in its effects to being separated, divorced or widowed with children. As a result, these categories were combined into a single category. The categories 'single, no children, private renting' and 'single, no children, social renting' were also combined into a single category because they were similar in their effects and because the distinction between them was not considered crucial.

Domestic * Sex (interaction terms between domestic circumstances and sex)

*Note*: no interaction term was included for single, with children because very few men were in this situation (282 out of 289 cases were female).

*Stage 4: Lifestyle*

Evenings out in the previous week

- Six or seven
- Four or five
- Two or three – weekdays and weekends
- Two – weekend only

- Two – weekdays only
- One – weekend
- One – weekday
- None (reference)

*Note*: weekdays were defined as Monday to Thursday; weekends as Friday to Sunday.

Frequency with which usually go out after dark

- Once a week (reference)
- At least once a fortnight
- At least once a month
- Less than once a month
- Never

Evenings visited pub in last month

- Almost every day
- About three times a week
- Once or twice a week
- Less than once a week
- None (reference)

Visits to a nightclub or disco in last month

- At least once a week
- Less than once a week
- None (reference)

Drinking style

- Habitual heavy drinker
- Habitual light drinker
- Frequent heavy binger
- Frequent binger
- Frequent moderate drinker
- Frequent light drinker
- Regular binger
- Regular moderate drinker
- Regular light drinker
- Occasional moderate drinker
- Occasional light drinker
- Non-drinker (reference)

*Note*: see main text for details

**Table A1.1 Cannabis life-course model – regression coefficients (BCS)**

| | *Past use v never used* | *Recent use v never used* |
|---|---|---|
| *Age (27–30 years)* | | |
| 16–17 years | 0.23 | 1.13** |
| 18–22 years | 0.36* | 0.92** |
| 23–26 years | 0.03 | 0.49** |
| *Sex (Male)* | | |
| Female | –0.52** | –1.42** |
| *Ethnicity (White)* | | |
| Black Caribbean | –1.42* | –0.29 |
| Black African | –2.51* | –1.94** |
| Indian, Pakistani or Bangladeshi | –0.68 | –0.93* |
| *Social class (Unskilled)* | | |
| Managerial or technical | 0.37* | 0.42* |
| Skilled manual | 0.36* | 0.15 |
| None given | –0.37 | –0.44* |
| *Parents' social class (Professional, managerial or technical)* | | |
| Skilled non-manual | 0.71* | –0.09 |
| None given | 0.70* | 0.34 |
| *Household income (< £10,000)* | | |
| £20,000–29,000 | 0.04 | –0.01 |
| £30,000 or more | 0.12 | –0.06 |
| Not given | –0.93* | –0.47 |
| £20,000–29,000 * living w. parents | 0.89* | 0.21 |
| £30,000 or more * living w. parents | 1.29* | 0.83* |
| Not given * living w. parents | 1.39* | 0.51 |
| *Health status (Very good)* | | |
| Good | 0.32** | 0.38** |
| Fair to very bad | 0.19 | 0.54** |
| *Region (North)* | | |
| East Midlands | 0.41* | 0.18 |
| South East | 0.36* | 0.21 |
| London | 0.19 | 0.49** |
| *Type of neighbourhood (Thriving)* | | |
| Expanding | –0.26 | –0.63** |
| Rising | 0.14 | 0.53** |
| *Economic status (Working full-time)* | | |
| Unemployed or other | 0.31 | 0.51** |

**Table A1.1 Cannabis life-course model – regression coefficients (BCS)** – *continued*

| | *Past use v never used* | *Recent use v never used* |
|---|---|---|
| *Domestic status (Married with children)* | | |
| Divorced, separated or widowed | 0.30 | 1.32** |
| Cohabiting | | |
| – with children | 0.69** | 0.98** |
| – no children, buying own home | 0.53* | 1.14** |
| – no children, not buying own home | 0.62* | 1.71** |
| Single | | |
| – with children | 1.08** | 2.19** |
| – no children, buying own home | –0.14 | 0.92** |
| – no children, renting | –0.23 | 1.28** |
| – no children, living with parents | –0.49 | 0.56** |
| – no children, buying own home * sex | 0.94* | 0.94* |
| – no children, renting * sex | 0.45 | 0.67* |
| – no children, living with parents * sex | 0.06 | 0.92** |
| *Others present (No one else present)* | | |
| Child household member present | –0.36 | –0.65* |
| *Completed (Self without discussion)* | | |
| Completed by interviewer or discussed with someone else | –0.26 | –0.87** |
| Constant | –1.95 | –2.47 |

n = 2,753    ** = $p < 0.01$    * = $p < 0.05$    Psuedo $R^2 = 0.11$

*Note*: non-significant variables were included in the model if they formed part of a statistically significant interaction effect.

**Table A1.2 Cannabis lifestyle model – regression coefficients (BCS)**

| | *Past use v never used* | *Recent use v never used* |
|---|---|---|
| *Age (27–30 years)* | | |
| 16–17 years | 0.41 | 1.52** |
| 18–22 years | 0.36* | 0.88** |
| 23–26 years | 0.07 | 0.46** |
| *Sex (Male)* | | |
| Female | –0.30 | –0.97** |
| *Ethnicity (White)* | | |
| Black Caribbean | –1.18* | 0.17 |
| Black African | –2.32* | –1.40* |
| *Social class (Unskilled)* | | |
| Managerial or technical | 0.38* | 0.40* |
| Skilled manual | 0.47* | 0.23 |
| *Parents' social class (Professional, managerial or technical)* | | |
| Skilled non-manual | 0.76* | –0.07 |
| None given | 0.62* | 0.26 |
| *Household income (< £10,000)* | | |
| £20,000–29,000 | –0.02 | –0.07 |
| £30,000 or more | –0.02 | –0.36 |
| Not given | –0.85 | –0.40 |
| £20,000–29,000 * living w. parents | 0.85* | 0.07 |
| £30,000 or more * living w. parents | 1.26* | 0.76* |
| Not given * living w. parents | 1.29* | 0.43 |
| *Health status (Very good)* | | |
| Good | 0.30* | 0.35** |
| Fair to very bad | 0.29 | 0.68** |
| *Region (North)* | | |
| South East | 0.35* | 0.28 |
| London | 0.24 | 0.67** |
| *Type of neighbourhood (Thriving)* | | |
| Expanding | –0.24 | –0.69** |
| Rising | 0.09 | 0.45* |
| *Community cohesiveness (Go own way)* | | |
| Help each other | –0.32* | –0.26 |
| *Economic status (Working full-time)* | | |
| Unemployed | 0.49 | 0.61* |
| Other | 0.31 | 0.67* |

**Table A1.2 Cannabis lifestyle model – regression coefficients (BCS)** *– continued*

| | *Past use v never used* | *Recent use v never used* |
|---|---|---|
| *Domestic status (Married with children)* | | |
| Divorced, separated or widowed | 0.26 | 1.14** |
| Cohabiting | | |
| – with children | 0.66** | 0.91* |
| – no children, buying own home | 0.42 | 0.91** |
| – no children, not buying own home | 0.52 | 1.58** |
| Single | | |
| – with children | 0.93** | 1.88** |
| – no children, buying own home | –0.29 | 0.49 |
| – no children, renting | –0.25 | 1.01** |
| – no children, living with parents | –0.65 | 0.27 |
| – no children, buying own home * sex | 0.86 | 0.73 |
| – no children, living with parents * sex | –0.11 | 0.59* |
| *Evenings out in last week (None)* | | |
| Four or five | 0.11 | 0.46* |
| *Pub (Evenings in last month)* | | |
| Once or twice a week | 0.08 | 0.45** |
| About three times a week | 0.28 | 0.73** |
| Almost every day | 0.58* | 1.16** |
| *Drinking style (Non-drinker)* | | |
| Occasional or regular light drinker | 0.70* | 0.12 |
| Occasional moderate drinker | 0.88* | 0.59 |
| Regular moderate drinker | 0.73* | 0.62* |
| Regular binger | 1.30** | 0.97** |
| Frequent light drinker | 1.32** | 0.95** |
| Frequent moderate drinker | 1.20** | 1.10** |
| Frequent binger | 1.15** | 1.37** |
| Frequent heavy binger | 1.66** | 1.65** |
| Habitual light drinker | 1.22** | 1.53** |
| Habitual heavy drinker | 1.22** | 1.52** |
| *Others present (No one else present)* | | |
| Child household member present | –0.35 | –0.60* |
| *Completed (Self without discussion)* | | |
| Completed by interviewer or discussed with someone else | –0.17 | –0.71* |
| Constant | –2.97 | –3.60 |

n = 2,722 ** = $p < 0.01$ * = $p < 0.05$ Psuedo $R^2 = 0.14$

*Note*: 1) Non-significant variables were included in the model if they formed part of a statistically significant interaction effect; 2) Single, no children, home owner * sex was included in the model because it was very close to meeting the criteria for inclusion ($p = 0.05$ on past use v never used).

**Table A2.1 Hallucinants life-course model – regression coefficients (BCS)**

| | *Past use v never used* | *Recent use v never used* |
|---|---|---|
| *Age (27–30 years)* | | |
| 16–17 years | –0.20 | 0.90* |
| 18–22 years | 0.42* | 1.00** |
| 23–26 years | 0.28* | 0.65** |
| *Sex (Male)* | | |
| Female | –0.89** | –1.06** |
| *Ethnicity (White)* | | |
| Black Caribbean | –0.28 | –2.38* |
| Black African, Indian, Pakistani or Bangladeshi | –1.38** | –1.34* |
| *Social class (Unskilled)* | | |
| Managerial or technical | 0.40* | 0.08 |
| None given | –0.76** | –0.71* |
| *Household income (< £10,000)* | | |
| £30,000 or more | –0.39* | –0.15 |
| £30,000 or more * living w. parents etc | 1.03** | 0.72 |
| *Financial difficulty (Not low-income household)* | | |
| Extreme difficulty | 0.34* | 0.47* |
| *Health status (Very good)* | | |
| Good | 0.31** | 0.38* |
| Fair to very bad | 0.28 | 0.77** |
| *Region (North)* | | |
| East Anglia | –1.02* | 0.07 |
| *Type of neighbourhood (Thriving)* | | |
| Expanding | –0.13 | –0.90** |
| *Community cohesiveness (Go own way)* | | |
| Help each other | –0.05 | –0.74** |
| *Economic status (Working full-time)* | | |
| Unemployed or other | 0.39* | 0.16 |
| *Domestic status (Married with children)* | | |
| Married no children | –0.68* | 0.26 |
| Divorced, separated or widowed | –0.43 | 1.53** |
| Cohabiting | | |
| – with children or no children, buying own home | 0.25 | 1.78** |
| – no children, not buying own home | 0.41 | 1.67** |
| – with children or no children, buying own home * sex | –0.01 | –2.09** |

**Table A2.1 Hallucinants life-course model – regression coefficients (BCS)** – *continued*

| | *Past use v never used* | *Recent use v never used* |
|---|---|---|
| Single | | |
| – with children | 0.81** | 1.67** |
| – no children, buying own home | –0.27 | 1.81** |
| – no children, renting | 0.21 | 1.81** |
| – no children, living with parents | –0.68* | 0.77 |
| – no children, buying own home * sex | 0.87* | –0.34 |
| – no children, living with parents * sex | 0.66* | 0.48 |
| Constant | –1.22 | –3.32 |

n = 2,734 ** = $p < 0.01$ * = $p < 0.05$ Psuedo $R^2 = 0.10$

*Note*: non-significant variables were included in the model if they formed part of a statistically significant interaction effect.

**Table A2.2 Hallucinants lifestyle model – regression coefficients (BCS)**

| | *Past use v never used* | *Recent use v never used* |
|---|---|---|
| *Age (27–30 years)* | | |
| 16–17 years | –0.02 | 1.16** |
| 18–22 years | 0.34* | 0.76** |
| 23–26 years | 0.26 | 0.53* |
| *Sex (Male)* | | |
| Female | –0.53** | –0.85** |
| *Ethnicity (White)* | | |
| Black Caribbean, Black African, Indian, Pakistani or Bangladeshi | –0.44 | –1.13* |
| *Health status (Very good)* | | |
| Good | 0.33** | 0.41* |
| Fair to very bad | 0.36 | 0.85** |
| *Social class (Unskilled)* | | |
| Managerial or technical | 0.44** | 0.05 |
| None given | –0.61* | –0.18 |
| *Household income (< £10,000)* | | |
| £30,000 or more | –0.51** | –0.35 |
| £30,000 or more * living w. parents etc | 1.02** | 0.71 |
| *Financial difficulty (Not low-income household)* | | |
| Extreme difficulty | 0.36* | 0.58* |
| *Region (North)* | | |
| East Anglia | –0.93* | 0.23 |
| *Type of neighbourhood (Thriving)* | | |
| Expanding | –0.14 | –1.06** |
| *Community cohesiveness (Go own way)* | | |
| Help each other | –0.12 | –0.80** |
| *Economic status (Working full-time)* | | |
| Student | –0.23 | –0.77* |
| Unemployed or other | 0.45* | 0.20 |
| *Domestic status (Married with children)* | | |
| Married no children | –0.65* | 0.28 |
| Divorced, separated or widowed | –0.65 | 1.13* |
| Cohabiting | | |
| – with children or no children, buying own home | 0.29 | 1.60** |
| – no children, not buying own home | 0.34 | 1.49** |
| – with children or no children, buying own home * sex | –0.20 | –2.06** |

**Table A2.2 Hallucinants lifestyle model – regression coefficients (BCS)** *– continued*

| | *Past use v never used* | *Recent use v never used* |
|---|---|---|
| Single | | |
| – with children | 0.61** | 1.29** |
| – no children, buying own home | –0.12 | 1.05* |
| – no children, renting | –0.09 | 1.16** |
| – no children, living with parents | –0.62* | 0.45 |
| *Pub (No. of evenings during last month)* | | |
| Once or twice a week | –0.11 | 0.53* |
| About three times a week | 0.57** | 0.75** |
| Almost every day | 0.38 | 1.18** |
| *Club (No. of evenings during last month)* | | |
| Less than once a week | 0.14 | 0.49** |
| Once a week or more | 0.31 | 1.03** |
| *Drinking style (Non-drinker)* | | |
| Regular moderate drinker | 0.62* | 0.10 |
| Regular binger | 0.96** | 0.74* |
| Frequent light drinker | 0.52** | 0.13 |
| Frequent moderate drinker | 0.75** | 0.58* |
| Frequent binger | 0.73** | 0.54* |
| Frequent heavy binger | 1.33** | 0.99** |
| Habitual heavy drinker | 0.85** | 0.76* |
| Constant | –1.96 | –4.01 |

n = 2,730 ** = $p < 0.01$ * = $p < 0.05$ Psuedo $R^2 = 0.14$

*Note*: non-significant variables were included in the model if they formed part of a statistically significant interaction effect.

**Table A3.1 Cocaine life-course model – regression coefficients (BCS)**

| | *Past use v never used* | *Recent use v never used* |
|---|---|---|
| *Age (27–30 years)* | | |
| 23–26 years | 0.88** | 0.22 |
| 23–26 years * sex | –1.25* | 0.85 |
| *Sex (Male)* | | |
| Female | –0.40 | –3.30** |
| *Ethnicity (White)* | | |
| Black Caribbean, black African, Indian, Pakistani or Bangladeshi | 0.80 | –2.35* |
| *Financial difficulty (Not low-income household)* | | |
| Extreme difficulty | 0.64* | 0.49 |
| Little difficulty | 1.17* | 0.18 |
| *Region (North)* | | |
| East Anglia | 0.83 | 1.67** |
| South East | 0.36 | 1.14** |
| Greater London | 0.56 | 1.77** |
| *Type of neighbourhood (Thriving)* | | |
| Expanding | –0.70 | –2.12* |
| *Economic status (Working full-time)* | | |
| Other | 0.85* | –0.57 |
| *Domestic status (Married with children)* | | |
| Cohabiting | | |
| – no children, buying own home | 0.43 | 1.96** |
| – no children, not buying own home | 0.83 | 1.72* |
| Single | | |
| – with children | 0.70 | 2.16* |
| – no children, buying own home or renting | 0.44** | 1.84** |
| – no children, living with parents | –0.05* | 0.78 |
| – no children, buying own home or renting * sex | –0.23 | 2.34** |
| – no children, living with parents * sex | 0.06 | 2.95** |
| Constant | –3.87 | –4.99 |

n = 2,788 ** = $p < 0.01$ * = $p < 0.05$ Psuedo $R^2 = 0.14$

*Note*: non-significant variables were included in the model if they formed part of a statistically significant interaction effect.

**Table A3.2 Cocaine lifestyle model – regression coefficients (BCS)**

| | *Past use v never used* | *Recent use v never used* |
|---|---|---|
| *Age (27–30 years)* | | |
| 23–26 years | 0.90** | 0.29 |
| 23–26 years * sex | –1.22* | 0.73 |
| *Sex (Male)* | | |
| Female | –0.27 | –2.82** |
| *Financial difficulty (Not low-income household)* | | |
| Extreme difficulty | 0.66* | 0.66 |
| Little difficulty | 1.22* | 0.36 |
| *Region (North)* | | |
| East Anglia | 1.07* | 2.15** |
| South East | 0.43 | 1.23** |
| Greater London | 0.59 | 1.88** |
| *Type of neighbourhood (Thriving)* | | |
| Expanding | –0.76 | –2.19* |
| *Economic status (Working full-time)* | | |
| Other | 0.85* | –0.56 |
| *Domestic status (Married with children)* | | |
| Cohabiting – no children, buying own home or renting | 0.65 | 1.73** |
| Single | | |
| – with children | 0.67 | 1.92 |
| – no children, buying own home or renting | 0.23 | 1.45* |
| – no children, living with parents | –0.14 | 0.53 |
| – no children, buying own home or renting * sex | 0.30 | 1.94* |
| – no children, living with parents * sex | –0.02 | 2.57** |
| *Pub (No. of evenings during last month)* | | |
| Almost every day | 0.76 | 0.81* |
| *Club (No. of evenings during last month)* | | |
| Once a week or more | 0.28 | 1.05** |
| *Drinking style (Non-drinker)* | | |
| Regular or frequent moderate drinker | 0.03 | 1.17** |
| Frequent binger | 0.04 | 1.22** |
| Frequent heavy binger | 0.99** | 1.54** |
| Habitual light drinker | 0.40 | 1.80** |
| Habitual heavy drinker | 0.96* | 1.21* |
| Constant | –4.24 | –6.27 |

n = 2,783 ** = $p < 0.01$ * = < 0.05 Psuedo $R^2 = 0.18$

*Note*: 1) Non-significant variables were included in the model if they formed part of a significant interaction effect; 2) 'Single with children' was included in the model because it was very close to meeting the criteria for inclusion (p = 0.054 on recent use v never used).

## YLS models

Variables were included in the multivariate models in the following format:

*Preliminary stage*

Inner city

- Lives in inner city area (reference)
- Does not live in inner city area

Number of adults in household (continuous variables)

Others present during the self-completion exercise

- Parent(s) or guardian
- Sibling
- Some other adult
- Some other child
- Someone else

Sample

- Part of core sample (reference)
- Part of booster sample – not high crime area
- Part of booster sample – high crime area

*Stage one: Demographics*

Age

- 16–17 years
- 18–22 years
- 23–26 years
- 27–30 years (reference)

Sex

- Male (reference)
- Female

Age * Sex (interaction terms between age and sex)

Ethnicity

- White (reference)
- Black Caribbean
- Black African
- Indian
- Pakistani or Bangladeshi
- Other

*Note*: Pakistani and Bangladeshi were combined because they contained a small number of cases and because they share a similar religious and socio-economic profile (Modood et al., 1997).

Social class

- Professional
- Intermediate
- Skilled non-manual
- Skilled manual
- Partly skilled
- Unskilled (reference)
- Unclassified

*Note*: respondents were classified according to their current or most recent job.

Parents' social class

- Professional (reference)
- Intermediate
- Skilled non-manual
- Skilled manual
- Partly skilled or unskilled

*Note*: this classification was based on father's or mother's job when the respondent was 15 years old. Where both parents had been working, the highest occupational class was selected. Unskilled was combined with partly skilled because only 31 respondents were included in the former category.

Disposable income

- Less than £20 (reference)
- £20–30
- £31–40
- £41–50
- £51–70
- £71–100
- £101–132
- £133 or more

*Note*: based on the amount of money respondents had to spend each week once they had paid their rent, mortgage or housing costs and bills.

*Stage two: Deprivation area of residence*

To make this stage more manageable variables were entered into the model in two groups. Variables which measured individual or household characteristics were entered before those that measured neighbourhood or area characteristics.

Unemployment

- Currently unemployed (long-term)
- Currently unemployed (not long-term)
- Unemployed in past (long-term) but not now
- Unemployed in past (not long-term) but not now
- Never unemployed (reference)

*Note*: long-term unemployment was defined as that which had lasted for one year or more. Never unemployed refers to those who were not currently unemployed and never had been for more than six months. Respondents who were studying full-time were not asked about past periods of unemployment and were classified as never unemployed.

Qualifications

- Has formal qualifications (reference)
- Does not have formal qualifications

*Note*: respondents who were 16 years of age may not have reached the official school leaving age and were included in the no qualifications category only if they had no qualifications and appeared to have left school.

Financial difficulty

- Not low-income (reference)
- Low-income, no apparent difficulty
- Low-income, slight difficulty
- Low-income, moderate difficulty
- Low-income, extreme difficulty
- Low-income, very extreme difficulty

*Note*: low income was defined as less than £20 a week after rent, mortgage or housing costs and bills. The proportion of young adults in this category was almost identical to the proportion in the BCS living in a household with an annual income of less than £10,000 (25 per cent compared with 26 per cent).

Financial difficulty was assessed on the basis of the number of items that respondents could not afford to buy. Respondents were asked which of the following, if any, they (and the people they live with) have to go without because they cannot afford them: holiday; somewhere larger to live; personal hobby; eating out; video recorder; records, cassettes or CDs; going out; food for themselves; food for their family; clothes for themselves; clothes for their family; a place to live. Excluding items relating to 'their family' (these items were not relevant to everybody) left a total of ten items. Those who had to go without seven or more of the listed items were considered to be in very extreme difficulty; those who had to go without five or six of the listed items were considered to be in extreme difficulty; those who had to go without three or four of the listed items were considered to be in moderate difficulty; those who had to go without one or two of the listed items were considered to be in slight difficulty; and those who did not have to go without any of the listed items were considered to be in no apparent difficulty.

Parental economic activity

- Both parents economically active or single parent and economically active (reference)
- One parent economically active and other had been in the past
- One parent economically active and other never had been
- Neither parent economically active or one parent and not economically active but had been in the past

- Neither parent economically active or one parent and never had been
- Unclassified

Parental unemployment

- Neither parent had been long-term unemployed or single parent and not been long-term unemployed (reference)
- One parent had been long-term unemployed and one had not
- Both parents had been long-term unemployed or single parent and had been long-term unemployed
- Unclassified

*Notes*: 1) Questions about parental economic activity and unemployment asked about the situation when the respondent was 15 years old; (2) In relation to parents, long-term unemployment was defined as that which lasted two years or more; (3) Parental unemployment and parental economic inactivity were closely related to one another and only one of these variables was included per model. Each variable was entered into the model separately and that which was associated with the most powerful model, as indicated by the pseudo $R^2$, was retained.

Region

- North (reference)
- Yorkshire/Humberside
- North West
- East Midlands
- West Midlands
- Wales
- East Anglia
- South East
- South West
- Greater London

Type of neighbourhood

- Thriving (reference)
- Expanding
- Rising
- Settling
- Aspiring
- Striving

*Note*: see note for BCS.

Inner city (already entered in the preliminary stage).

*Stage three: Life-course*

Work status

- Working full-time (reference)
- Working part-time
- Studying

- Looking after the home
- Unemployed
- Other

Domestic circumstances

- Married with children (reference)
- Married, no children
- Separated, divorced or widowed (with or without children)
- Cohabiting with children
- Cohabiting, no children, buying own home
- Cohabiting, no children, not buying own home
- Single with children
- Single, no children, buying own home
- Single, no children, renting
- Single, no children, living with parents

*Note*: as with the BCS, the number of separated, divorced or widowed respondents who did not have children was fairly small (n = 26) and the multivariate models indicated that this position was very similar in its effects to being separated, divorced or widowed with children. As a result, these categories were combined into a single category. The categories 'single, no children, private renting' and 'single, no children, social renting' were also combined into a single category because they were similar in their effects and because the distinction between them was not considered to be crucial.

Domestic * Sex (interaction terms between domestic circumstances and sex)

*Note*: all possible interaction effects between domestic situation and sex were included in the analysis.

*Stage four: Lifestyle*

Religiosity
- Not religious (reference)
- Religious but not actively so
- Actively religious

*Note*: respondents were asked 'what, if any, is your religion or church?' and were given a range of options including Buddhism, Islam, Sikhism, Hinduism, Christianity and none. They were also asked whether they had 'attended a religious service, meeting or some other religious activity' in the last month. Respondents were considered not at all religious if they did not identify with a particular religion; as religious but not actively so if they identified with a particular religion but had not recently attended a service; and as actively religious if they identified with a particular religion and had recently attended a service.

Number of evenings go out

- Every evening (reference)
- About every other evening
- At least once a week

- At least once a fortnight
- At least once a month
- Less than once a month
- Never

Time spent with friends

- Very often (reference)
- Often
- Occasionally
- Rarely
- Never

*Note*: separate questions were asked about time spent with a group of friends and a particular close friend. These measures were strongly associated with one another and only one was included in each model – time spent with a close friend was included in all the models because it was a consistently more powerful predictor than time spent with a group of friends (as indicated by the Psuedo $R^2$).

Street

- Hung around high street, town or city centre during the last month
- Not hung around high street, town or city centre during the last month (reference)

Pub/Club

- Been to a pub and a nightclub, party, dance or disco in the last month
- Been to a nightclub etc but not to a pub in the last month
- Been to a pub but not a nightclub etc in the last month
- Not been to a pub or nightclub etc in the last month (reference)

Drinking style

- Habitual heavy drinker (reference)
- Habitual moderate drinker
- Frequent very heavy binger
- Frequent heavy binger
- Frequent binger
- Frequent moderate drinker
- Regular moderate drinker
- Occasional moderate drinker
- Non-drinker – desister
- Non-drinker – abstainer

*Note*: See main text for details. Non-drinkers – abstainer was initially selected as the reference but did not provide a stable comparison group (the standard errors were large) and was consequently replaced by regular heavy drinkers.

Frequency of drunkenness in the last year

- At least once a week
- Several times a month

- Once or twice a month
- Every couple of months
- Less often
- Not at all (reference)

*Note*: the YLS also included a measure of how frequently respondents had been hungover in the last year. Frequency of drunkenness was used as the preferred measure because it was consistently associated with the most powerful model, as indicated by the Psuedo $R^2$.

Smoking habits

- Moderate to heavy smoker
- Light smoker
- Occasional smoker
- Ex-smoker
- Experimenter
- Abstainer (reference)

*Note*: moderate to heavy smokers smoked every day or more than ten cigarettes a week; light smokers smoked between one and ten cigarettes a week; occasional smokers smoked, but not every week; ex-smokers used to smoke, but do not anymore; experimenters only ever smoked once or twice; and abstainers had never smoked.

Age first drank or smoked

- Less than ten years old (reference)
- 10–13 years old
- 14–15 years old
- 16 years or older/never

*Note*: those who had never drunk or smoked were initially set up as a distinct category, but the models could not estimate the effects associated with this category because no-one in it had ever used cannabis, the hallucinants or cocaine. As a result 'never having smoked or drunk' was combined with the 'first drunk or smoked when 16 years or older' category to form a non-starter/late-starter category.

**Table A4.1 Cannabis life-course model – regression coefficients (YLS)**

| | *Past use v never used* | *Recent use v never used* |
|---|---|---|
| *Age (27–30 years)* | | |
| 16–17 years | –0.42 | 0.49** |
| 18–22 years | 0.09 | 0.74** |
| 23–26 years | 0.13 | 0.30* |
| *Sex (Male)* | | |
| Female | –0.31** | –0.65** |
| *Ethnicity (White)* | | |
| Black Caribbean | –0.92* | –1.08** |
| Black African | –2.46* | –1.37* |
| Indian | –1.32** | –1.98** |
| Pakistani or Bangladeshi | –2.13** | –2.01** |
| Other | –0.41 | –0.66* |
| *Social class (Unskilled)* | | |
| Intermediate | 0.34* | 0.05 |
| *Parents' social class (Professional)* | | |
| Intermediate or skilled non-manual | –0.15 | –0.49* |
| Skilled manual | –0.47 | –0.60** |
| Partly skilled or unskilled | –0.31 | –0.76** |
| Unclassified | –0.23 | –0.61** |
| *Unemployment (Never unemployed)* | | |
| Currently unemployed (long-term) | 0.13 | 0.54* |
| Currently unemployed (not long-term) | 0.16 | 0.55* |
| Unemployed in past (long-term) but not now | 0.27 | 0.49** |
| Unemployed in past (not long term) but not now | 0.43* | 0.29 |
| *Parental unemployment (Neither parent etc)* | | |
| Both parents or single parent long-term unemployed | 0.48* | –0.10 |
| *Financial difficulty (Not low-income household)* | | |
| No apparent difficulty | –0.29 | –0.68** |
| Slight difficulty | –0.63** | –0.45* |
| No information | –0.41 | –0.97* |
| *Region (North)* | | |
| Wales | –0.14 | –0.57** |
| *Type of neighbourhood (Thriving)* | | |
| Rising | 0.26 | 0.47** |
| *Economic status (working full-time)* | | |
| Other | 0.88** | 1.04** |

**Table A4.1 Cannabis life-course model – regression coefficients (YLS)** *– continued*

| | *Past use v never used* | *Recent use v never used* |
|---|---|---|
| *Domestic status (Married with children)* | | |
| Divorced, separated or widowed | 0.10 | 0.76* |
| Cohabiting | | |
| – with children | 0.46* | 0.81** |
| – no children, buying own home | 0.47 | 1.36** |
| – no children, not buying own home | 0.17 | 1.80** |
| Single | | |
| – with children | 0.43* | 1.63** |
| – no children, buying own home | 0.35 | 1.25** |
| – no children, renting | 0.25 | 1.68** |
| – no children, living with parents | –0.31 | 1.11** |
| *Sample (core)* | | |
| Booster – high crime area | 0.31* | 0.34** |
| *Who else was present during the interview* | | |
| Parents/guardians (versus not present) | –0.65** | –0.43** |
| Other adult (versus not present) | 0.06 | 0.40** |
| Other children (versus not present) | –0.11 | –0.42* |
| Constant | –0.66 | –1.22 |

n = 3,422 ** = $p < 0.01$ * = $p < 0.05$ Psuedo $R^2 = 0.10$

**Table A4.2 Cannabis lifestyle model – regression coefficients (YLS)**

| | *Past use v never used* | *Recent use v never used* |
|---|---|---|
| *Age (27–30 years)* | | |
| 16–17 years | –0.74** | –0.10 |
| 18–22 years | 0.05 | 0.50** |
| 23–26 years | 0.16 | 0.40* |
| *Sex (Male)* | | |
| Female | –0.34** | –0.59** |
| *Social class (Unskilled)* | | |
| Partly skilled | –0.40* | –0.02 |
| *Parents' social class (Professional)* | | |
| Intermediate | –0.35 | –0.84** |
| Skilled non-manual | –0.32 | –1.10** |
| Skilled manual | –0.72* | –1.13** |
| Partly skilled or unskilled | –0.59 | –1.20** |
| Unclassified | –0.53 | –1.17** |
| *Qualifications (Got qualifications)* | | |
| No qualifications | –0.44* | –0.51* |
| *Unemployment (Never unemployed)* | | |
| Unemployed in past (not long-term) but not now | 0.41* | 0.29 |
| *Parental unemployment (neither parent etc)* | | |
| Both parents or single parent long-term unemployed | 0.55* | –0.01 |
| *Financial difficulty (Not low-income household)* | | |
| Extreme or very extreme difficulty | 0.51* | 0.58* |
| *Region (North)* | | |
| North West | 0.27 | 0.45* |
| Wales | –0.16 | –0.69** |
| London | 0.30 | 0.39* |
| *Type of neighbourhood (Thriving)* | | |
| Expanding | –0.43* | –0.42* |
| Aspiring | –0.39* | –0.20 |
| *Economic status (Working full-time)* | | |
| Other | 0.90* | 1.21** |
| *Domestic status (Married with children)* | | |
| Cohabiting | | |
| – no children, buying own home | 0.43 | 1.17** |
| – no children, not buying own home | 0.04 | 1.65** |

**Table A4.2 Cannabis lifestyle model – regression coefficients (YLS)** – *continued*

| | *Past use v never used* | *Recent use v never used* |
|---|---|---|
| Single | | |
| – with children | 0.09 | 0.95** |
| – no children, buying own home | 0.20 | 0.86** |
| – no children, renting | 0.00 | 1.20** |
| – no children, living with parents | –0.32 | 0.82** |
| *Street (Not 'hung around' on street in last month)* | | |
| Hung around on street in last month | 0.15 | 0.78** |
| *Religion (Not religious)* | | |
| Religious, active in last month | –0.57** | –0.89** |
| Religious, not active in last month | –0.45** | –0.46** |
| *Time spent with friends (Very often)* | | |
| Occasionally or rarely | –0.18 | –0.34** |
| Never or does not apply | –0.35 | –1.55** |
| *Drinking style (Habitual heavy drinker)* | | |
| Non-drinker (abstainer) | –2.53* | –0.95 |
| Non-drinker (desister) or occasional moderate drinker | –0.09 | –0.65** |
| Regular moderate drinker | –0.15 | –0.87** |
| Frequent moderate drinker | –0.05 | –0.58** |
| Frequent binger or frequent heavy binger | 0.51* | –0.23 |
| *Drunkenness (Not at all in last year)* | | |
| At least once a week | 0.64* | 1.25** |
| Several times a month | 0.59* | 1.41** |
| Once or twice a month | 0.95** | 1.51** |
| Every couple of months | 0.62** | 1.02** |
| Less than once every couple of months | 0.59** | 0.96** |
| *Smoking habits (Abstainer)* | | |
| Moderate to heavy smoker | 2.34** | 3.95** |
| Light smoker | 2.32** | 3.71** |
| Occasional smoker | 2.13** | 3.44** |
| Experimenter | 2.47** | 2.81** |
| Ex-smoker | 1.09** | 1.83** |
| *Age first drank or smoked (Less than 10 years old)* | | |
| 10–13 years old | –0.45 | –0.52* |
| 14–15 years old | –0.86** | –1.30** |
| 16 years or older/never | –1.33** | –1.89** |
| *Who else was present during the interview* | | |
| Parents/guardians (versus not present) | –0.58* | –0.32 |
| Other adult (versus not present) | 0.09 | 0.45* |
| Constant | –1.06 | –2.11 |

n = 3,363 ** = $p < 0.01$ * = $p < 0.05$ Psuedo $R^2 = 0.29$

**Table A5.1 Hallucinants life-course model – regression coefficients (YLS)**

| | *Past use v never used* | *Recent use v never used* |
|---|---|---|
| *Age (27–30 years)* | | |
| 16–17 years | –0.84** | –0.03 |
| 18–22 years | 0.06 | 1.02** |
| 23–26 years | 0.37** | 0.37* |
| 16–17 years * sex | 0.82* | 1.27** |
| 18–22 years * sex | 0.59** | 0.12 |
| *Sex (Male)* | | |
| Female | –0.80** | –1.05** |
| *Ethnicity (White)* | | |
| Black Caribbean | –0.87* | –2.00** |
| Black African, Indian, Pakistani or Bangladeshi | –3.20** | –2.63** |
| Other | –0.75 | –0.75 |
| *Social class (Unskilled)* | | |
| Skilled non–manual | 0.01 | –0.39* |
| Unclassified | –0.40** | –0.54** |
| *Parents' social class (Professional)* | | |
| Skilled manual | –0.32** | –0.03* |
| *Weekly spending money (Less than £20)* | | |
| £51–70 | 0.37* | 0.47* |
| £101–132 | –0.14 | 0.55* |
| *Unemployment (Never unemployed)* | | |
| Currently unemployed (long-term) | 0.33 | 0.88** |
| Currently unemployed (not long-term) | 0.28 | 0.82** |
| Unemployed in past (long-term) but not now | 0.53* | 0.84** |
| Unemployed in past (not long-term) but not now | 0.51* | 0.36 |
| *Parental unemployment (Neither parent etc)* | | |
| One parent long-term unemployed and one not | 0.14 | 0.56** |
| *Financial difficulty (Not low-income)* | | |
| No apparent difficulty | –0.64* | –0.17 |
| Extreme or very extreme difficulty | 0.43* | –0.22 |
| No information | –1.22** | –1.29* |
| *Region (North)* | | |
| North West | 0.20 | 0.37* |
| East Anglia | –0.58* | 0.20 |
| *Economic status (Working full-time)* | | |
| Other | 0.80** | 0.85** |

**Table A5.1 Hallucinants life-course model – regression coefficients (YLS)** *– continued*

| | *Past use v never used* | *Recent use v never used* |
|---|---|---|
| *Domestic status (Married with children)* | | |
| Divorced, separated or widowed | 0.13 | 1.57** |
| Cohabiting | | |
| – with children | 0.32 | 1.00* |
| – no children, buying own home | 0.18 | 1.72** |
| – no children, not buying own home | 0.67* | 2.30** |
| Single | | |
| – with children | 0.39 | 2.37** |
| – no children, buying own home | 0.16 | 1.77** |
| – no children, renting | 0.14 | 2.12** |
| – no children, living with parents | –0.26 | 1.58** |
| *Sample (core)* | | |
| Booster – high crime area | 0.27* | 0.23** |
| *Who else was present during the interview* | | |
| Parents/guardians (versus not present) | –0.41 | –0.46** |
| Constant | –0.85 | -3.25 |

n = 3,426 ** = $p < 0.01$ * = < 0.05 Psuedo $R^2 = 0.12$

*Note*: the ethnic 'other' category has been included in the model even though it was not statistically significant because it had a sizeable effect; because excluding it would have masked some of the other effects associated with minority groups; and because it was close to the cut-off point for significance (for past use versus never used $p = 0.06$ and for recent use versus never used $p = 0.10$).

**Table A5.2 Hallucinants lifestyle model – regression coefficients (YLS)**

| | *Past use v never used* | *Recent use v never used* |
|---|---|---|
| *Age (27–30 years)* | | |
| 16–17 years | –1.45** | –0.82* |
| 18–22 years | –0.25 | 0.52 |
| 23–26 years | 0.11 | –0.02 |
| 16–17 years * sex | 0.90* | 1.30** |
| 18–22 years * sex | 0.74** | 0.40 |
| 23–26 years * sex | 0.48 | 0.80* |
| *Sex (Male)* | | |
| Female | –0.88** | –1.16** |
| *Ethnicity (White)* | | |
| Black Caribbean, Black African, Indian, Pakistani or Bangladeshi | –1.04** | –1.32* |
| *Social class (Unskilled)* | | |
| Professional | –0.86* | –1.02 |
| Skilled non-manual | 0.06 | –0.40* |
| Unclassified | –0.35* | –0.41* |
| *Parents' social class (Professional)* | | |
| Skilled manual | –0.33** | –0.07 |
| *Unemployment (Never unemployed)* | | |
| Currently unemployed (long-term) | 0.55 | 0.95** |
| Currently unemployed (not long-term) | 0.31 | 0.63* |
| Unemployed in past (long-term) but not now | 0.43* | 0.77** |
| Unemployed in past (not long-term) but not now | 0.59** | 0.60* |
| *Parental unemployment (Neither parent etc)* | | |
| One parent long-term unemployed and one not | 0.14 | 0.57** |
| *Financial difficulty (Not low-income household)* | | |
| Very extreme difficulty | 0.73* | 0.36 |
| No information | –1.18** | –1.20 |
| *Region (North)* | | |
| North West | 0.28 | 0.54** |
| East Anglia | –0.73** | –0.03 |
| *Economic status (Working full-time)* | | |
| Other | 0.80* | 0.86* |
| *Domestic status (Married with children)* | | |
| Cohabiting | | |
| – no children, homeowner | 0.01 | 0.98* |
| – no children, not homeowner | 0.52 | 1.61** |

**Table A5.2 Hallucinants lifestyle model – regression coefficients (YLS)** – *continued*

| | *Past use v never used* | *Recent use v never used* |
|---|---|---|
| Single | | |
| – with children | 0.16 | 1.41** |
| – no children, buying own home | –0.09 | 0.94** |
| – no children, renting | –0.21 | 1.05** |
| – no children, living with parents | –0.48** | 0.67* |
| *Street (Not 'hung around' on street in last month)* | | |
| Hung around on street in last month | 0.36 | 0.44* |
| *Religion (Not religious)* | | |
| Religious, active in last month | –0.43* | –0.93* |
| *Time spent with friends (Very often)* | | |
| Occasionally | –0.15 | –0.36* |
| Never or does not apply | –0.49 | –1.88** |
| *Pub/club (Not been to pub or club in last month)* | | |
| Been to pub and club in last month | 0.18 | 0.46** |
| *Drinking style (Habitual heavy drinker)* | | |
| Non-drinker (abstainer or desister) | –1.01* | 0.29 |
| Occasional or regular moderate drinker | –0.20 | –0.57** |
| Frequent moderate drinker | –0.22 | –0.53** |
| *Drunkenness (Not at all in last year)* | | |
| At least once a week | 0.51* | 1.64** |
| Several times a month | 1.28** | 1.63** |
| Once or twice a month | 0.81** | 1.57** |
| Every couple of months | 0.45* | 0.95** |
| Less than once every couple of months | 0.31 | 0.70** |
| *Smoking habits (Abstainer)* | | |
| Moderate to heavy smoker | 1.31** | 1.75** |
| Light smoker | 1.38** | 1.51** |
| Occasional smoker | 1.07** | 1.14** |
| Ex-smoker | 1.09* | 0.56* |
| *Age first drank or smoked (Less than 10 years old)* | | |
| 14–15 years old | –0.52** | –0.82** |
| 16 years or older/never | –1.24** | –1.68** |
| Constant | –1.16 | –3.39 |

n = 3,372 ** = $p < 0.01$ * = < 0.05 Psuedo $R^2 = 0.25$

*Note*: non-significant variables have been included in the model if they were part of a significant interaction effect.

**Table A6.1 Cocaine life-course model – regression coefficients (YLS)**

| | *Past use v never used* | *Recent use v never used* |
|---|---|---|
| *Age (27–30 years)* | | |
| 16–17 years | –1.08 | –1.40* |
| 18–22 years | –0.27 | 0.67** |
| 16–17 years * sex | –0.82 | 2.14** |
| *Sex (Male)* | | |
| Female | –0.59* | –1.14** |
| *Ethnicity (White)* | | |
| Black Caribbean, Black African, Indian, Pakistani or Bangladeshi | –1.18* | –2.89** |
| *Parents' social class (Professional)* | | |
| Skilled non manual or skilled manual | –0.42* | –0.14 |
| *Qualifications (Got qualifications)* | | |
| No qualifications | –0.10 | 0.64* |
| *Unemployment (Never unemployed)* | | |
| Currently unemployed (long-term) | 1.25** | 0.69 |
| Unemployed in past (long-term) but not now | 0.58 | 0.94** |
| Unemployed in past (not long-term) but not now | 0.46 | 0.66* |
| *Parental economic activity (Both parents active etc)* | | |
| One parent economically active and other had been in the past | 0.96** | –0.12 |
| One parent economically active and other never had been | 0.34 | –0.69* |
| *Region (North)* | | |
| North West | 0.58 | 1.14** |
| East Anglia | 0.81* | 1.22** |
| South East | 0.56* | 0.47 |
| London | 0.89** | 1.46** |
| *Type of neighbourhood (Thriving)* | | |
| Rising | 0.03 | 0.77** |
| *Economic status (Working full-time)* | | |
| Student | –0.42 | –0.63* |
| *Domestic status (Married with children)* | | |
| Cohabiting | | |
| – no children, buying own home | 0.14 | 1.76** |
| – no children, not buying own home | 0.93 | 1.68** |

**Table A6.1 Cocaine life-course model – regression coefficients (YLS)** – *continued*

| | *Past use v never used* | *Recent use v never used* |
|---|---|---|
| Single | | |
| – with children | 2.07** | 2.19** |
| – no children, buying own home | 0.94* | 1.09 |
| – no children, renting | 0.49 | 2.22** |
| – no children, living with parents | 0.56 | 1.84** |
| – with children * sex | –1.29* | –0.76 |
| – no children, buying own home * sex | –0.56 | 1.46* |
| *Who else was present during the interview* | | |
| Parents/guardians (versus not present) | –1.07* | –1.42** |
| Constant | –3.51 | –4.81 |

n = 3,443 ** = $p < 0.01$ * = $p < 0.05$ Psuedo $R^2 = 0.15$

**Table A6.2 Cocaine lifestyle model – regression coefficients (YLS)**

| | *Past use v never used* | *Recent use v never used* |
|---|---|---|
| *Age (27–30 years)* | | |
| 16–17 years | –2.03** | –2.05** |
| 18–22 years | –0.66* | 0.19 |
| 16–17 years * sex | –0.61 | 1.75* |
| *Sex (Male)* | | |
| Female | –0.58** | –0.81** |
| *Ethnicity (White)* | | |
| Other | 0.13 | 1.20* |
| *Unemployment (Never unemployed)* | | |
| Unemployed (long-term) | 1.31** | 0.74* |
| Unemployed in past (long-term or not) but not now | 0.39 | 0.38** |
| *Parental economic activity (Both parents active etc)* | | |
| One parent economically active and other had been in past | 0.79** | 0.04 |
| *Region (North)* | | |
| North West | 0.45 | 1.11** |
| London | 0.85** | 1.65** |
| *Domestic status (Married with children)* | | |
| Cohabiting | | |
| – no children, buying own home | –0.11 | 1.58** |
| – no children, not buying own home | 0.54 | 1.47* |
| Single | | |
| – with children | 0.80* | 1.11* |
| – no children, buying own home | 0.74 | 1.46** |
| – no children, renting | 0.14 | 1.64** |
| – no children, living with parents | 0.34 | 1.32** |
| *Street (Not 'hung around' on street in last month)* | | |
| Hung around on street in last month | 0.66 | 0.62* |
| *Religion (Not religious)* | | |
| Religious, active in last month | –0.12 | –1.48* |
| *Time spent with friends (Very often)* | | |
| Rarely, never or does not apply | –0.42 | –1.73** |
| *Drinking style (Habitual heavy drinker)* | | |
| Occasional moderate drinker | –0.24 | –1.52** |
| Regular moderate drinker | –1.12* | –1.00* |

**Table A6.2 Cocaine lifestyle model – regression coefficients (YLS)** – *continued*

| | *Past use v never used* | *Recent use v never used* |
|---|---|---|
| *Drunkenness (Not at all in last year)* | | |
| At least once a week | 0.73* | 1.46** |
| Several times a month | 0.79* | 1.21** |
| Once or twice a month | 0.89** | 1.09** |
| Every couple of months | 0.39 | 0.75* |
| *Smoking habits (Abstainer)* | | |
| Moderate to heavy smoker | 1.65** | 1.69** |
| Light smoker | 0.95 | 1.33** |
| Occasional smoker | 1.66** | 1.38** |
| Ex-smoker | 1.49** | 0.12 |
| *Age first drank or smoked (Less than 10 years old)* | | |
| 14–15 years old | –0.26 | –0.77** |
| 16 years or older/never | –1.03** | –1.45** |
| *Who else was present during the interview* | | |
| Parents/guardians (versus not present) | –0.92 | –1.45** |
| Constant | –4.35 | –5.44 |

n = 3,386 ** = p < 0.01 * = < 0.05 Psuedo $R^2$ = 0.25

# Notes

## Chapter 1

1 This is a good point at which to discuss my own terminology. I have used 'late industrial' and 'late modern' interchangeably to describe the distinct social arrangements that came to characterise many of the world's advanced capitalist economies during the second half of the twentieth century: arrangements that were driven by the restructuring of the global economy and the collapse of the traditional manufacturing base in what is sometimes described as the 'economic north'. The nature of the late industrial or late modern condition has been discussed at length elsewhere (see Garland, 2001; Reiner, 2000; Young, 1999) and will be considered at several points in the following chapters. Although similar in their meaning 'late industrial' and 'late modern' carry different connotations and my preference is for the former: the term 'late industrial' has the advantage that it places the focus firmly on patterns of social organisation (albeit ones that exist at a certain juncture of time and place) rather than on time. 'Modernity', and by implication late modernity, are often thought of as a project – that is, as a distinct set of aims, beliefs and methods – but the term still retains inevitable connotations of recency. Such connotations are particularly problematic given the historic dimensions of the analysis presented in this book. History, after all, attaches no particular significance to the present, seeing it as little more than the past in waiting.

2 The detailed survey analysis is based on the 1998 British Crime Survey and the 1998/9 Youth Lifestyles Survey, with some additional use of further sweeps of the British Crime Survey. The full bibliographic references are as follows:

Home Office Crime and Criminal Justice Unit, Office of Population Censuses and Surveys Social Survey Division, British Crime Survey, 1994 [computer file]. Colchester, Essex: The Data Archive [distributor], 4 November 1996. SN: 3591.

Home Office Research and Statistics Directorate, Social and Community Planning Research, British Crime Survey, 1996 [computer file]. Colchester, Essex: The Data Archive [distributor], 16 June 1998. SN: 3832.

Home Office Research and Statistics Directorate and Social and Community Planning Research, British Crime Survey, 1998 [computer file]. London: Research, Development and Statistics Directorate [distributor], November 1999.

Home Office Crime and Criminal Justice Unit and Social and Community Planning Research, Youth Lifestyles Survey, 1998–1999 [computer file]. London: Research, Development and Statistics Directorate [distributor], October 1999.

Home Office Research, Development and Statistics Directorate and BMRB. Social Research, British Crime Survey, 2002–2003 [computer file]. 6th Edition. Colchester, Essex: UK Data Archive [distributor], October 2007. SN: 5059.

Home Office Research, Development and Statistics Directorate and BMRB. Social Research, British Crime Survey, 2006–2007 [computer file]. 4th Edition. Colchester, Essex: UK Data Archive [distributor], March 2008. SN: 5755.

3 The terms problem drug use and recreational drug use help to distinguish between different patterns of use even though the distinction between them may be blurred. Recreational drug use describes that which is geared towards pleasure or leisure and is often used to denote the use of ecstasy and other 'dance' drugs. Problem use is that which results in social, psychological, physical or legal problems due to intoxication, regular excessive consumption or dependence (Lloyd, 1998). This term tends to be used in connection to the most harmful drugs, particularly heroin and crack cocaine.

4 The term hallucinant refers to hallucinogens and stimulants, including amphetamines, ecstasy, LSD, magic mushrooms and amyl nitrate (Ramsay and Percy, 1996).

## Chapter 2

1 The term marihuana or marijuana is generally used in the United States to describe what is known as cannabis in Britain and elsewhere. My preferred term is cannabis though I have used the term marihuana when this has been used by other authors, whose work I am describing.

2 Harm reduction describes an approach to working with drug users that focuses on minimising the potential for harm rather than on eradicating use. Such an approach was endorsed in Britain by the Advisory Council on the Misuse of Drugs (1984) and provides the basis for some 'treatment' interventions such as the provision of clean injecting equipment.

3 The 1992/3 YLS was based on paper aided personal interviewing (PAPI), while the 1998/9 survey was based on computer aided self-completion interviewing (CASI). This presents a problem if comparisons are to be made as CASI is generally considered to elicit higher rates of disclosure. In order for trends to be assessed, 804 respondents to the 1998/9 survey were given the same paper questionnaire that was used in 1992/3. These comparisons confirmed that offending behaviour was generally disclosed at a higher rate by CASI respondents. Unfortunately, drug use was excluded from the analysis which compared results from the two surveys based on the PAPI responses (Stratford and Roth, 1999; Flood-Page et al., 2000).

## Chapter 3

1 Prime Minister Gordon Brown announced his intention to return cannabis to Class B in 2008 against the advice of the relevant advisory bodies and in a move that was widely interpreted as an example of political posturing (*The Guardian*, May 8 2008). Reclassification to Class B came into force in January 2009 (http://www.homeoffice.gov.uk/).

2 With reclassification, powers of arrest and imprisonment were retained for cannabis possession offences, though there was to be a presumption against arrest in favour of street warnings and the maximum penalty was reduced from five to two years custody. The maximum penalty for supplying Class C drugs, by contrast, was increased from five to 14 years imprisonment,

which meant, in effect, that the penalty for supplying cannabis remained unchanged (Trace et al., 2004; May et al., 2007).

3 The Independent Inquiry explicitly stated that alcohol and tobacco could reasonably be placed in Class A and B respectively. This view was endorsed by the second group of experts despite some reservations about the efficacy of a class based system (Nutt et al., 2007). The results from this group were said not to justify the existing three-class system because they did not reveal any obvious discontinuities. There was the hint of a transition, however, which led the authors to suggest that if the three-way classification is to be retained, one possible interpretation is that drugs with harm scores equal to that of alcohol and above might be Class A, cannabis and those below might be Class C, and drugs in between might be Class B. On this basis alcohol and tobacco would have harm ratings comparable with Class A and B drugs respectively.

4 The harmfulness of cocaine depends in part on the form in which it is used. Freebase cocaine or 'crack' poses greater risks of physical harm than powder cocaine and has a greater dependence potential, which is reflected in the involvement of crack users in drug-related crime (Best et al., 2001; Bennett and Holloway, 2005).

5 Unless otherwise stated the 'average' refers to the median, which has been used as the preferred measure of central tendency where there is evidence of a departure from the Normal distribution.

6 The number of respondents who had used heroin, methadone or crack was insufficient for meaningful analysis and these substances were excluded from that presented here.

7 Each pair of correlations from the 1998 BCS was compared to its equivalent from the YLS and the remaining sweeps of the BCS included in the analysis (i.e. 1994, 2003/4 and 2006/7). The sum of the absolute differences was divided by the number of pairs to produce an average (mean) difference. This figure indicated that the average difference from the 1998 BCS lay in the range of 0.04 to 0.06 for each of the other surveys. Unless otherwise stated the figures cited throughout this chapter are based on the 1998 BCS and 1998/9 YLS.

8 Ecstasy provided the only slight exception to this general rule as the 1998/9 YLS indicated it was most strongly associated with cocaine, though the 1998 BCS indicated it was most strongly associated with LSD.

9 The proportion of cocaine users who had also used crack remained fairly stable at 10 per cent in 1994, 13 per cent in 1998 (15 per cent according to the YLS), 13 per cent in 2002/3 and 11 per cent in 2006/7.

10 Analyses relating to age of first use were based exclusively on the YLS because the relevant information was not contained in the BCS. Given suggestions that drug use is starting at an ever younger age, these analyses were based on the full age range included in the YLS (i.e. 12–30 years old). Less than 10 per cent of users fell into the 12–15 age band, however, and their inclusion made very little difference to the results. For ten of the 13 specific substances, the median age of first use was the same regardless of whether it was estimated on the basis of 12–30 year olds or 16–30 year olds. In the three remaining cases the figures were one year apart. It should also be noted that inclusion of older respondents made little difference to the results.

For ten of the specific substances, analyses based on 16–30 year olds and 16–22 year olds produced estimates that were within a year of one another and for the remaining case figures were two years apart. Moreover, in 11 cases the estimate based on one of these age-ranges was included in the 95 per cent confidence interval for the estimate based on the other.

11 Substances were generally only grouped together when there were no statistically significant differences between them. The only exception to this related to cocaine and crack. While cocaine tended to be used significantly earlier than crack (on average by 1.5 years), neither of these substances was first used significantly earlier than either heroin or methadone. Consequently, all of these substances were grouped together. Where substances have been grouped, the values given in Figure 3.1 represent the average (mean) of the individual comparisons. Gaps between the age of first use for all of the drugs shown here were assessed on the basis of a non-parametric test (Wilcoxon matched pairs) as, for most comparisons, there was evidence of significant departure from the Normal distribution. In illustrating these gaps, however, the mean, and not the median, has been used because of the particular difficulties associated with constructing confidence intervals for the difference between medians (Altman, 1991).

12 Although solvents were most closely associated with LSD this association was relatively weak (0.18 according to the BCS and 0.17 according to the YLS).

13 Young adults who had taken illicit drugs were included in the analysis because they were crucial in establishing the degree to which various considerations acted as a deterrent. Illicit drug users may be viewed as those for whom deterrents have proved ineffective.

## Chapter 4

1 The BCS and YLS both indicated that parental occupational class was, at most, only weakly associated with cannabis use or cocaine use (Cramer's V was no greater than 0.10) and was not significantly associated with hallucinant use ($p > 0.05$).

2 Recent estimates based on surveys of users throughout the United Kingdom, indicate that cannabis costs between £10 to £20 an eighth depending on the type, amphetamines cost approximately £9 a gram, ecstasy costs approximately £3 per tab and cocaine cost approximately £43 a gram (see http://www.idmu.co.uk/).

3 Regardless of whether young adults were living independently or with parents, the BCS indicated that household income was only weakly associated with cannabis use and hallucinant use (Kendall's tau was no greater than 0.13) and was not significantly associated with cocaine use ($p > 0.05$). The YLS also indicated that disposable income was only weakly associated with each of these categories of drug use (Kendall's tau was no greater than 0.07).

4 Multivariate models were respecified with 'used in the last year' as the reference category. By directly comparing the probability of past use with the probability of recent use these models indicated the effect of sex – as well as the other independent variables – on desistance. The models based on both surveys indicated that being female increased the probability of desistance in

relation to cannabis but not the hallucinants. The situation regarding cocaine was less clear cut: the BCS indicated that being female significantly increased the probability of desistance, but the YLS revealed no such effect.

5 A logistic regression model was specified with drug use as the dependent variable and age and sex as the independent variables. An interaction term was included between the independent variables, which showed that the effects of sex did not vary significantly by age or vice versa. Young people aged 16 to 19 years were excluded from the analysis because rates of drug use do not peak until the late teens or early twenties. Excluding those below 20 years of age helped to separate out cohort effects from age effects, though it had very little impact on the results of the analysis.

6 Religiosity continued to reduce the probability of drug use even when young adults from black and minority ethnic groups were excluded from the models. Indeed, the effects of religiosity in these respecified models were not significantly different from the effects contained in the original models based on all young adults.

7 Actively religious young adults abstained from drinking alcohol in much larger numbers than those who were not at all religious (13 per cent compared with one per cent) and considerably fewer of them had been 'very drunk' in the last year (56 per cent compared with 76 per cent). Actively religious young adults also abstained from smoking in much larger numbers than those who were not at all religious (29 per cent compared with 15 per cent) and considerably fewer of them smoked on a daily basis or thereabouts (18 per cent compared with 40 per cent). $p < 0.01$ (drinking style by religiosity; frequency of drunkeness by religiosity; and smoking habits by religiosity).

8 The YLS included a range of potential risk factors and has been used to examine drug use among vulnerable young people (Goulden and Sondhi, 2001). These indicators were not included in the analysis described here because they are not suited to multivariate procedures – the number of respondents affected was relatively small, with the result that it is not always possible to control for other, potentially confounding, factors (Goulden and Sondhi, 2001). There was also an issue of consistency because the BCS did not include comparable indicators.

9 Respondents were considered to be otherwise marginalised from the labour market if they were not studying full-time, were not working full-time or part-time and were not looking after the home or family. They were, in the main, on a government Youth Training Scheme, classified as long-term or permanently sick or disabled or studying part-time.

## Chapter 5

1 Clinically, binge drinking refers to continuous drinking over a day or more to the point of unconsciousness, but the term is now used more generally to describe heavy drinking sessions. The amount of alcohol involved is a matter of debate though British studies tend to define binge drinkers as men who consume at least eight units and women at least six units in a day. This definition has been challenged by some commentators who favour subjective approaches which define binge drinking as that resulting in at least partial drunkenness (Institute of Alcohol Studies, 2005).

2 Based largely on comparisons with commercial sales figures it has long been suspected that self-report measures routinely underestimate the amount people drink. While the possibility of under-reporting remains, recent international studies have concluded that the self-report methodology provides a reasonably reliable measure of alcohol consumption both within the general population and among adolescents (Gruenewald and Johnson, 2006).

3 Current Department of Health (1995) advice is that men who consistently drink four or more units of alcohol a day and women who consistently drink three or more units a day face progressive health risks. According to previous guidance, drinking less than 21 units of alcohol per week for men and 14 units per week for women is unlikely to damage health.

4 Weekly totals were estimated by multiplying the number of drinks consumed per drinking day by the number of days that alcohol was usually consumed.

5 According to the BCS, Kendall's tau = 0.25 for cannabis use by drinking style, 0.18 for hallucinant use by drinking style and 0.04 for cocaine use by drinking style. The YLS produced similar figures for cannabis and the hallucinants, at 0.26 and 0.22 respectively, but suggested a stronger relationship with cocaine use (0.11). The association between frequency of drunkenness and illicit drug use was 0.32 for cannabis, 0.27 for the hallucinants and 0.11 for cocaine. $p < 0.01$ in all cases.

6 The frequency with which people get drunk implies a certain drinking style and these variables were fairly strongly associated with one another (Kendall's tau = 0.46, $p < 0.01$), which meant considerable care was required when entering them into the models. For each category of drug use two models were developed – one which included drinking style and drunkenness as separate variables and one which combined them into a single variable. The Pseudo $R^2$ statistic indicated that for each category of drug use the two models were virtually identical. Where both variables were included separately the models were able to isolate the effects associated with each and provided robust estimates of the effects (the standard errors were not particularly large). These models were preferred on the grounds that the effects of drinking style could be compared to the effects of drunkenness.

7 Information on smoking habits was provided by the YLS, but not the BCS. According to the YLS Kendall's tau = 0.44 (cannabis use by smoking habits); 0.33 (hallucinants by smoking habits); and 0.12 (cocaine by smoking habits). $p < 0.01$ in all cases.

8 This analysis was based on the age at which respondents said they first tried alcohol, tobacco and illicit drugs. Statistical tests revealed no significant differences between the reported age at which young adults started to drink and smoke, but did reveal significant differences between the age at which they first drank or smoked and the age at which they first tried illicit drugs. None of the young adults included in the survey had used drugs without also smoking or drinking and the vast majority (88 per cent) were older when they first tried drugs than when they had their first proper alcoholic drink or first tried smoking. Slightly less than one-in-ten (eight per cent) started to drink and/or smoke at the same age that they first tried drugs, which left a very small proportion (two per cent) who used drugs before they tried drinking and/or smoking.

9 The vast majority of young adults had their first 'proper' alcoholic drink and/or first tried smoking when they were between 10 and 15 years old: slightly more than one-in-three had done so when they were 10 to 13 and a similar proportion had done so when they were 14 or 15. This left fewer than one-in-ten who drank and/or smoked before their 10th birthday and approximately one-in-five who did not drink or smoke until after their 15th birthday. A very small proportion (two per cent) had abstained from both drinking and smoking.

10 Kendall's tau = 0.13 (drinking style by smoking habits); 0.18 (drunkenness by smoking habits); 0.16 (drinking style by age at which first drank and/or smoked); 0.19 (drunkenness by age at which first drank and/or smoked); and 0.28 (smoking by age at which first drank and/or smoked). In all cases, $p < .01$.

11 Kendall's tau = 0.15 (cannabis use by time spent with a close friend); 0.10 (hallucinant use by time spent with a close friend); and 0.07 (cocaine use by time spent with a close friend). $P < 0.01$ in all cases. Very similar figures were produced in relation to time spent with a group of friends.

12 Cramer's V = 0.15, $p < .01$ (cannabis use by hanging around on the street); 0.08, $p < .01$ (hallucinant use by hanging around on the street); and 0.08, $p < .05$ (cocaine use by hanging around on the street).

## Chapter 6

1 According to the BCS, Kendall's tau = 0.47 (marital status by parental status); 0.53 (marital status by housing status); and 0.41 (parental status by housing status). According to the YLS, Kendall's tau = 0.46 (marital status by parental status); 0.48 (marital status by housing status); and 0.41 (parental status by housing status). $P < .01$ in all cases.

2 All things being equal, the BCS indicated that recent cannabis use and recent hallucinant use were most likely among 16 to 17 year olds, while the YLS indicated that they were most likely among 18 to 22 year olds. This apparent discrepancy was linked to the influence of lifestyle indicators, however, and was largely an artefact of the modelling process. The BCS indicated that being 16 or 17 years old substantially increased the probability of recent cannabis use and recent hallucinant use only when lifestyle indicators had been added to the models, which is notable because those in this age group spent relatively few evenings in the pub and tended to be concentrated among non-drinkers and occasional drinkers. Thus, the BCS models indicate that recent cannabis use and recent hallucinant use are more prevalent among 16 and 17 year olds than we would expect based on their drinking styles and time spent in pubs. The YLS produced a different set of results because the influence of drinking style and use of pubs was largely eclipsed by the frequency of drunkenness. Despite their more moderate drinking style, 16 and 17 year olds got drunk fairly frequently and the rates of drug use they reported were broadly consistent with the frequency with which they got drunk.

3 The multivariate models generally showed that the effect of being a student, looking after the home or working part-time was not significantly different from that of working full-time. There was some suggestion from the YLS that being a student reduced the probability of cocaine use but this effect ceased

to be significant once lifestyle factors had been taken into account (see Technical Appendix for details).

4 In most of the life-course and lifestyle models being single with children did not have a significantly different effect on recent use from being a single home owner or being single and living independently in rented accommodation. The only models where this was not the case were the BCS cannabis models. In all models, being a single home owner did not have a significantly different effect from being single and living independently in rented accommodation.

5 For all the claims that have been made about the normalisation of drug use and the closing of the gender gap, the *North West Cohort Study* actually found that differences between the sexes began to emerge as members of the cohort entered early adulthood (Parker et al., 1998; Williams and Parker, 2001). At 14 and 15 years of age the proportion of males and females who had used illicit drugs in the last month was very similar, but notable differences began to emerge thereafter. At 18 years of age, 45 per cent of males and 28 per cent of females had used drugs in the last month and at 22 years of age 39 per cent and 25 per cent had done so respectively.

6 The Licensing Act 2003 makes it a criminal offence to sell alcohol to anyone below the age of 18 years or to allow an unaccompanied child under 16 years to be on premises that are exclusively or primarily used for the supply of alcohol for consumption on site. In practice many clubs and pubs pursue a policy of not admitting anybody below the age of 18 years.

7 These differences persisted even when the influence of age was taken into account. Almost all the lifestyle indicators included in the analysis were significantly linked to domestic circumstances among 18 to 22 year olds, 23 to 26 year olds and 27 to 30 year olds. Although such links were less evident among 16 to 17 year olds, this is unsurprising given that the vast majority were single, childless and living with their parents.

## Chapter 7

1 Economic motives have been heavily implicated in rising crime rates and considerable emphasis has been placed on the way in which widening social divisions and new forms of social exclusion have fuelled recent trends (Young, 1999; Reiner, 2007; Garland, 2001). Although economic motives are most obviously applicable to acquisitive offences, deprivation and social exclusion have been linked to the dramatic increase in problematic drug use since the early 1980s (ACMD, 1998; Seddon, 2005). These factors have a much weaker relationship with recreational drug use, however, and have a much more limited role in explaining related trends.

# References

D. Abdulrahim (1998) 'Power, Culture and the Hard to Reach', in R. Barbour and G. Huby (eds) *The Social Construction of Post Aids Knowledge* (London: Routledge).

M.A. Abrams (1959) *The Teenage Consumer* (London: London Press Exchange).

E.M. Adlaf, P. Begin and E. Sawka (2005) *Canadian Addiction Survey (CAS): A National Survey of Canadians' Use of Alcohol and Other Drugs: Prevalence of Use and Related Harms: Detailed Report* (Ottawa: Canadian Centre on Substance Abuse).

Advisory Council on the Misuse of Drugs (ACMD) (1984) *Prevention* (London: HMSO).

Advisory Council on the Misuse of Drugs (ACMD) (1998) *Drug Misuse and the Environment* (London: The Stationary Office).

Advisory Council on the Misuse of Drugs (ACMD) (2000) *Reducing Drug Related Deaths* (London: The Stationary Office).

Advisory Council on the Misuse of Drugs (ACMD) (2002) *The Classification of Cannabis Under the Misuse of Drugs Act 1971* (London: Home Office).

Alcohol Concern (2003) *Binge Drinking*, Factsheet 20 (London: Alcohol Concern).

D.G. Altman (1991) *Practical Statistics for Medical Research* (London: Chapman and Hall).

J.J. Arnett (2004) *Emerging Adulthood: The Winding Road Through the Late Teens to the Twenties* (Oxford and New York: Oxford University Press).

R. Aust and N. Smith (2003) *Ethnicity and Drug Use: Key Findings from the 2001/2002 British Crime Survey* (London: Home Office).

J.G. Bachman, P.M. O'Malley and L.D. Johnston (1984) 'Drug Use Among Young Adults: The Impacts of Role Status and Social Environments', *Journal of Personality and Social Psychology*, 47: 629–45.

J.G. Bachman, K.N. Wadsworth, P.M. O'Malley, L.D. Johnston and J.E. Schulenberg (1997) *Smoking, Drinking, and Drug Use in Young Adulthood: The Impacts of New Freedoms and New Responsibilities* (Mahwah, NJ: Lawrence Erlbaum Associates).

J.G. Bachman, P.M. O'Malley, J.E. Schulenberg, L.D. Johnston, A.L. Bryant and A.C. Merline (2002) *The Decline of Substance Use in Young Adulthood: Changes in Social Activities, Roles, and Beliefs* (Mahwah, NJ: Lawrence Erlbaum Associates).

S.L. Bailey (1992) 'Adolescents' Multisubstance Use Patterns: The Role of Heavy Alcohol and Cigarette Use', *American Journal of Public Health*, 82(9): 1220–4.

A. Barton (2003) *Illicit Drugs: Use and Control* (London: Routledge).

A. Bauman and P. Phongsavan (1999) 'Epidemiology of Substance Use in Adolescence: Prevalence, Trends and Policy Implications', *Drug and Alcohol Dependence*, 55(3): 187–207.

P. Bean (2002) *Drugs and Crime* (Cullompton, Devon: Willan).

U. Beck (1992) *Risk Society: Towards a New Modernity* (London: Sage).

U. Beck (1997) *The Reinvention of Politics: Rethinking Modernity in the Global Social Order* (Cambridge: Polity Press).

H.S. Becker (1955) 'Marihuana Use and Social Control', *Social Problems*, 3: 35–44.

H.S. Becker (1963) *Outsiders: Studies in the Sociology of Deviance* (New York: The Free Press).

T. Bennett and K. Holloway (2005) *Understanding Drugs, Alcohol and Crime* (Maidenhead: Open University).

D. Best, L. Vingoe and J. Strang (2001) *Dangerousness of Drugs* (London: National Addiction Centre/Department of Health).

H.L. Binnie and G. Murdock (1969) 'The Attitudes to Drugs and Drugtakers of Students of the University and Colleges of Higher Education in an English Midland City', University of Leicester, *Vaughan Papers*, 14: 1–29.

S. Blackman (2004) *Chilling Out: The Cultural Politics of Substance Consumption, Youth and Drug Policy* (Maidenhead: Open University Press).

D. Blaze-Temple and S.K. Lo (1992) 'Stages of Drug Use: A Community Survey of Perth Teenagers', *British Journal of Addiction*, 87(2): 215–25.

R. Boreham and S. McManus (2003) *Drug Use, Smoking and Drinking among Young Teenagers in 2003* (London: The Stationary Office).

H. Bradby (2007) 'Watch Out for the Aunties! Young British Asians' Accounts of Identity and Substance Use', *Sociology of Health and Illness*, 29(5): 656–72.

J. Braithwaite (1989) *Crime, Shame and Reintegration* (Cambridge: Cambridge University Press).

British Medical Association (2003) *Adolescent Health* (London: BMA).

Y. Bromley and O. Shkaratan (1972) 'The General and the Particular in Historical, Ethnographical and Sociological Research', *Current Anthropology*, 13(5): 569–74.

R. Bunton, S. Nettleton and R. Burrows (1995) *The Sociology of Health Promotion: Critical Analyses of Consumption, Lifestyle and Risk* (London and New York: Routledge).

J. Burgoyne (1991) 'Does the Ring Make a Difference? Couples and the Private Face of a Public Relationship in Post-War Britain?', in D. Clarke (ed.) *Marriage, Domestic Life and Social Change* (London and New York : Routledge).

C.O. Butts III, G.B. Stefano, G.L. Fricchione and E. Salamon (2003) 'Religion and its Effects on Crime and Delinquency', *Med Sci Monit*, 9(8): SR79–82.

E.H. Carr (1961) *What is History?* (London: Macmillan).

B. Carrington and B. Wilson (2002) 'Global Clubcultures: Cultural Flows and Late Modern Dance Music Cultures', in M. Cieslik and G. Pollock (eds) *Young People in Risk Society* (Aldershot: Ashgate).

C. Cassidy, R. O'Connor and N. Dorrer (2006) *Young People's Experiences of Transitions to Adulthood: A Study of Minority Ethnic and White Young People* (York: Joseph Rowntree Foundation).

S. Cavan (1966) *Liquor License* (Chicago: Aldine).

D. Cheal (2002) *Sociology of Family Life* (Basingstoke: Palgrave).

L. Chisholm and K. Hurrelmann (1995) 'Adolescence in Europe: Pluralised Transition Patterns and their Implications for Personal and Social Risk', *Journal of Adolescence*, 18(2): 129–58.

F. Coffield and L. Gofton (1994) *Drugs and Young People* (London: Institute for Public Policy Research).

N. Coggans and S. McKellar (1994) 'Peer Pressure: A Convenient Explanation', *Druglink: The Journal on Drug Misuse in Britain*, 9: 16–18.

S. Cohen (1971) *Images of Deviance* (Harmondsworth: Penguin).

S. Cohen (1972) *Folk Devils and Moral Panics: The Creation of the Mods and Rockers* (London: MacGibbon and Kee).

S. Cohen (2002) *Folk Devils and Moral Panics: The Creation of the Mods and Rockers* (London: Routledge).

J.C. Coleman and L. Hendry (1999) *The Nature of Adolescence* (London: Routledge).

B. Coles (1995) *Youth and Social Policy* (London: UCL Press).

M. Collin with J. Godfrey (1997) *Altered State: The Story of Ecstasy Culture and Acid House* (London: Serpent's Tail).

C.C.H. Cook (2006) *Alcohol, Addiction and Christian Ethics* (Cambridge: Cambridge University Press).

D.T. Courtwright (2001) *Forces of Habit: Drugs and the Making of the Modern World* (Cambridge, Mass: Harvard University Press).

G. Crow (2002) 'Families, Moralities, Rationalities and Social Change', in A. Carling, S. Duncan and R. Edwards (eds) *Analysing Families: Morality and Rationality in Policy and Practice* (London: Routledge).

F. Davis (1970) 'Focus on the Flower Children: Why All of Us May Be Hippies Someday', in J.D. Douglas (ed.) *Observation of Deviance* (London: Random House).

J. Davis (1990) *Youth and the Condition of Britain* (London: Athlone Press).

L. Degenhardt, W.T. Chiu, N. Sampson, R.C. Kessler, J.C. Anthony, M. Angermeyer, R. Bruffaerts, G. Girolamo, O. Gureje, Y. Huang, A. Karam, S. Kostyuchenko, J.P. Lepine, M.E.M. Mora, Y. Neumark, J.H. Ormel, A. Pinto-Meza, J. Posada-Villa, D.J. Stein, T. Takeshima and J.E. Wells (2008) 'Toward a Global View of Alcohol, Tobacco, Cannabis, and Cocaine Use: Findings from the WHO World Mental Health Surveys', *PLoS Medicine*, 5(4): 1053–67.

M. DeKoven (2004) *Utopia Limited: The Sixties and the Emergence of the Postmodern* (Durham: Duke University Press).

Department of Health (1995) *Sensible Drinking: The Report of an Inter-Departmental Working Group* (London: Department of Health).

Department of Health (2001) *Statistical Bulletin: Statistics on Alcohol – England 1978 Onwards* (London: HMSO).

D.J. DeWit, D.R. Offord and M. Wong (1997) 'Patterns of Onset and Cessation of Drug Use Over the Early Part of the Life Course', *Health Education and Behavior*, 24(6): 746–58.

L. Dillon, N. Chivite Matthews, I. Greval, R. Brown, S. Webster, E. Weddell, G. Brown and N. Smith (2007) *Risk and Protective Factors and Resilience to Drug Use* (London: Home Office).

N. Dodd (1999) *Social Theory and Modernity* (Cambridge: Polity).

M. Donnelly (2005) *Sixties Britain* (London: Pearson/Longman).

N. Dorn and M. Lee (1999) 'Drugs and Policing in Europe', in N. South (ed.) *Drugs: Cultures, Controls and Everyday Life* (London: Sage).

D. Downes (1988) 'The Sociology of Crime and Social Control in Britain, 1960–1987', *British Journal Criminology*, 28(2): 175–87.

D. Downes and P. Rock (2007) *Understanding Deviance: A Guide to the Sociology of Crime and Rule Breaking* (Oxford and New York: Oxford University Press).

S.C. Duncan, T.E. Duncan and H. Hops (1998) 'Progressions of Alcohol, Cigarette, and Marijuana Use in Adolescence', *Journal of Behavioral Medicine*, 21(4): 375–88.
G.J. Duncan, B. Wilkerson and P. England (2006) 'Cleaning Up Their Act: The Effects of Marriage and Cohabitation on Licit and Illicit Drug Use', *Demography*, 43(4): 691–710.
T. Duster (1970) *The Legalisation of Morality* (New York: Free Press).
L. Ellis (1985) 'Religiosity and Criminality: Evidence and Explanation of Complex Relationships', *Sociological Perspectives*, 28: 501–20.
M. Elvins (2003) *Anti-Drugs Policies of the European Union: Transnational Decision-Making and the Politics of Expertise* (Basingstoke and New York: Palgrave Macmillan).
European Monitoring Centre for Drugs and Drug Addiction (EMCDDA) (1999) *Drugs Problems in the European Union: Annual Report* (Lisbon: EMCDDA).
European Monitoring Centre for Drugs and Drugs Addiction (EMCDDA) (2002) *Drugs in Focus: Recreational Drug Use – A Key EU Challenge* (Italy: Office for Official Publication of the European Communities).
European Monitoring Centre for Drugs and Drug Addiction (EMCDDA) (2007) *The State of the Drug Problem in Europe: Annual Report 2007* (Luxembourg: Office for Official Publications of the European Communities).
European Monitoring Centre for Drugs and Drugs Addiction (EMCDDA) (2008) *The State of the Drug Problem in Europe: Annual Report 2008* (Luxembourg: Office for Official Publications of the European Communities).
E.J. Evans (1983) *The Forging of the Modern State: Early Industrial Britain, 1783–1870* (London: Longman).
S. Farrall and B. Bowling (1999) 'Structuration, Human Development and Desistance from Crime', *British Journal of Criminology*, 39(2): 253–68.
C.E. Faupel, A.M. Horowitz and G.S. Weaver (2004) *The Sociology of American Drug Use* (New York: McGraw Hill).
H. Finestone (1964) 'Cats, Kicks and Colour', in H. Becker (ed.) *The Other Side* (New York: Free Press).
F. Fish, B. Wells, G. Bindeman, J. Bunney and M. Jordan (1974) 'Prevalence of Drug Misuse Amongst Young People in Glasgow 1970–1972', *British Journal of Addiction*, 69: 231–6.
J. Flight (2005) *Substance Use by Canadian Youth – A National Survey of Canadians' Use of Alcohol and Other Drugs*, Canadian Addiction Survey (CAS) (Ottawa: Health Canada).
C. Flood-Page, S. Campbell, V. Harrington and J. Miller (2000) *Youth Crime Findings from the 1998/1999 Youth Lifestyles Survey* (London: Home Office).
J. Fountain, H. Bartlett, P. Griffiths, M. Gossop, A. Boys and J. Strang (1999) 'Why Say No? Reasons Given by Young People for Not Using Drugs', *Addiction Research*, 7(4): 339–53.
J. Fountain, J. Bashford, M. Winters and K. Patel (2003) *Black and Minority Ethnic Communities in England: A Review of the Literature on Drug Use and Related Service Provision* (London/Preston: National Treatment Agency for Substance Misuse and the Centre for Ethnicity and Health).
D. Fowler (1995) *The First Teenagers: The Lifestyle of Young Wage-Earners in Interwar Britain* (London: Woburn Press).
B. Fox (1997) 'Reproducing Difference: Changes in the Lives of Partners Becoming Parents', in M. Luxton (ed.) *Feminism and Families* (Halifax, NS: Fernwood).

S. Frith (1985) 'The Sociology of Youth', in M. Haralambos (ed.) *Sociology: New Directions* (Ormskirk, Lancashire: Causeway Books).
E. Fuller (2005) *Drug Use, Smoking and Drinking among Young People in England in 2005* (London: The Information Centre).
A. Furlong and F. Cartmel (2007) *Young People and Social Change: New Perspectives* (Buckingham: Open University Press).
T. Futing Liao (1994) *Interpreting Probability Models: Logit, Probit and Other Generalized Linear Models* (Thousand Oaks, CA: Sage).
D. Gadd and S. Farrall (2004) 'Criminal Careers, Desistance and Subjectivity', *Theoretical Criminology*, 8(2): 123–56.
L.M. Galanti, P. Manigart and P. Dubois (1998) 'Tobacco Smoking and Alcohol and Drug Consumption in a Large, Young Healthy Population', *Archives of Environmental Health*, 53(2): 156–60.
D. Garland (2001) *The Culture of Control: Crime and Social Order in Contemporary Society* (Oxford and New York: Oxford University Press).
J. Gershuny (2000) *Changing Times: Work and Leisure in Postindustrial Society* (Oxford and New York: Oxford University Press).
C. Gibbins and G. Julian (2006) *Family Spending: A Report on the 2004–05 Expenditure and Food Survey* (Basingstoke and New York: Palgrave Macmillan).
A. Giddens (1976) *New Rules of Sociological Method: A Positive Critique of Interpretative Sociologies* (London: Hutchinson).
A. Giddens (1984) *The Constitution of Society: Outline of the Theory of Structuration* (Cambridge: Polity Press).
A. Giddens (1990) *The Consequences of Modernity* (Cambridge: Polity Press).
A. Giddens (1991) *Modernity and Self-Identity* (Cambridge: Polity Press).
A. Giddens (1998) *The Third Way: The Renewal of Social Democracy* (Cambridge: Polity Press).
M.M. Glatt (1977) 'The English Drink Problem: Its Rise and Fall Through the Ages', *Proceedings of the Royal Society of Medicine*, 70(3): 202–6.
M.D. Glantz and R.W. Pickens (1992) *Vulnerability to Drug Abuse* (Washington DC: American Psychological Association).
E. Goddard (2006) *Smoking and Drinking Among Adults, 2006* (London: National Statistics).
A. Golub and B.D. Johnson (2001) 'Variation in Youthful Risks of Progression from Alcohol and Tobacco to Marijuana and to Hard Drugs Across Generations', *American Journal of Public Health*, 91(2): 225–32.
M. Gossop (1996) *Living with Drugs* (Arena: Aldershot).
M.R. Gottfredson and T. Hirschi (1990) *A General Theory of Crime* (Stanford, California: Stanford University Press).
A. Gould and N. Stratford (2002) 'Illegal Drugs: Highs and Lows', *British Social Attitudes, The 19th Report* (London: Sage).
C. Goulden and A. Sondhi (2001) *At the Margins: Drug Use by Vulnerable Young People in the 1998/9 Youth Lifestyles Survey* (London: Home Office).
M. Gourley (2004) 'A Subcultural Study of Recreational Ecstasy Use', *Journal of Sociology*, 40(1): 59–73.
J. Graham and B. Bowling (1995) *Young People and Crime* (London: Home Office).
J. Grube (2005) *Youth Drinking Rates and Problems: A Comparison of European Countries and the United States* (Washington: Office of Juvenile Justice and Delinquency Prevention).

P.J. Gruenewald and F.W. Johnson (2006) 'The Stability and Reliability of Self-Reported Drinking Measures', *Journal of Studies on Alcohol*, 67(5): 738–45.

J. Hales and N. Stratford (1999) *1998 British Crime Survey: Technical Report* (London: Social Community Planning Research).

M. Hallstone (2002) 'Updating Howard Becker's Theory of Using Marijuana for Pleasure', *Contemporary Drug Problems*, 29(4): 821–46.

A. Hamid (2002) *The Ganja Complex: Rastafari and Marijuana* (Oxford: Lexington Books).

T. Hammer and P. Vaglum (1990) 'Use of Alcohol and Drugs in the Transitional Phase from Adolescence to Young Adulthood', *Journal of Adolescence*, 13(2): 129–42.

R. Hammersley, L. Marsland and M. Reid (2003) *Substance Use by Young Offenders: The Impact of the Normalisation of Drug Use in the Early Years of the 21st Century* (London: Home Office).

L.D. Harrison (1997) 'The Validity of Self-Reported Drug Use in Survey Research', in L.D. Harrison and A. Hughes (eds) *The Validity of Self-Reported Drug Use: Improving the Accuracy of Survey Estimates* (Washington, DC: National Institute on Drug Abuse).

Health Advisory Service (1996) *Children and Young People, Substance Misuse Services – The Substance of Young Needs* (London: HMSO).

S. Heath and E. Cleaver (2003) *Young, Free and Single? Twenty-Somethings and Household Change* (Basingstoke and New York: Palgrave Macmillan).

A. Heath and J. Payne (2000) 'Social Mobility', in A.H. Halsey with J. Webb (eds) *Twentieth Century British Trends* (London: Macmillan).

F. Heidensohn (1989) *Crime and Society* (London: Macmillan).

S. Henderson (1997) *Ecstasy: Case Unsolved* (London: Pandora).

S. Henderson (1999) 'The Question of Gender', in N. South (ed.) *Drugs: Cultures, Controls and Everyday Life* (London: Sage).

S. Hinchcliff (2001) 'The Meaning of Ecstasy Use and Clubbing to Women in the Late 1990s', *International Journal of Drug Policy*, 12: 455–68.

T. Hirschi (1969) *Causes of Delinquency* (Berkeley: University of California Press).

T. Hirschi and M.R. Gottfredson (1983) 'Age and the Explanation of Crime', *American Journal of Sociology*, 89: 552–84.

J. Hirst and A. McCamley-Finney (1994) *The Place and Meaning of Drugs in the Lives of Young People* (Sheffield: Sheffield Hallam University).

D. Hobbs, P. Hadfield, S. Lister and S. Winlow (2003) *Bouncers: Violence and Governance in the Night-time Economy* (Oxford and New York: Oxford University Press).

Home Office (1979) *Report on a Review of the Classification of Controlled Drugs and Penalties under Schedules 2 and 4 of the Misuse of Drugs Act 1971* (London: Home Office).

Home Office (2000) *Time for Reform: Proposals for the Modernisation of our Licensing Laws* (London: Home Office).

M. Hough (2001) 'Balancing Public Health and Criminal Justice Interventions', *International Journal of Drug Policy*, 12: 429–33.

House of Commons Science and Technology Committee (2006) *Drug Classification: Making a Hash of It?* (London: The Stationary Office).

G. Hunt and K. Evans (2003) 'Dancing and Drugs: A Cross-National Perspective', *Contemporary Drug Problems*, 30: 779–814.

A. Huxley (1959) *The Doors of Perception and Heaven and Hell* (London: Penguin).
Institute for the Study of Drug Dependency (ISDD) (1993) *National Audit of Drug Misuse in Britain* (London: ISDD).
Institute for the Study of Drug Dependency (ISDD) (1994) *Drug Misuse in Britain – 1994* (London: ISDD).
Institute of Alcohol Studies (2005) *Binge Drinking: Nature Prevalence and Causes* (IAS: St Ives, Cambs).
Institute of Alcohol Studies (2007) *Alcohol: Price, Legal Availability and Expenditure* (IAS: St Ives, Cambs).
Institute of Alcohol Studies (2008) *Drinking in Great Britain* (IAS: St Ives, Cambs).
M. Jackson, J.H. Goldthorpe and C. Mills (2005) 'Education, Employers and Class Mobility', in K. Leicht (ed). *Research in Social Stratification and Mobility Volume 23* (Amsterdam: Elsevier).
P. Jha and F.J. Chaloupka (1999) *Curbing the Epidemic: Governmentality and the Economics of Tobacco Control* (Washington: World Bank).
P.B. Johnson, S.M. Boles and H.D. Kleber (2000) 'The Relationship Between Adolescent Smoking and Drinking and Likelihood Estimates of Illicit Drug Use', *Journal of Addictive Diseases*, 19(2): 75–81.
B.D. Johnson, F. Bardhi, S.J. Sifaneck and E. Dunlop (2006) 'Marijuana Argot as Subculture Threads: Social Constructions by Users in New York City', *British Journal of Criminology*, 46(1): 46–77.
L. Johnston, R. MacDonald, P. Mason, L. Ridley and C. Webster (2000) *Snakes and Ladders: Young People, Transitions and Social Exclusion* (Bristol: Policy Press).
L.D. Johnston, P.M. O'Malley, J.G. Bachman and J.E. Schulenberg (2007) *Monitoring the Future National Survey Results on Drug Use, 1975–2006* (Bethesda, MD: National Institute on Drug Abuse).
G. Jones (1995) *Leaving Home* (Buckingham: Open University Press).
G. Jones and D. Martin (1997) *The Social Context of Spending in Youth*, Centre for Educational Sociology (Edinburgh: Edinburgh University).
D. Kandel and R. Faust (1975) 'Sequence and Stages in Patterns of Adolescent Drug Use', *Archives of General Psychiatry*, 32(7): 923–32.
J. Katz (1988) *Seductions of Crime* (New York: Basic Books).
K. Khan (1999) *Race, Drugs, Europe: Action Points for Change* (Race and Drugs Project: T3E/University of Middlesex).
K.E. Kiernan (1986) 'Leaving Home: A Comparative Analysis of Six Western European Countries', *European Journal of Population*, 2: 177–84.
M. Kohn (1992) *Dope Girls: The Birth of the British Drug Underground* (London: Lawrence and Wishart).
A. Kosviner and D. Hawks (1977) 'Cannabis Use Among British University Students, II. Patterns of Use and Attitudes to Use', *British Journal of Addiction*, 72: 41–58.
P. Larkin (1990) *Collected Poems* (London: Marvell and Faber and Faber).
J.H. Laub and R.J. Sampson (2003) *Shared Beginnings, Divergent Lives: Delinquent Boys to Age 70* (Cambridge, Massachusetts: Harvard University Press).
M. Leitner, J. Shapland and P. Wiles (1993) *Drug Usage and Drug Prevention: The Views and Habits of the General Public* (London: HMSO).
E. Lemert (1948) 'Some Aspects of a General Theory of Sociopathic Behaviour', *Proceedings of the Pacific Sociological Society*, XVI: 23–9.
E. Lemert (1951) *Social Pathology* (New York: McGraw-Hill).

K.E. Leonard and G.G. Homish (2005) 'Changes in Marijuana Use Over the Transition into Marriage', *Journal of Drug Issues*, 35: 409–30.
J. Lewis (2001) *The End of Marriage? Individualism and Intimate Relations* (Cheltenham: Edward Elgar).
A. Lindesmith (1965) *The Addict and the Law* (London: Indiana University Press).
C. Lloyd (1998) 'Risk Factors for Problem Drug Use: Identifying Vulnerable Groups', *Drugs, Education, Prevention and Policy*, 5(3): 217–31.
R.J. MacCoun and P. Reuter (2001) *Drug War Heresies: Learning from Other Vices, Times and Places* (Cambridge and New York: Cambridge University Press).
Z. MacDonald (1999) 'Illicit Drug Use in the UK: Evidence from the British Crime Survey', *British Journal of Criminology*, 39(4): 585–608.
S. Machin and A. Vignoles (2005) *What's the Good of Education?: The Economics of Education in the UK* (Princeton, N.J.: Princeton University Press).
P. Marks et al. (1973) *Public Attitudes to Drug Taking: A Short Report on Work Carried Out through the OPCS for the Home Office* (London: Office of Population Censuses and Surveys).
D. Martin (1999) *Clubbing: Dancing, Ecstasy and Vitality* (New York: Routledge).
M. Martinic and F. Measham (2008) *Swimming with Crocodiles: The Culture of Extreme Drinking* (London: Routledge).
A. Marsh and S. McKay (1994) *Poor Smokers* (London: Policy Studies Institute).
S. Maruna (2001) *Making Good: How Ex-Convicts Reform and Rebuild Their Lives* (Washington, DC: American Psychological Association).
A. Marwick (1998) *The Sixties: Cultural Revolution in Britain, France, Italy, and the United States* (Oxford and New York: Oxford University Press).
K. Marx (1864) 'Letter to Frederick Engels, November 4, 1864', in V. Adoratsky (1945) *Karl Marx: Selected Works in Two Volumes, Vol. II* (London: Lawrence and Wishart).
D. Matza (1964) *Delinquency and Drift* (New York: John Wiley and Sons).
D. Matza (1969) *Becoming Deviant* (Englewood Cliffs, NJ: Prentice-Hall).
D. Matza and G.M. Sykes (1961) 'Juvenile Delinquency and Subterranean Values', *American Sociological Review*, 26: 712–19.
T. May, H. Warburton, P.J. Turnbull and M. Duffy (2002) *Times They Are A-Changing: Cannabis Use and Cannabis Policing* (York: Joseph Rowntree Foundation).
T. May, H. Warburton, M. Duffy and M. Hough (2007) *Policing Cannabis as a Class C Drug: An Arresting Change?* (York: Joseph Rowntree Foundation).
B.I. Mawby and I.D. Batta (1980) *Asians and Crime: The Bradford Experience* (Middlesex: Scope Communications).
A.J. McKay, V.M. Hawthorne and H.N. McCartney (1973) 'Drugtaking Among Medical Students at Glasgow University', *British Medical Journal*, 1(5852): 540–3.
D. McVicar and P. Rice (2001) 'Participation in Further Education in England and Wales: An Analysis of Post-War Trends', *Oxford Economic Papers*, 53: 47–66.
S. McVie and P. Bradshaw (2005) *Adolescent Smoking, Drinking and Drug Use* (Edinburgh: Centre for Law and Society, University of Edinburgh).
F. Measham, R. Newcombe and H. Parker (1994) 'The Normalization of Recreational Drug Use Amongst Young People in North-West England', *British Journal of Sociology*, 45(2): 287–312.

F. Measham, H. Parker and J. Aldridge (1998) 'The Teenage Transition: From Adolescent Recreational Drug Use to the Young Adult Dance Culture in Britain in the Mid 1990s', *Journal of Drug Issues*, 28(1): 9–32.

F. Measham, J. Aldridge and H. Parker (2001) *Dancing on Drugs: Risk, Health, Hedonism in the British Club Scene* (London: Free Association Books).

F. Measham and M. Shiner (2008) 'The Baby, the Bathwater and the Legacy of Normalisation: The Role of Classical and Contemporary Criminological Theory in Understanding Young People's Drug Use', Paper Presented to the *International Society for the Study of Drug Policy Conference*, Lisbon. http://www.issdp.org/lisbon2008_public/shinermeasham_BabyandBathwater.pdf

R. Miliband (1978) 'A State of De-subordination', *British Journal of Sociology*, 29(4): 399–409.

M. Millman (1982) 'Images of Deviant Men and Women', in M. Evans (ed.) *The Women Question* (London: Fontana).

T. Modood, R. Berthoud, J. Lakey, J. Nazroo, P. Smith, S. Virdee and S. Beishon (1997) *Ethnic Minorities in Britain: Diversity and Disadvantage* (London: Policy Studies Institute).

M. Moloney, G. Hunt, N. Bailey and G. Erez (2009) 'New Forms of Regulating the Nighttime Economy: The Case of San Francisco', in P. Hadfield (ed.) *Nightlife and Crime: Social Order and Governance in an International Perspective* (Oxford and New York: Oxford University Press).

J. Mott and C. Mirrlees-Black (1995) *Self-Reported Drug Misuse in England and Wales: Findings from the 1992 British Crime Survey*, Research and Planning Unit Paper 89 (London: Home Office).

K. Murji (1999) 'White Lines: Cultures, Race and Drugs', in South, N. (ed.) *Drugs: Cultures, Controls and Everyday Life* (London: Sage).

R. Murphy and S. Roe (2007) *Drug Misuse Declared: Results of the 2006/07 British Crime Survey* (London: Home Office).

F. Musgrove (1964) *Youth and the Social Order* (London: Routledge and Kegan Paul).

National Institute on Alcohol Abuse and Alcoholism (NIAAA) (2003) *International Comparisons of Alcohol Consumption* (Maryland: NIAAA).

T. Newburn (2002) 'Young People, Crime, and Youth Justice', in M. Maguire, R. Morgan and R. Reiner (eds) *The Oxford Handbook of Criminology* (Oxford and New York: Oxford University Press).

T. Newburn and M. Shiner (2005) *Dealing with Disaffection: Young People, Mentoring and Social Inclusion* (Cullompton, Devon: Willan).

NOP Market Research Ltd (1982) *Survey of Drug Use in the 15–21 Age Group Undertaken by the Daily Mail* (London: NOP).

D. Nutt, L.A. King, W. Saulsbury and C. Blakemore (2007) 'Development of a Rational Scale to Assess Harm of Drugs of Potential Misuse', *Lancet*, 24, 369(9566): 1047–53.

Office for National Statistics (2008) 'Deaths Related to Drug Poisoning in England and Wales, 2003–07', *Health Statistics Quarterly*, 39: 82–8.

J. Orford (1985) *Excessive Appetites: A Psychological View of Addictions* (Chichester: Wiley and Sons).

B. Osgerby (1998) *Youth in Britain Since 1945* (Oxford: Blackwell).

H. Parker, K. Bakx and R. Newcombe (1988) *Living with Heroin* (Milton Keynes: Open University).

H. Parker, F. Measham and J. Aldridge (1995) *Drugs Futures: Changing Patterns of Drug Use Amongst English Youth* (London: Institute for the Study of Drug Dependence).

H. Parker, J. Aldridge and F. Measham (1998) *Illegal Leisure: The Normalization of Adolescent Recreational Drug Use* (London: Routledge).

H. Parker, L. Williams and J. Aldridge (2002) 'The Normalization of Sensible Recreational Drug Use: Further Evidence from the North West England Longitudinal Study', *Sociology*, 36(4): 941–64.

K. Patel, C. Bamhrah and G. Singh (1996) *Drug Use in the Asian Community* (Preston: Lancashire Drug Action Team).

G. Pearson (1983) *Hooligan: A History of Respectable Fears* (London: Macmillan).

G. Pearson (1987) *The New Heroin Users* (Oxford: Blackwell).

G. Pearson and K. Patel (1998) 'Drugs, Deprivation and Ethnicity: Outreach Among Asian Drug Users in a Northern English City', *Journal of Drug Issues*, 28(1): 199–224.

G. Pearson and M. Shiner (2002) 'Rethinking the Generation Gap: Attitudes Towards Illicit Drugs Among Young People and Adults', *Criminal Justice*, 2(1): 71–86.

R. Peto, R. Darby, H. Deo, P. Silcocks, E. Whitley and R. Doll (2000) 'Smoking, Smoking Cessation and Lung Cancer in the UK Since 1950: Combination of National Statistics with Two Case Control Studies', *British Medical Journal*, 321(7257): 323–9.

A. Petridis (1996) 'How Much Ecstasy Do The British Really Take?', *Mixmag*, 2(62): 98–100.

H. Pilkington (2005) *'Everyday' but not 'Normal': Drug Use and Youth Cultural Practice in Russia*, End of Award Report (Swindon: Economic and Social Research Council).

M. A. Plant (1973) *Young People at Risk: A Study of the 17–24 Age Group* (Cheltenham: Cheltenham Youth Trust).

M. Plant (1975) *Drug-takers in an English Town* (London: Tavistock).

M. Plant and M. Plant (1992) *Risk-takers: Alcohol, Drugs, Sex and Youth* (London: Routledge).

K. Plummer (1979) 'Misunderstanding Labelling Perspectives', in D. Downes and P. Rock (eds) *Deviant Interpretations* (Oxford: Martin Robertson).

Police Foundation (2000) *Drugs and the Law: Report of the Independent Inquiry into the Misuse of Drugs Act 1971* (London: Police Foundation).

M. Ramsay and A. Percy (1996) *Drug Misuse Declared: Results of the 1994 British Crime Survey* (London: Home Office).

M. Ramsay and J. Spiller (1997) *Drug Misuse Declared: Results of the 1996 British Crime Survey* (London: Home Office).

M. Ramsay and S. Partridge (1999) *Drug Misuse Declared in 1998: Results From the British Crime Survey* (London: Home Office).

M. Ramsay, P. Baker, C. Goulden, C. Sharp and A. Sondhi (2001) *Drug Misuse Declared in 2000: Results From the British Crime Survey* (London: Home Office).

W.C. Reckless (1967) *The Crime Problem* (New York: Appleton Century Crofts).

S. Redhead (1993) *Rave Off: Politics and Deviance in Contemporary Youth Culture* (Aldershot: Avebury).

S. Redhead (1997) *Subculture to Clubcultures: An Introduction to Popular Cultural Studies* (Oxford: Blackwell).

R. Reiner (2000) 'Crime and Control in Britain', *Sociology*, 34(1): 71–94.

R. Reiner (2007) *Law and Order: An Honest Citizen's Guide to Crime and Control* (Cambridge: Polity Press).
A. Reiss (1951) 'Delinquency as the Failure of Personal and Social Controls', *American Sociological Review*, 16: 196–207.
Release (1997) *Release Drugs and Dance Survey* (London: Release).
L. Rickards, K. Fox, C. Roberts, L. Fletcher and E. Goddard (2004) *Living in Britain: Results from the 2002 General Household Survey* (London: Stationary Office).
M. Roberts, C. Turner, S. Greenfield and G. Osborn (2006) 'A Continental Ambience? Lessons Managing Alcohol-related Evening time Entertainment from Four European Capitals', *Urban Studies*, 43(7): 1105–25.
P. Rock (1973) *Deviant Behaviour* (London: Hutchinson).
P. Rock (2005) 'Chronocentricism and British Criminology', *The British Journal of Sociology*, 56(3): 473–91.
S. Roe and L. Man (2006) *Drug Misuse Declared: Findings from the 2005/06 British Crime Survey* (London: Home Office).
S. Rolles, D. Kushlick and M. Jay (2004) *After the War on Drugs: Options for Control* (Bristol: Transform).
J. Ross (2007) *Illicit Drug Use in Australia: Epidemiology, Use Patterns and Associated Harm* (Sydney: National Drug and Alcohol Research Centre).
Royal College of Psychiatrists (2000) *Drugs, Dilemmas and Choices* (London: Gaskell).
V. Ruggiero (1999) 'The Legalisation of Illicit Substances', in N. South (ed.) *Drugs: Cultures, Controls and Everyday Life* (London: Sage).
V. Ruggiero and N. South (1995) *Eurodrugs: Drug Use, Markets and Trafficking in Europe* (London: University College Press).
M. Rutter, H. Giller and A. Hagell (1998) *Antisocial Behaviour by Young People* (Cambridge: Cambridge University Press).
R.J. Sampson and J.H. Laub (1993) *Crime in the Making: Pathways and Turning Points Through Life* (Cambridge, Massachusetts: Harvard University Press).
R.J. Sampson and J.H. Laub (2005) 'A Life-Course View of the Development of Crime', ANNALS, *AAPSS*, 602, November: 12–44.
D. Sangster, M. Shiner, K. Patel and N. Sheikh (2002) *Delivering Drug Services to Black and Minority Ethnic Communities* (London: Home Office).
D.A. Santor, D. Messervey and V. Kusumakar (2000) 'Measuring Peer Pressure, Popularity and Conformity in Adolescent Boys and Girls: Predicting School Performance, Sexual Attitudes and Substance Abuse', *Journal of Youth and Adolescence*, 29(2): 163–82.
N. Saunders (1993) *E for Ecstasy* (London: Neal's Yard Desk Top Publishing).
N. Saunders (1995) *Ecstasy and the Dance Culture* (London: Neal's Yard Desk Top Publishing).
H. Schmid, T.T. Bogt, E. Godeau, A. Hublet, S.F. Dias and A. Fotiou (2003) 'Drunkenness Among Young People: A Cross-National Comparison', *Journal of Studies on Alcohol*, 64(5): 650–61.
J.E. Schulenberg, J.L. Maggs and K. Hurrelmann (1997) *Health Risks and Developmental Transitions During Adolescence* (Cambridge: Cambridge University Press).
J.E. Schulenberg, P.M. O'Malley, J.G. Bachman and L.D. Johnston (2005) 'Early Adult Transitions and Their Relation to Well-Being and Substance Use', in R.A. Settersten, Jr., F.F. Frustenberg, Jr., and R.G. Rambaut (eds) *On the Frontier*

*of Adulthood: Theory, Research and Public Policy* (Chicago: University of Chicago Press).
E. Schur (1963) *Narcotic Addiction in Britain and America* (London: Tavistock).
E. Schur (1965) *Crimes Without Victims* (Englewood Cliffs: Prentice Hall).
E. Schur (1969) *Our Criminal Society: The Social and Legal Sources of Crime in America* (Englewood Cliffs: Prentice Hall).
A. Schutz (1966) 'Some Structures of the Life World', in *Collected Papers, 3, Studies in Phenomenological Philosophy* (The Hague: Martinus Nijhoff).
A. Schutz (1972) 'Choice and the Social Sciences', in L.E. Embree (ed.) *Life-world and Consciousness: Essays for Aron Gurwitsch* (Illinois: Northwestern University Press).
T. Seddon (2005) 'Drugs, Crime and Social Exclusion: Social Context and Social Theory in British Drugs-Crime Research', *British Journal of Criminology*, 46(4): 680–703.
T. Seddon, R. Ralphs and L. Williams (2008) 'Risk, Security and the "Criminalization" of British Drug Policy', *British Journal of Criminology*, 48: 818–34.
Select Committee on Home Affairs (2002) *The Government's Drugs Policy: Is it Working?* (London: The Stationary Office).
A. Self and L. Zealey (2008) Social Trends (London and New York: Palgrave Macmillan).
T. Sellin (1938) *Culture Conflict and Crime* (New York: Social Science Research Council).
H. Shapiro (1990) *Waiting for the Man* (London: Helter Skelter Publishing).
H. Shapiro (1999) *Dances with Drugs: Pop Music, Drugs and Youth Culture,* in N. South (ed.) *Drugs: Cultures, Controls and Everyday Life* (London: Sage).
T. Shildrick (2002) 'Young People, Illicit Drug Use and the Question of Normalization', *Journal of Youth Studies*, 5(1): 35–48.
M. Shiner and T. Newburn (1996) *Young People, Drugs and Peer Education* (London: Home Office).
M. Shiner and T. Newburn (1997) 'Definitely, Maybe Not: The Normalisation of Recreational Drug Use Amongst Young People', *Sociology*, 31(3): 511–29.
M. Shiner and T. Newburn (1999) 'Taking Tea with Noel: The Place and Meaning of Drug Use in Everyday Life', in N. South (ed.) *Drugs: Cultures, Controls and Everyday Life* (London: Sage).
M. Shiner (2000) *Doing it for Themselves: An Evaluation of Peer Approaches to Drug Prevention* (London: Home Office).
M. Shiner (2003) 'Out of Harm's Way? Illicit Drug Use, Medicalisation and the Law', *British Journal of Criminology*, 43(4): 772–96.
M. Shiner (2006) 'A Dubious Equality? Drug Use and the Discovery of Gender', in F. Heidensohn (ed.) *Gender and Justice: New Concepts and Approaches* (Cullompton, Devon: Willan).
R.K. Siegel (2005) *Intoxication: The Universal Drive for Mind-Altering Substances* (Rochester, Vermont: Park Street Press).
W. Sigle-Rushton (2008) 'England and Wales: Stable Fertility and Pronounced Social Status Differences', *Demographic Research*, 19: 455–502.
R.K. Silbereisen, R. Robins and M. Rutter (1995) 'Secular Trends in Substances Use: Concepts and Data on the Impact of Social Change on Alcohol and Drug Abuse', in M. Rutter and D. Smith (eds) *Psychosocial Disorders in Young People: Time Trends and Their Causes* (Chichester: Wiley).

J. Simon (2007) *Governing through Crime: How the War on Crime Transformed American Democracy and Created a Culture of Fear* (Oxford and New York: Oxford University Press).
P. 6, B. Jupp, H. Perry and K. Laskey (1997) *The Substance of Youth* (York: Joseph Rowntree Foundation).
C. Skinner (1994) *Sample Models and Weights: Unpublished Paper Presented at Joint Statistical Meetings, Toronto* (University of Southampton: Centre for Survey Data Analysis).
S. Smallwood and B. Wilson (2007) *Focus on Families* (Basingstoke and New York: Palgrave Macmillan).
A.J. Smith (1992) 'The Third Generation', *New Statesman and Society*, (September), 31–2.
D.J. Smith (2002) 'Crime and the Life-course', in M. Maguire, R. Morgan and R. Reiner (eds) *The Oxford Handbook of Criminology* (Oxford: Oxford University Press).
R.J. Smith and T. Maughan (1998) 'Youth Culture and the Making of the Post-Fordist Economy: Dance Music in Contemporary Britain', *Journal of Youth Studies*, 1(2): 211–28.
N. South (1994) 'Drugs: Control, Crime, and Criminological Studies', in M. Maguire, R. Morgan and R. Reiner (eds) *The Oxford Handbook of Criminology* (Oxford: Clarendon).
N. South (1997) 'Drugs: Use, Crime and Control', in M. Maguire, R. Morgan and R. Reiner (eds) *The Oxford Handbook of Criminology* (Oxford: Clarendon).
N. South (1999) *Drugs: Cultures, Controls and Everyday Life* (London: Sage).
N. South (2002) 'Drugs, Alcohol and Crime', in Maguire, M., Morgan, R. and R. Reiner (eds) *The Oxford Handbook of Criminology* (Oxford: Clarendon).
H.B. Spear and J. Mott (2002) *Heroin Addiction Care and Control: The British System 1916–1984* (London: Drugscope).
I. Srubar (1993) 'On the Limits of Rational Choice', *Rationality and Society*, 5(1): 32–46.
P. Stares (1996) *Global Habit: The Drug Problem in a Borderless World* (Washington DC: The Brookings Institute).
STATA (1999) *STATA: Release 6*, College Station (Texas: STATA Press).
N. Stefanogiannis, K. Mason and L.C. Yeh (2007) *Drug Use in New Zealand: Analysis of the 2003 New Zealand Health Behaviours Survey – Drug Use* (Wellington: Ministry of Health).
N. Stratford and W. Roth (1999) *The 1998 Youth Lifestyles Survey: Technical Report* (London: National Centre for Social Research).
Substance Abuse Mental Health Services Administration (SAMHSA) (2007) *Results from the 2006 National Survey on Drug Use and Health: National Findings* (Rockville, MD: SAMHSA).
C. Sumner (1994) *The Sociology of Deviance: An Obituary* (Buckingham: Open University Press).
E.H. Sutherland (1939) *Principles of Criminology* (Philadelphia: Lippincott).
G.M. Sykes and D. Matza (1957) 'Techniques of Neutralization', *American Sociological Review*, 22: 664–70.
F. Tannenbaum (1938) *Crime and the Community* (New York: Colombia University Press).

S. Taylor (2002) 'Jock Young on The Drugtakers', *The Classic Collection* (London: Halovine).

K. Thompson (1998) *Moral Panics* (London: Routledge).

S. Thornton (1995) *Club Cultures: Music, Media and Subcultural Capital* (Cambridge: Polity Press).

C.R. Tittle and M.R. Welch (1983) 'Religiosity and Deviance: Toward a Contingency Theory of Constraining Effects', *Social Forces*, 61: 653–82.

M.R. Torabi, W.J. Bailey and M. Majd-Jabbari (1993) 'Cigarette Smoking as a Predictor of Alcohol and Other Drug Use by Children and Adolescents: Evidence of the "Gateway Drug Effect"', *Journal of School Health*, 63(7): 302–6.

M. Trace, A. Klein and M. Roberts (2004) 'Reclassification of Cannabis in the United Kingdom', *The Beckley Foundation Drug Policy Programme*, Briefing Paper One (Oxfordshire: Beckley Foundation).

C. Turner, A. Russell and W. Brown (2003) 'Prevalence of Illicit Drug Use in Young Australian Women, Patterns of Use and Associated Risk Factors', *Addiction*, 98(10): 1419–26.

T. Tyler (1990) *Why People Obey The Law* (New Haven and London: Yale University Press).

United Nations (2007) *World Drug Report 2007* (Vienna: United Nations).

United Nations (2008) *World Drug Report 2008* (Vienna: United Nations).

T. Veblen (1899) *The Theory of the Leisure Class* (New York: The Macmillan Company).

W. Vega, S. Aguilar-Gaiola, L. Andrade, R. Bijil, G. Borges, J. Caraveo-Anduaga, D. DeWit, S. Heeringa, R. Kessler and B. Kolody (2002) 'Prevalence and Age of Onset for Drug Users in Seven International Sites: Results from the International Consortium of Psychiatric Epidemiology', *Drug and Alcohol Dependence*, 68(3): 285–97.

F.A. Wagner, H.E. Valesco-Mondragon, M. Herrera-Vazquez, G. Borges and E. Lazcano-Ponce (2005) 'Early Alcohol or Tobacco Onset and Transition to Other Drug Use Among students in the State of Morelos, Mexico', *Drug and Alcohol Dependence*, 77(1): 93–6.

K.D. Wald and A.C. Calhoun-Brown (2007) *Religion and Politics in the United States* (Lanham, MD: Rowman and Littlefield Publishers).

J.M. Jr. Wallace, T.N. Brown, J.G. Bachman and T.A. Lavesit (2003) 'The Influence of Race and Religion on Abstinence from Alcohol, Cigarettes and Marijuana Among Adolescents', *Journal of Studies on Alcohol*, 64: 843–8.

J. Ward, Z. Henderson and G. Pearson (2003) *One Problem Among Many: Drug Use Among Care Leavers in Transition into Independent Living* (London: Home Office).

C. Webster (1997) *Local Heroes: Racial Violence Among Asian and White Young People* (Leicester: Leicester University).

C. Wibberley and J. Price (2000) 'Young People's Drug Use: Facts and Feelings – Implications for the Normalization Debate', *Drugs: Education, Prevention and Policy*, 7(2): 147–62.

L. Wilkins (1964) *Social Deviance* (London: Tavistock).

L. Wilkins (1965) 'Some Sociological Factors in Drug Addiction Control', in D. Wilner and G. Kassebaum (eds) *Narcotics* (New York: McGraw-Hill).

F. Williams (2004) *Rethinking Families* (London: Gulbenkian Foundation).

L. Williams and H. Parker (2001) 'Alcohol, Cannabis, Ecstasy and Cocaine: Drugs of Reasoned Choice Among Young Adult Recreational Drug Users in England', *International Journal of Drug Policy*, 12: 397–413.

E. Wincup, G. Buckland and R. Bayliss (2003) *Youth Homelessness and Substance Use: Report to the Drugs and Alcohol Research Unit* (London: Home Office).

World Health Organisation (WHO) (1999) *Meeting Report on Religion and Health: Tobacco Free Initiative* (Geneva: World Health Organisation).

World Health Organisation (WHO) (2002) *The World Health Organisation Report: Reducing Risks to Health, Promoting Healthy Life* (Geneva: World Health Organisation).

World Health Organisation (WHO) (2004) *WHO Global Status Report on Alcohol 2004* (Geneva: World Health Organisation).

M.A. Wright (1998) 'The Great British Ecstasy Revolution', in G. McKay (ed.) *DIY Culture: Party and Protest in Nineties Britain* (London: Verso).

K. Yamaguchi and D.B. Kandel (1984) 'Patterns of Drug Use from Adolescence to Young Adulthood II: Sequences of Progression', *American Journal of Public Health*, 74(7): 668–72.

K. Yamaguchi and D.B. Kandel (1985) 'On the Resolution of Role Incompatibility: A Life Event History Analysis of Family Roles and Marijuana Use', *American Journal of Sociology*, 90: 1284–325.

R.K. Yin (2003) *Case Study Research: Design and Method* (Thousand Oaks: Sage).

J. Young (1971) *The Drugtakers: The Social Meaning of Drug Use* (London: MacGibbon and Kee).

J. Young (1999) *The Exclusive Society: Social Exclusion, Crime and Difference in Late Modernity* (London: Sage).

# Index

*Note*: Page numbers in italics refer to tables or figures.